David King
Publications 1977–2019

David King
Publications 1977–2019

Colpa Press / San Francisco Center for the Book

Contents

Introduction

Matt Borruso

David King (1948–2019) was an English artist, graphic designer, and musician best known for his design of the Crass symbol in 1977. That same year King moved from England to the United States, where he went on to create a huge body of work in numerous mediums over the next four decades. This book provides an introduction to some of the small press publishing projects, zines, and graphic design work King produced between 1977 and 2019.

King was born in Ilford, Essex, and grew up in Gants Hill and Chigwell. At 16 he enrolled at South-East Essex Technical College in Dagenham to study graphic design, where in 1964 he met Jeremy Ratter (aka Penny Rimbaud) and Gee Vaucher, who later went on to form the band Crass. After graduating in 1967, King spent the next 10 years working for a succession of London advertising agencies, first as a graphic designer and later as an art director.

In the late 1970s he left the advertising world to live at Dial House, the open-door home founded by Ratter and Vaucher on an isolated farm in the middle of an airfield in rural North Weald, Essex. There King designed a symbol for Penny Rimbaud's 1977 pamphlet *Christ's Reality Asylum*. This symbol—which we now know as the Crass symbol—was first spray-painted on this homemade pamphlet via a hand-cut stencil King made. Later that year it was adopted by the newly formed band Crass.

In the fall of 1977 King moved to New York, where he worked as freelance illustrator creating work for Danceteria, the Peppermint Lounge, the Museum of Modern Art, *The New York Times*, Pop Front, and many others. It was also in 1977 that he designed and illustrated his only known mass-market book cover, for Brian Aldiss' paperback *Non-Stop,* published by Pan Science Fiction.

His personal book work during this period was limited to small prototypes such as *Little People* and *Landescapes* which he would unsuccessfully attempt to sell to mainstream publishers. These prototypes were very much in line with the commercial illustration work he was producing at the time. One rejection letter from Universe Books connects *Landescapes* with Brian Rice and Tony Evans' *The English Sunrise* (1973), a small book of photographs of objects depicting the rising sun hiding in plain sight all over England in the form of signage, shop doors, and even biscuits. Though quite different from *Landescapes*, *The English Sunrise* does provide a rough model for the way King saw the world: through his humor; his photography; and the way he would catalog images and objects in his many collections, scrapbooks, and publications.

Soon after moving to New York, King, who had no musical background, began drumming for the no wave band Arsenal with Charlie Nash and Dione King. Through this band he began creating flyers for shows which were inexpensively reproduced on newly available consumer-grade copy machines. The technology of the photocopier seemed to open a floodgate of making, as King began producing dozens and dozens of flyers and artworks.

In 1980, the band moved to San Francisco and King's commercial design and illustration work slowed. Although he did design for *Details* magazine remotely in the 1990s, San Francisco, unlike New York, was never a print media capital. But it was in San Francisco that he began producing zines as a way to move through his graphic design concepts.

Many of these zines are only a few stapled pages with juxtaposed found images (most often from mainstream sources like *National Geographic* or the *San Francisco Chronicle*) and minimal text. Like the flyers, they were almost all created on a photocopier in the same letter-sized format. Cheap, and to the point.

This zine making runs parallel to King's musical projects with Arsenal, which would later become Sleeping Dogs and finally Brain Rust. Early zines like *Sleeping Dogs #1* and *#2* were thoroughly connected to the band in terms of political content and anarcho punk aesthetics. King had these issues printed on an offset press in larger editions, and they were distributed through Rough Trade.

The rest of his output was truly obscure; we really don't know how many copies of his zines he made or how they were distributed. *Suburbs of Hell* was a single issue—a short, illustrated, dystopian science fiction story somewhat indebted to J.G. Ballard—while the more purely visual *Beware* spanned 20 issues between 1981 and 1982. Others like *Too Many Zombies* and *No. One* were collaborations made using mail art practices and correspondence. Many of King's zines at this time featured local artists, poets, writers, and musicians from the San Francisco Bay Area.

In the late '80s the zines tapered off as King returned to school for his BFA at the San Francisco Art Institute. (Although he did make at least one poetry zine, *Poems!*, for a 1992 Diane di Prima class.) But for the most part the era of photocopied zines closed with the dissolution of Brain Rust and the end of King's active participation in the music scene.

The 2000s saw the rise of desktop self-publishing and print-on-demand books through companies like Shutterfly, Blurb, Apple, and others. King was an early adopter of these products and services, which are in some ways the next logical step after the copy shop, offering cheap-ish consumer-grade reproductions in book format via digital template platforms. These print-on-demand books have long been maligned by "serious" bookmakers and artists, but looking back it's easy to see their potential and appeal for someone like King.

He took his subjects—Ballard, rock formations, masked film characters, the Batman logo—and compiled them into brief volumes, often making just one or two copies. Many use very low-resolution cell phone images or photographs of television screens. These books, self published under his imprint MoST Books (Museum of Small Things), became printed extensions of his cut-and-paste scrapbooks or curated versions of his many sprawling collections.

Beginning in the 2010s, and until the end of his life in 2019, King grew more and more involved in the small DIY publishing world exploding at that time through the resurgence of zine making, Risograph printing, and Printed Matter's art book fairs in New York and Los Angeles. He produced numerous small-run books through Colpa Press and Goteblüd, as well as large-scale projects through &Pens Press and Gingko / Kill Yr Idols.

Like many artists, through these fairs and small presses, he found an opportunity to have his work seen outside of the more codified gallery structure. This new outlet allowed for a wave of bookmaking projects that reproduced the work he had been creating all of his life, but that was far less known than the Crass symbol. This activity lasted right up until his death, culminating in the publication of *David King Stencils: Past, Present and Crass!*, a full circle moment in terms of his published output.

This book is a companion to the exhibition *David King Publications 1977–2019*, held at the San Francisco Center for the Book October 25–December 22, 2024. The exhibition and book collect a chronological sampling of the publishing work that King made over his lifetime, in addition to flyers, photographs, and graphic design projects. But neither the show nor the book are in any way complete. We are still digging through King's archive, consistently finding new things that he made, and piecing together a better picture of his life and work.

Matt Borruso
February, 2024

Transferware

Experimental Jetset

Ways of transferring, transgressing, transforming, transporting, translating, and transcribing.

1.

Like many of our generation, we guess that our first experience with the *transfer* (in particular, *transfer printing*) was the iron-on shirt. We can still remember the many T-shirt stands that populated markets and fairs during our late-70s childhood years. You could pick a design from a large binder—a skull, a snake, a dagger, a pin-up, a dubious slogan, a band logo. This graphic was then transferred onto a T-shirt of your choice, using a large heated metal press (often a steaming, hissing machine—or perhaps that was our vivid imagination). The print on the shirt felt like a thick, shiny, cheap plastic layer—and after a few tumbles through the washing machine, you could peel it off, not unlike a Band-Aid. There was always something clandestine about those T-shirt parlors—you could sense that the graphics were pirated, the band logos were bootlegged, the quality of the shirts was inferior, and the prints would simply fall off. And yet, it was exactly this shady dimension that made it attractive to kids like us. Already then, we realized there was something *transgressive* about the process of transferring.

This shady notion (of bootlegging, of pirating) seems almost embedded in the method of transfer printing itself. Its history goes back to the pottery industry of the 1700s and 1800s, when transfer techniques were used to add complex decorations to cheap pottery. Imitating hand-painted ceramics, these 'transferwares' were made in bulk, and targeted at growing foreign markets. The iron-on shirts that we wore as children were direct descendants of this practice. Cheap graphic thrills for the masses.

As teenagers, we came across the notion of the transfer again—but now in the form of dry-transfer lettering. Companies like Letraset and Mecanorma were producing cheap sheets of rub-off/rub-on alphabets—perfect for the Xeroxed fanzines and mini-comics we produced during our high school days. Sure, dry-transfer lettering sheets were around since the early '60s, developed for the burgeoning advertising industry. But in the '70s and '80s, these sheets became a staple in DIY/punk circles (and in fact, we were still using these sheets up until the mid-90s). Again, there was something slightly transgressive about the use of these dry-transfer sheets—having the authority of established, commercial typefaces at your fingertips, while using them for subversive means. Rubbing them, scratching them, basically perverting them.

In that sense, you could argue the transfer (whether as transferware, iron-on shirts, or dry-transfer lettering) has always occupied an interesting space—between mass-market exploitation and low-tech bootlegging, between advertising and punk, between crass commercialism and just Crass.

2.

When thinking about the work of David King, we can't help but think about exactly this notion of the transfer. After all, his most iconic creation, the Crass symbol, was made to be stenciled, to be transferred. As Howard A. Rodman noted in his essay "Seven Theses on David King" (2019), a "stencil is, in effect, a machine [...] that enables its user to incite images." In other words, a stencil is a machine to transfer images, to transport images from one situation into another. And by transferring images, the image also gets

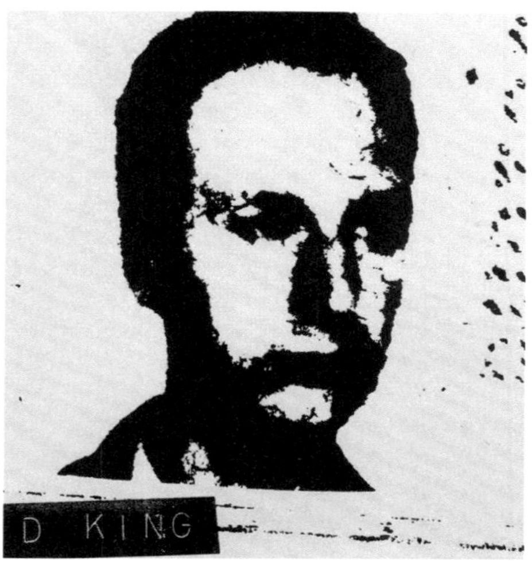

transformed. Every new surface or context changes something about the symbol—its shape, its meaning, its function.

And when it comes to the Crass symbol, there has been no bigger transformer than David King himself. King tirelessly used the circular mark as a platform for all kinds of versions and variations. In that sense, King became a stencil machine himself—creating and recreating the symbol in an ongoing series of ever-changing iterations, proving the point that Josef Albers once made, that "variants demonstrate, besides a sincere attitude, a healthy belief that there is no final solution in form; thus form demands unending performance and invites constant reconsideration."

But let's not forget that David King was not just the one doing the transferring—he was also the one being transferred. Throughout his life, he moved from subculture to subculture (from art school to advertising agency, from no wave to anarcho-punk), and from city to city (from London to New York to San Francisco). After all, to transfer is to transport—and King did transplant himself from situation to situation, while managing to bridge seemingly unbridgeable scenes. (In fact, he inhabited these different worlds almost simultaneously, living with Crass at the radically open Dial House right after working as a graphic designer and art director for multiple London advertising agencies.)

In this regard, it's also interesting to take into consideration the role that British art schools played in most of the post-war period (up until the end of the '80s). As Simon Frith and Howard Horne argued in *Art into Pop* (1987), state-funded art and design schools (linked to manufacturing industries) were widely seen as accessible alternatives to universities, and as such offered a sort of upward social mobility for working-class youth. In this way, the art school environment created not only a place where different social classes came together, but also enabled a synthesis of fine arts and applied arts. This milieu created the pop-art/punk continuum as we now know it (with Ian Dury being taught by Peter Blake, Bryan Ferry being a pupil of Richard Hamilton, etc.).

David King was a product of exactly this environment, this place where 'high' and 'low' arts (and with it, 'high' and 'low' classes) intermingled. In fact, in an unpublished interview (dated December 15, 2011, and archived at the David King Estate), King describes the architecture of the art school that he attended (the South-East Essex Technical College and School of Art) as "H-shaped, with the art school being on one side of of the 'H', and the trade school on the other side." According to King, "the bridge of the 'H' was where the café was, and where both sides met." It was exactly in this café, literally in the bridge between art and trade, where David King first met Penny Rimbaud and Gee Vaucher—who would later start Crass. It's hard to find a more fitting metaphor for the synthesis of 'high' and 'low' art than the bridge in that H-shaped building.

Within this environment, the notion of pop (and with it, the idea of the collage) is obviously very important, as it provides the conceptual framework in which advertising and punk can exist simultaneously. (An interesting case in point can be found in some of Gee Vaucher's pre-Crass work—in particular, the poster she designed in 1972 for the ICES 72 festival. Consisting of a motorik grid of 64 brightly colored logo-like ice creams, it's a work that provides an interesting pop subtext to her later political collages.)

In his essay "Essential Forms" (2019), Matt Borruso already placed David King within the tradition of pop, and compared the work of King (and his fascination with American visual culture) with that of artists who were part of (or close to) the Independent Group (in particular, J.G. Ballard, Eduardo Paolozzi and Richard Hamilton). In that sense, we regard King certainly as part of the pop-art/punk continuum that we mentioned earlier. Generally speaking, the collages of punk are often described as being rooted in the Dada collages of John Heartfield—dark, political, stern. But there is also something to be said for the idea of punk being rooted in the pop collages of Hamilton and Paolozzi—trashy, colorful, radiant.

Moreover, let's not forget that pop itself is a method in which images are being *transferred* from one sphere into another. In that sense, the many acts of transferral going on within the practice of David King are essentially pop gestures—attempts to transport symbols through different ambiences, with a certain ease and speed.

If that last sentence brings to mind Guy Debord's definition of the *dérive* ("a technique of rapid passage through varied ambiences"), we can assure you that this is not a coincidence. Because indeed, we would like to argue that David King's sense of transferability also finds a translation in his psychogeographical practice, as can be seen in the photos in which King transcribed his drifts through San Francisco—we are here particularly thinking of *Walking Photos* (published in 2019 by Colpa Press). In that particular publication, King shows the city as the sun-dazed collage that it is—and instead of letting the images do the traveling, it is indeed the walker (and reader) who travels through the images.

3.

There are many labels used to describe David King—fine artist, graphic designer, art director, illustrator, collagist, musician, photographer, zine maker, independent publisher. But being graphic designers ourselves, we would like to claim his practice as just that: graphic design. Then again, we employ a very loose, transdisciplinary (or perhaps anti-disciplinary) definition of graphic design—and the idea of the transfer is never far away in that definition. After all, what is graphic design but the transferral of language (or signs, or images) from one sphere into another? The transportation of knowledge, from one scene to another? And just as with the original notion of transferware, there will always be something shady about graphic design—a sense of piracy, of inauthenticity, of exploitation. After all, was the first actual piece of graphic design, the Gutenberg Bible (1450), not just an unauthorized bootleg project, as well as the first instance of mass production?

In our view, graphic design will forever exist in this shadowy intersection between mass-market exploitation and subversive distribution, between pop and punk, between crass commercialism and just Crass. And David King not only created an emblem that perfectly captures that paradoxical position—his practice as a whole was emblematic of it.

Experimental Jetset
Amsterdam
May 7, 2024

Early books, graphic design, flyers

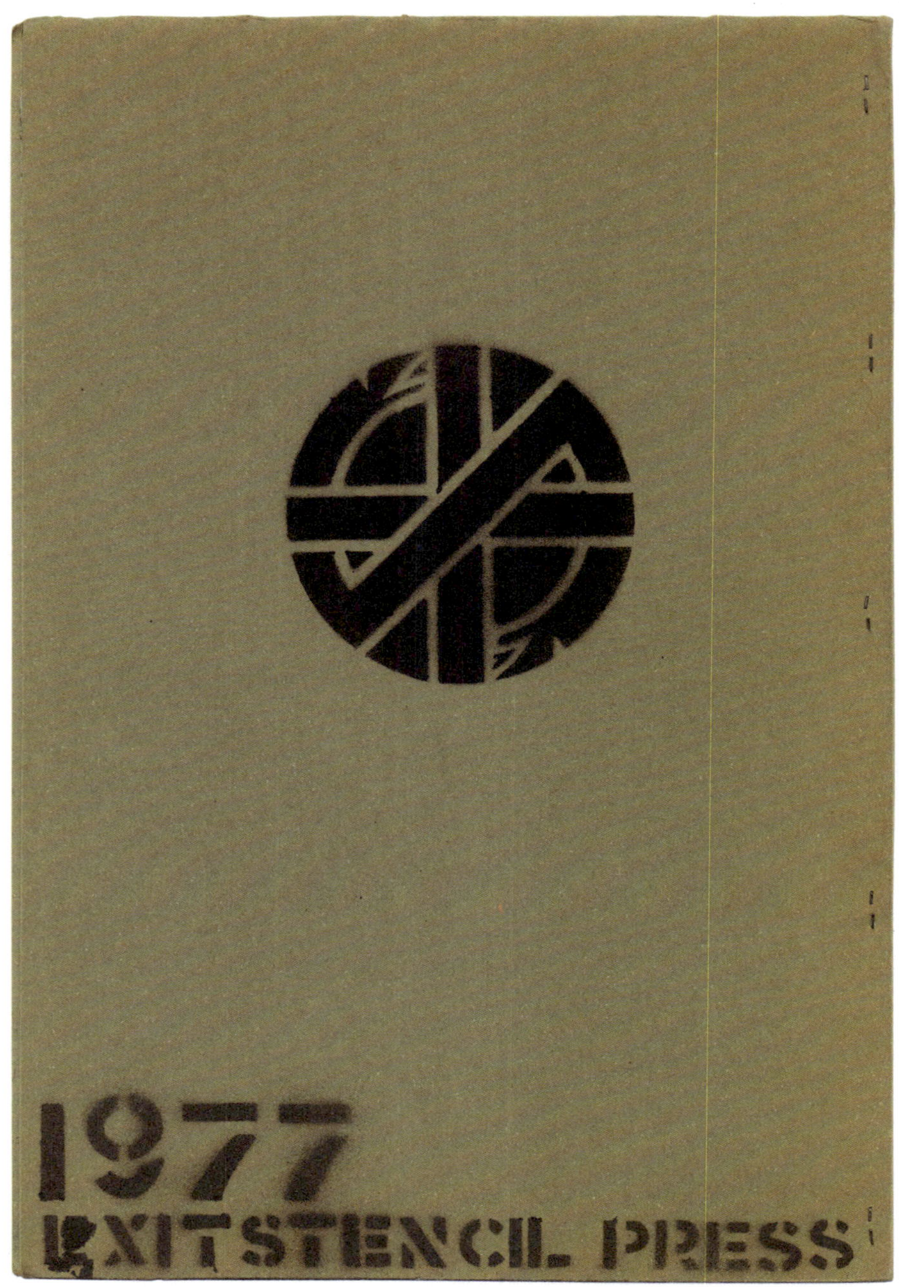
1977
EXITSTENCIL PRESS

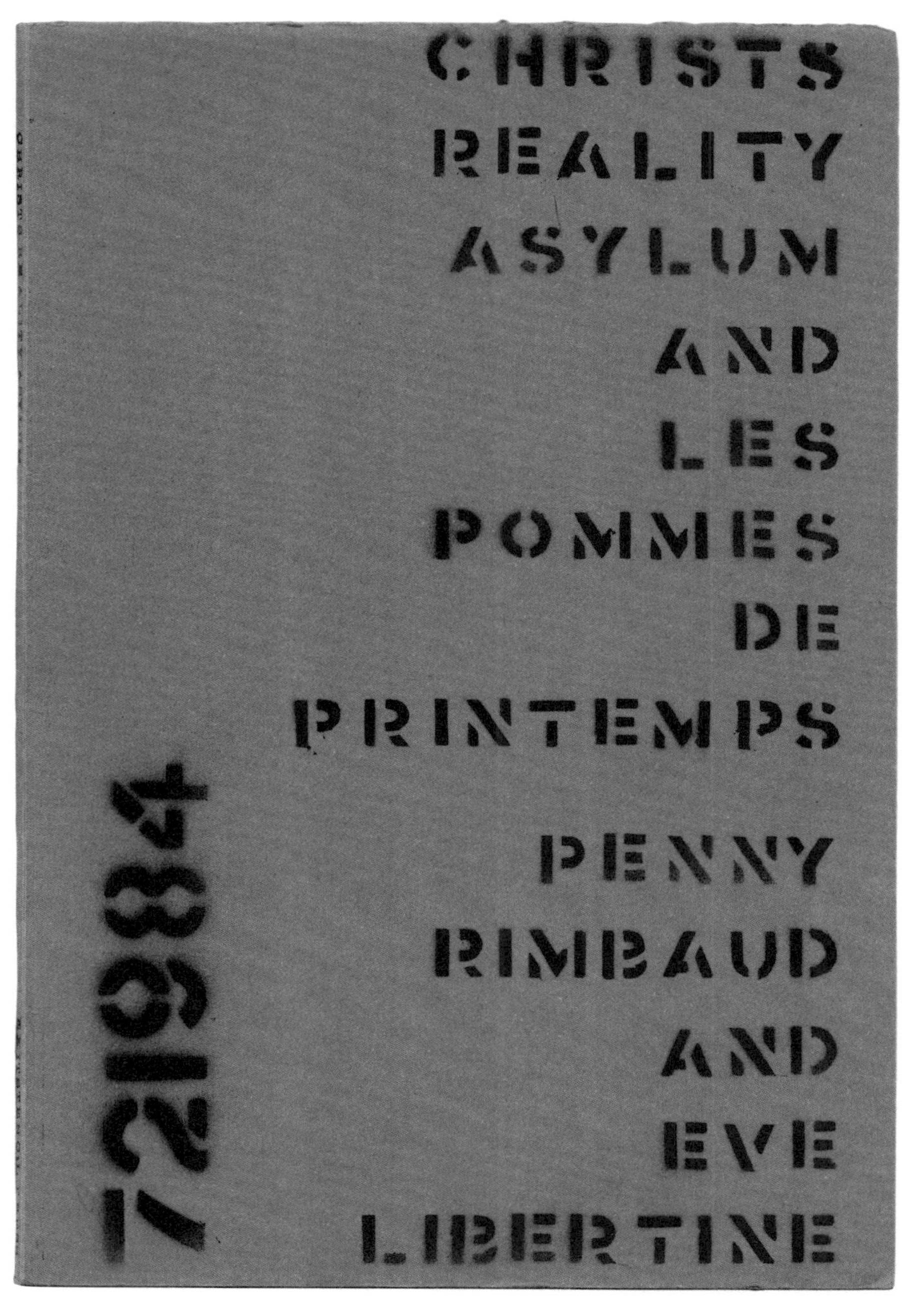

Christ's Reality Asylum and Les Pommes De Printemps
by Penny Rimbaud, Exitstencil Press, 1977
Mimeograph, stencil and spray paint, side stapled,
22 pages, 9.25 x 13.5 in. (23.5 x 34.3 cm)

Rimbaud's pamphlet marks the first appearance of what would later become known as the Crass symbol, designed by David King.

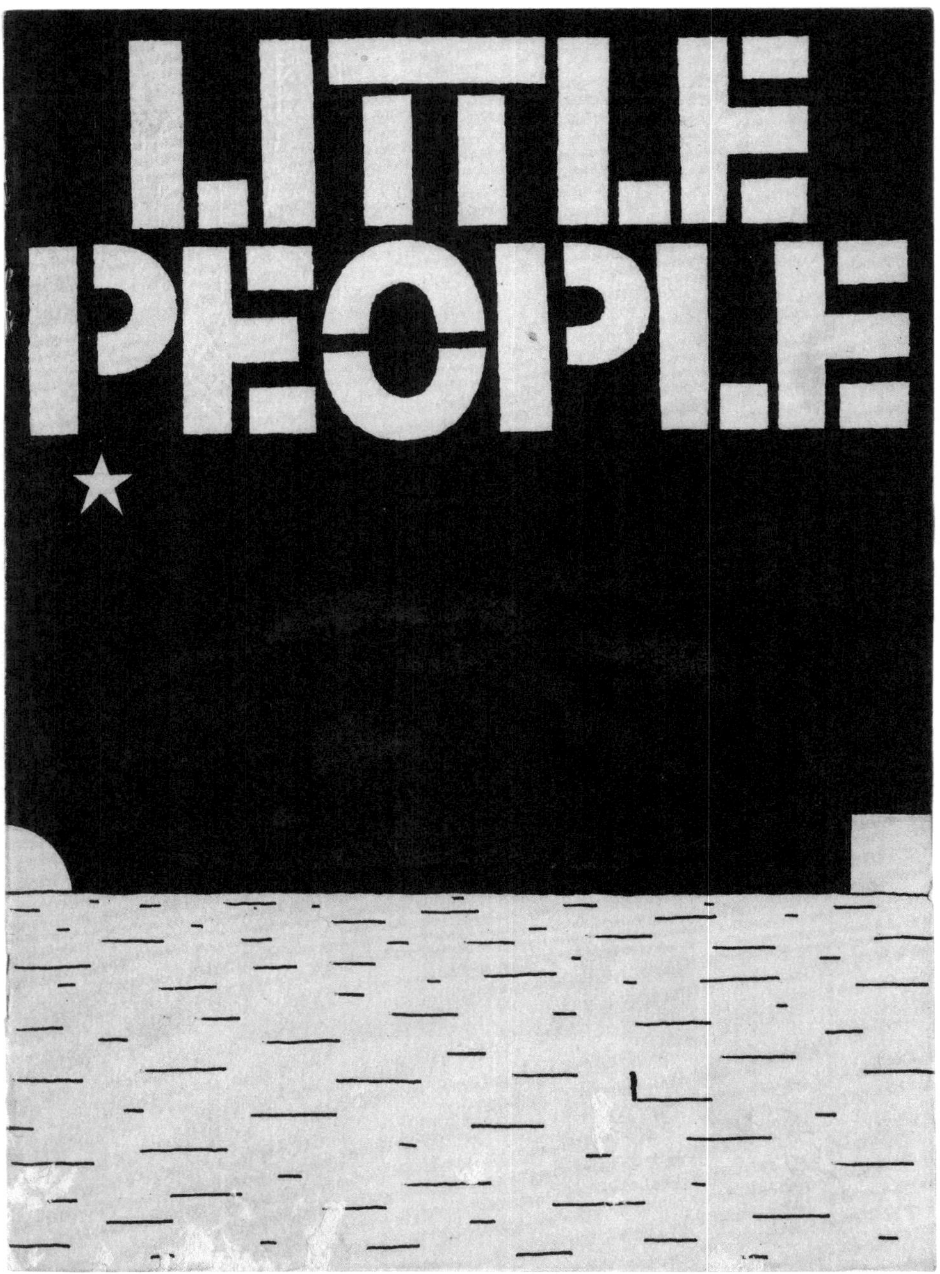
LITTLE
PEOPLE

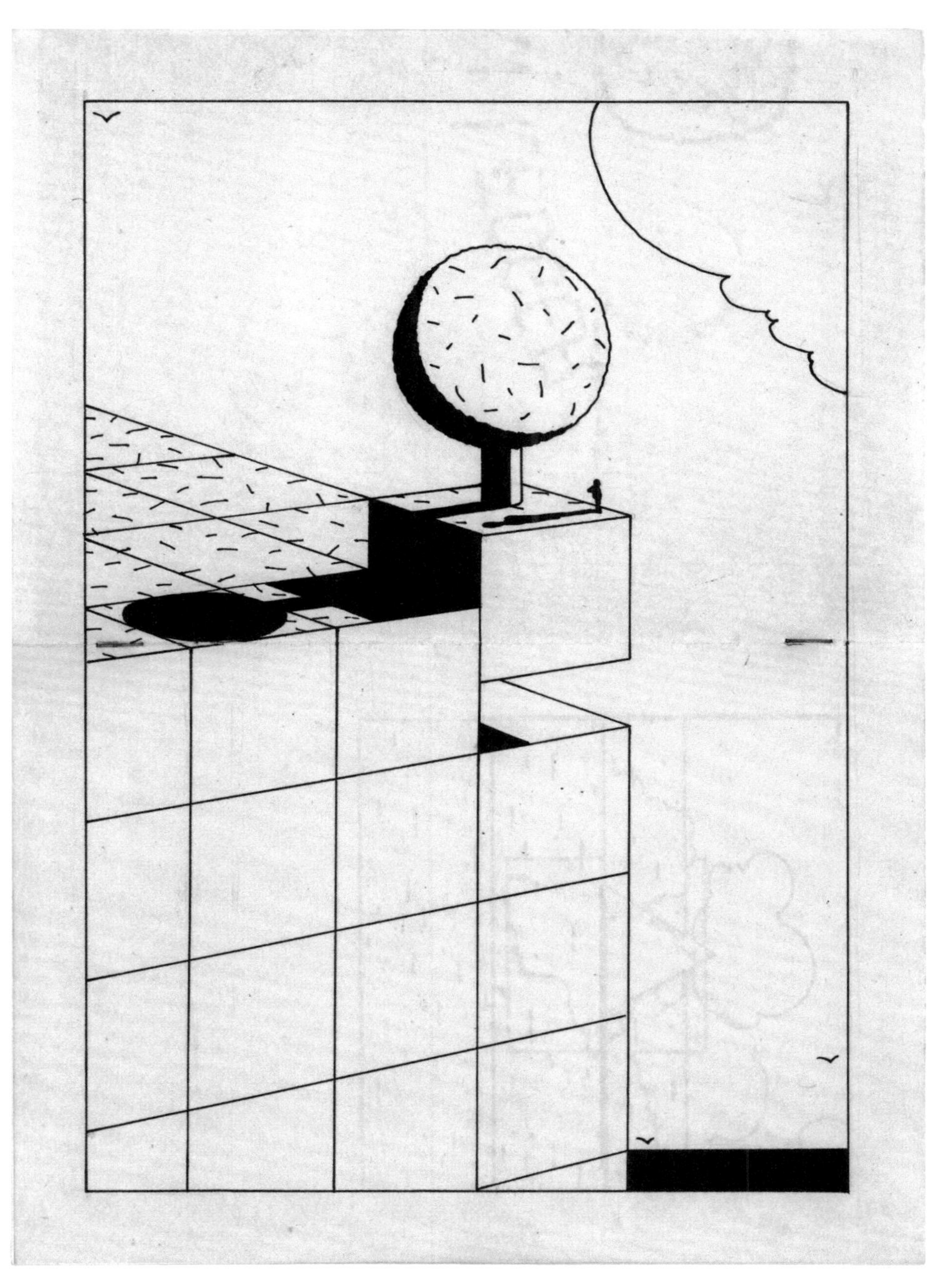

Little People, 1977/79
Pen and ink on paper, staple bound, 28 pages, unique, 5 x 7 in. (12.7 x 17.8 cm)

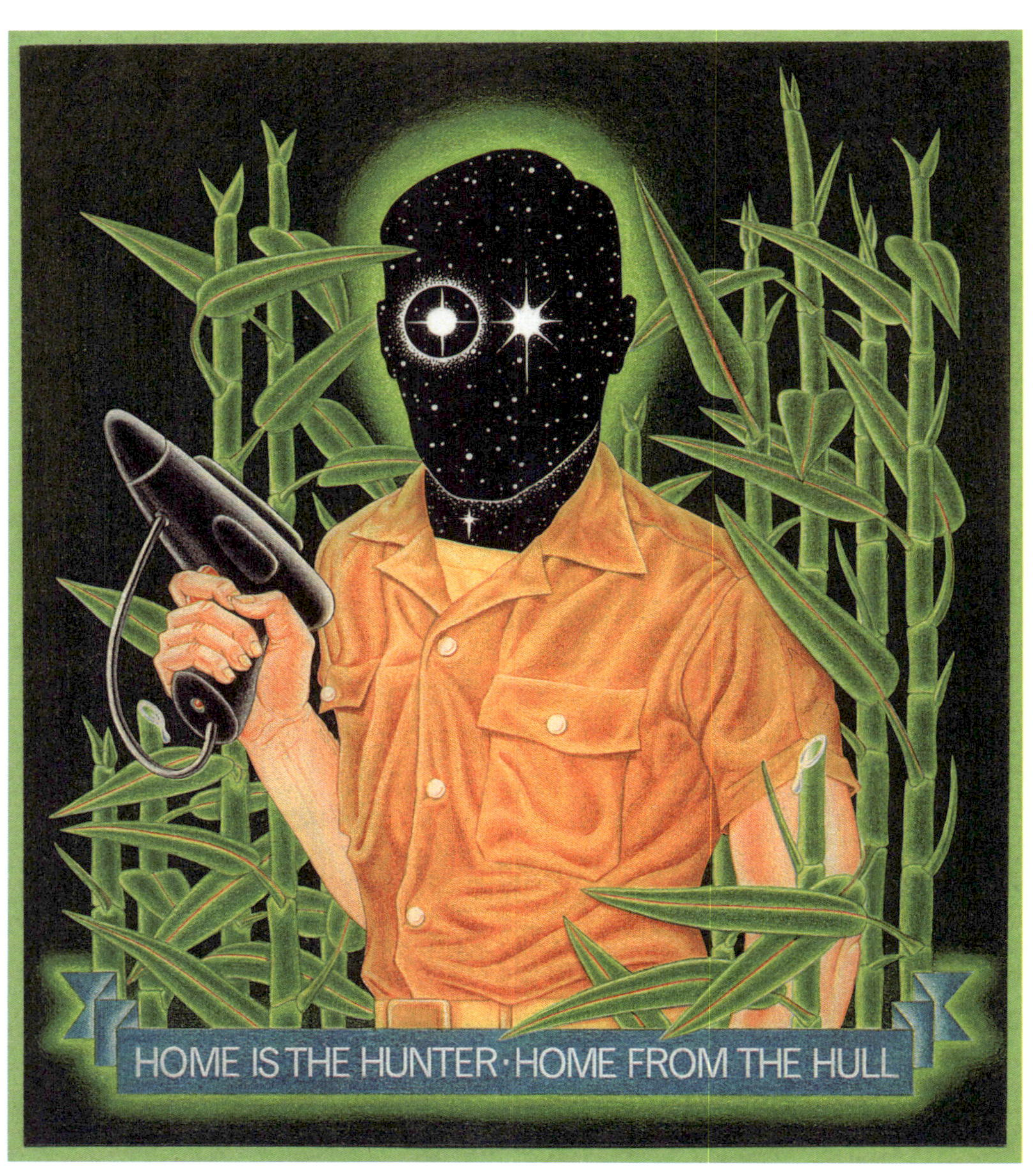

Original art for *Non-Stop* by Brian Aldiss, 1977
colored pencil, paint, cut paper,
and rub-down type on board,
11.75 x 16.5 in. (29.8 x 41.9 cm)

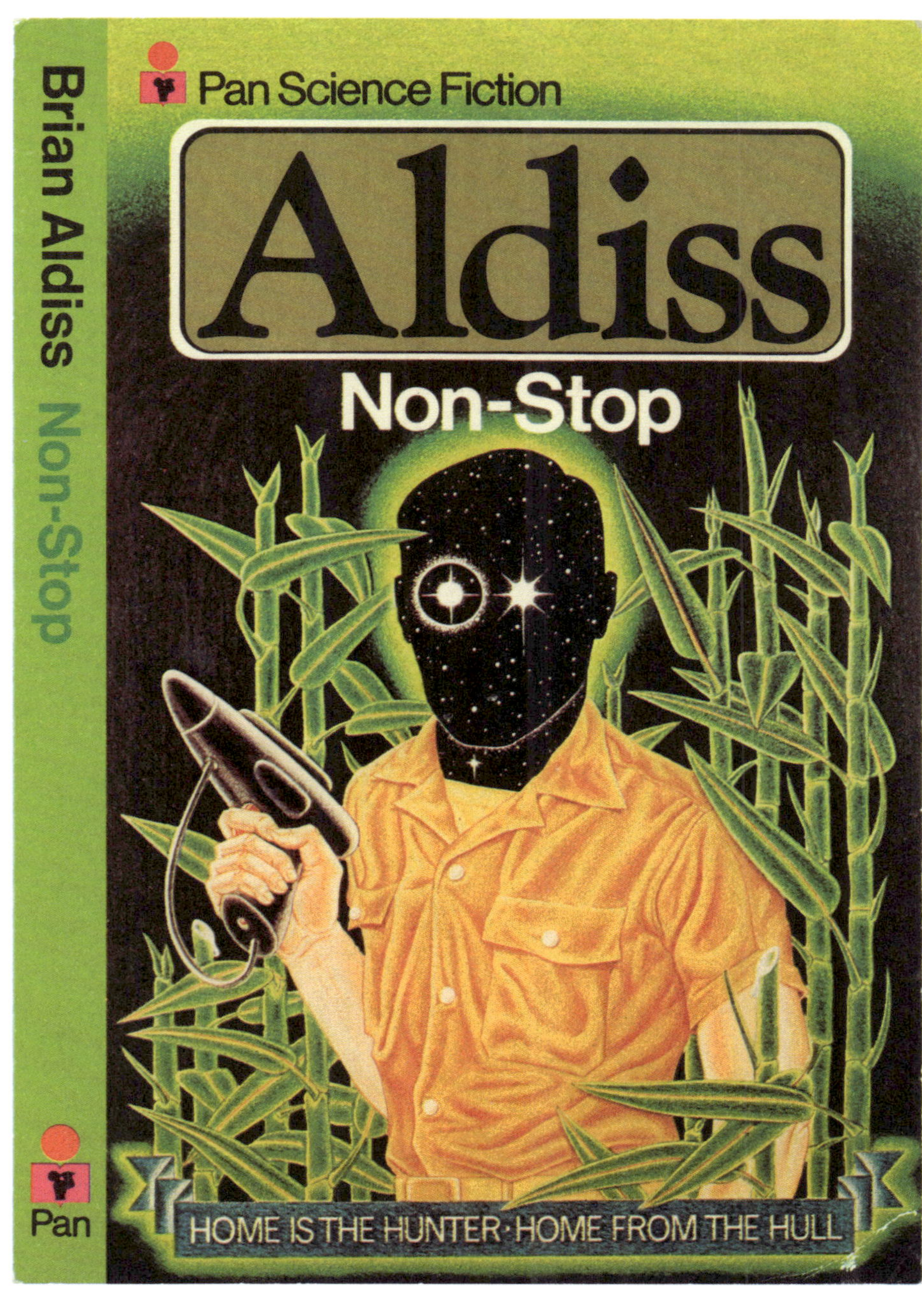

Non-Stop by Brian Aldiss, cover art by David King, Pan Books, 1977
Mass market paperback, 204 pages, 4.25 x 7 in. (10.8 x 17.8 cm)

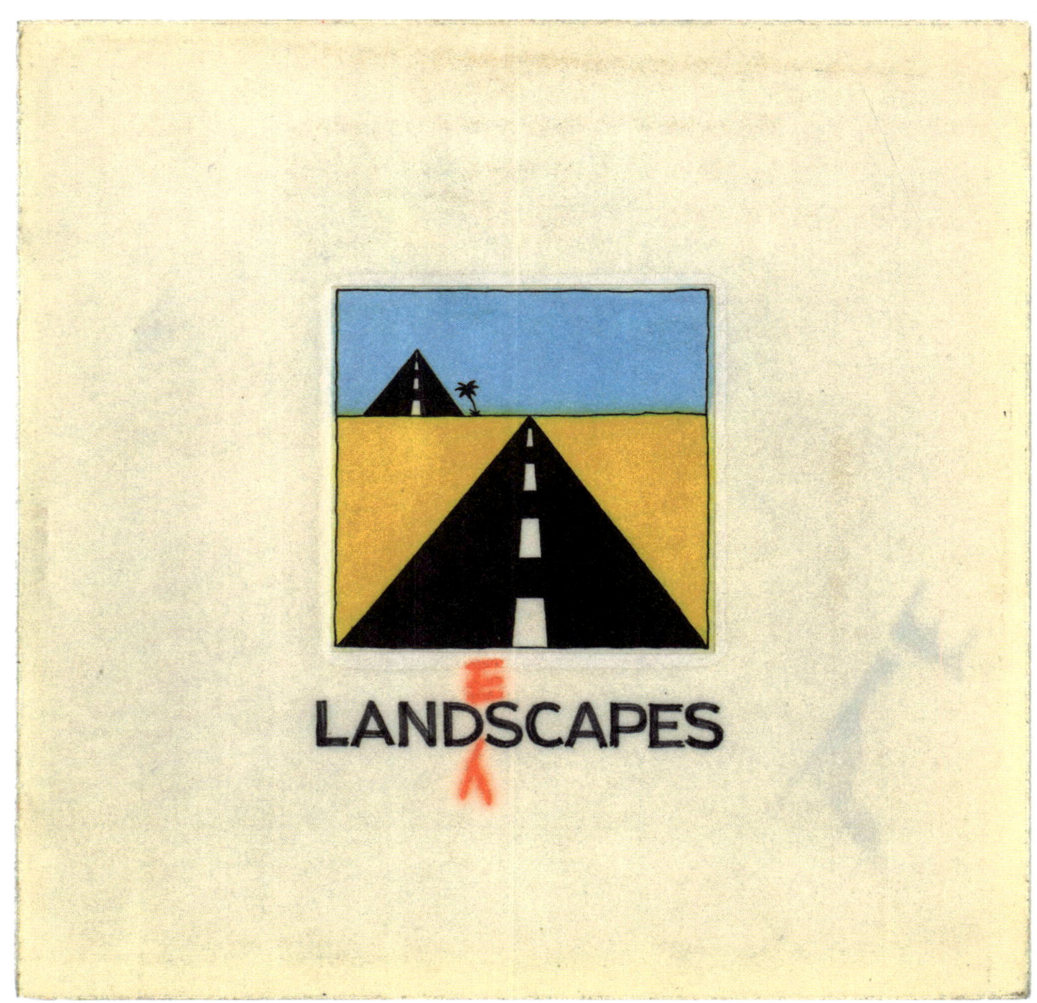
LANDSCAPES

Landescapes, 1977/79
Pen, ink, and marker on paper, staple bound, 12 pages, unique, 8.25 x 8.25 in. (21 x 21 cm)

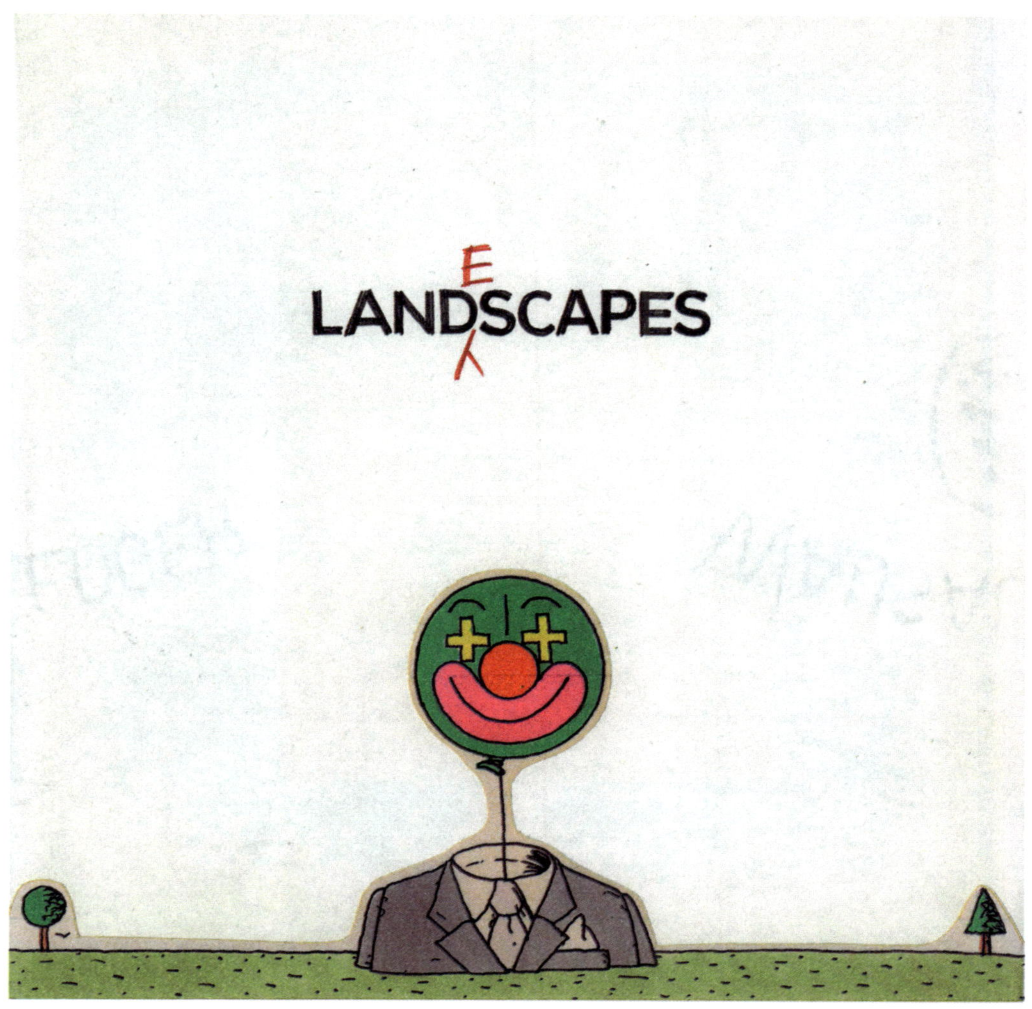

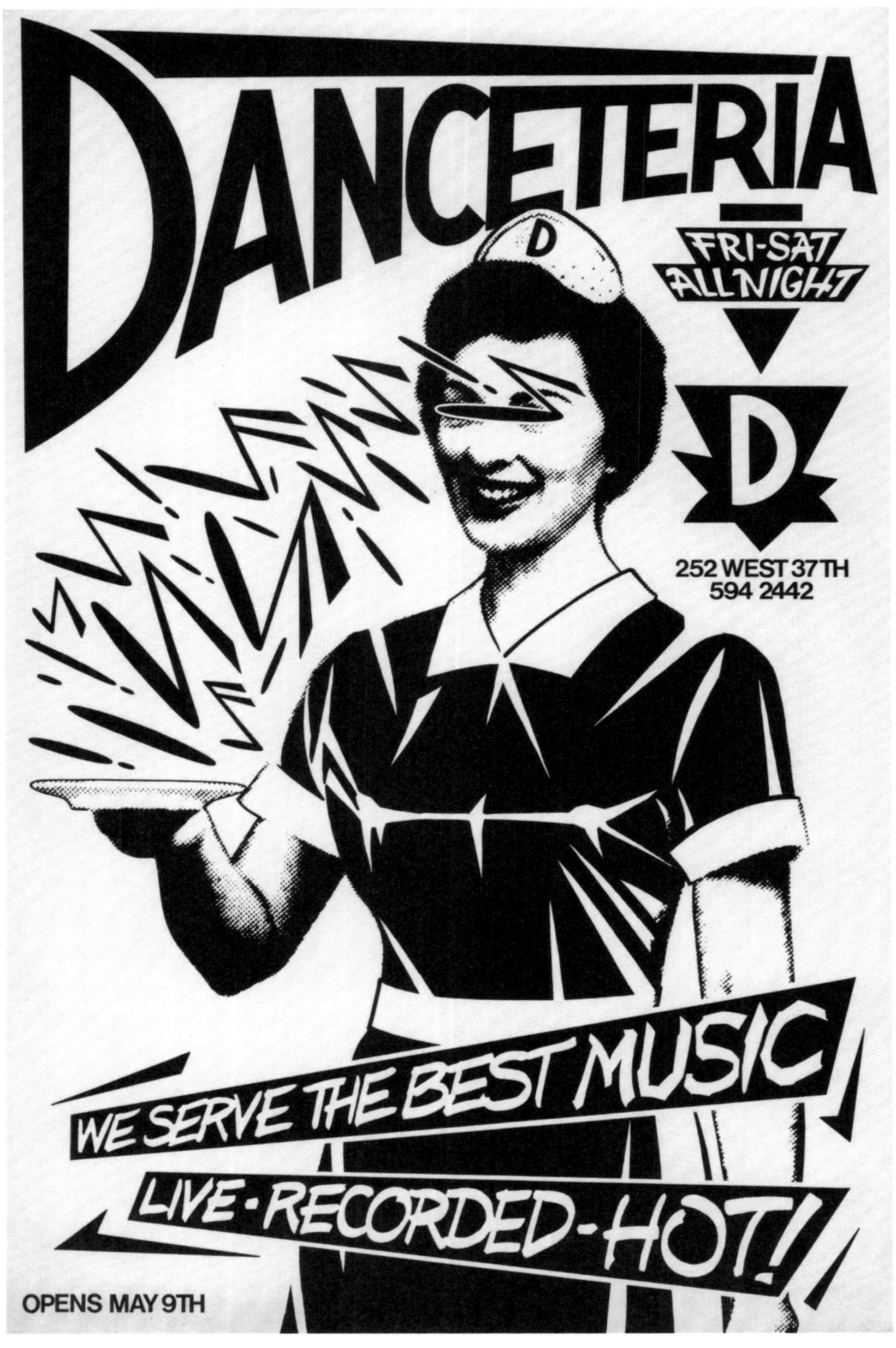
DANCETERIA
D
FRI-SAT
ALL NIGHT
D
252 WEST 37TH
594 2442
WE SERVE THE BEST MUSIC
LIVE-RECORDED-HOT!
OPENS MAY 9TH

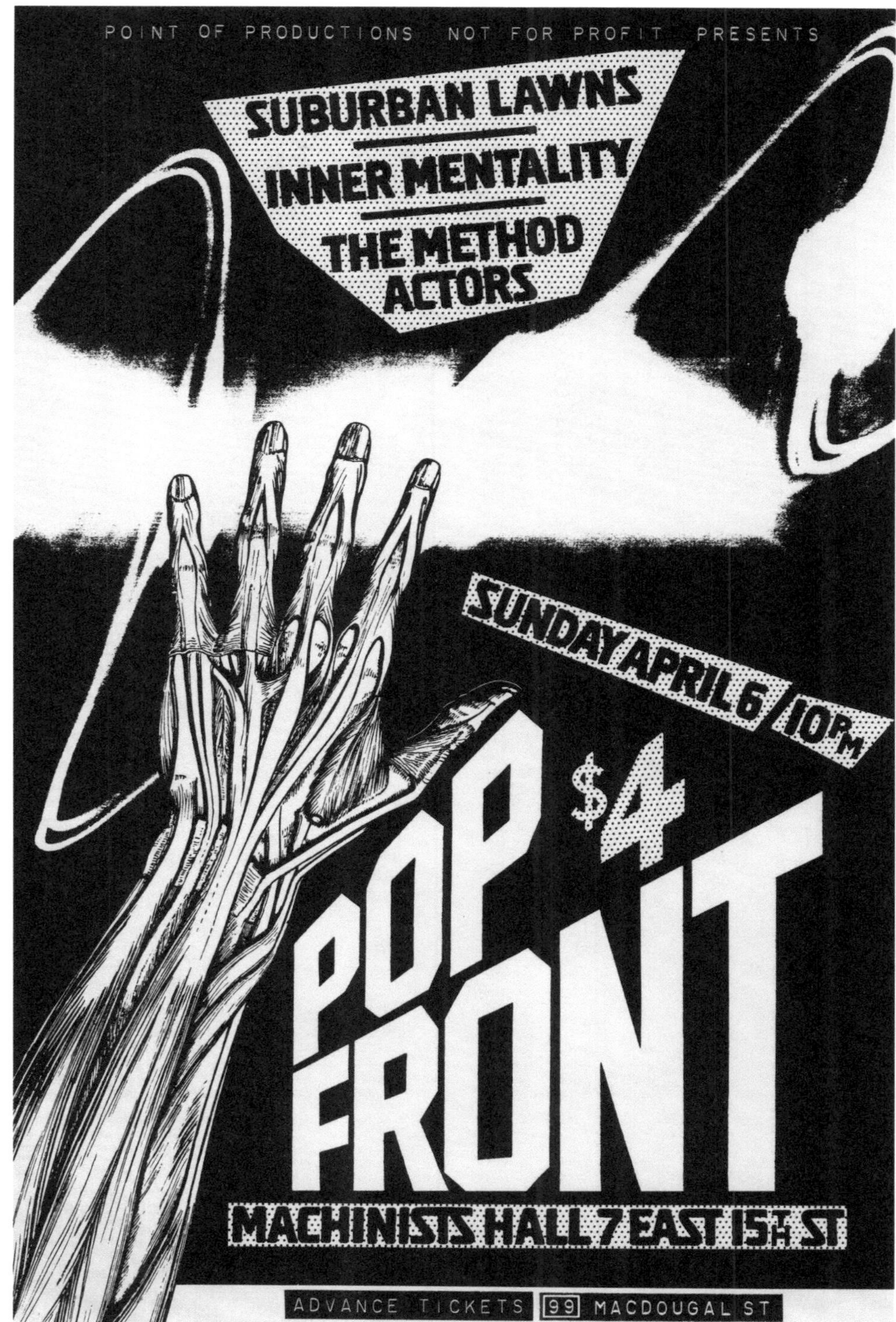
POINT OF PRODUCTIONS NOT FOR PROFIT PRESENTS
SUBURBAN LAWNS
INNER MENTALITY
THE METHOD ACTORS
SUNDAY APRIL 6 10PM
$4
POP FRONT
MACHINISTS HALL 7 EAST 15th ST
ADVANCE TICKETS 99 MACDOUGAL ST

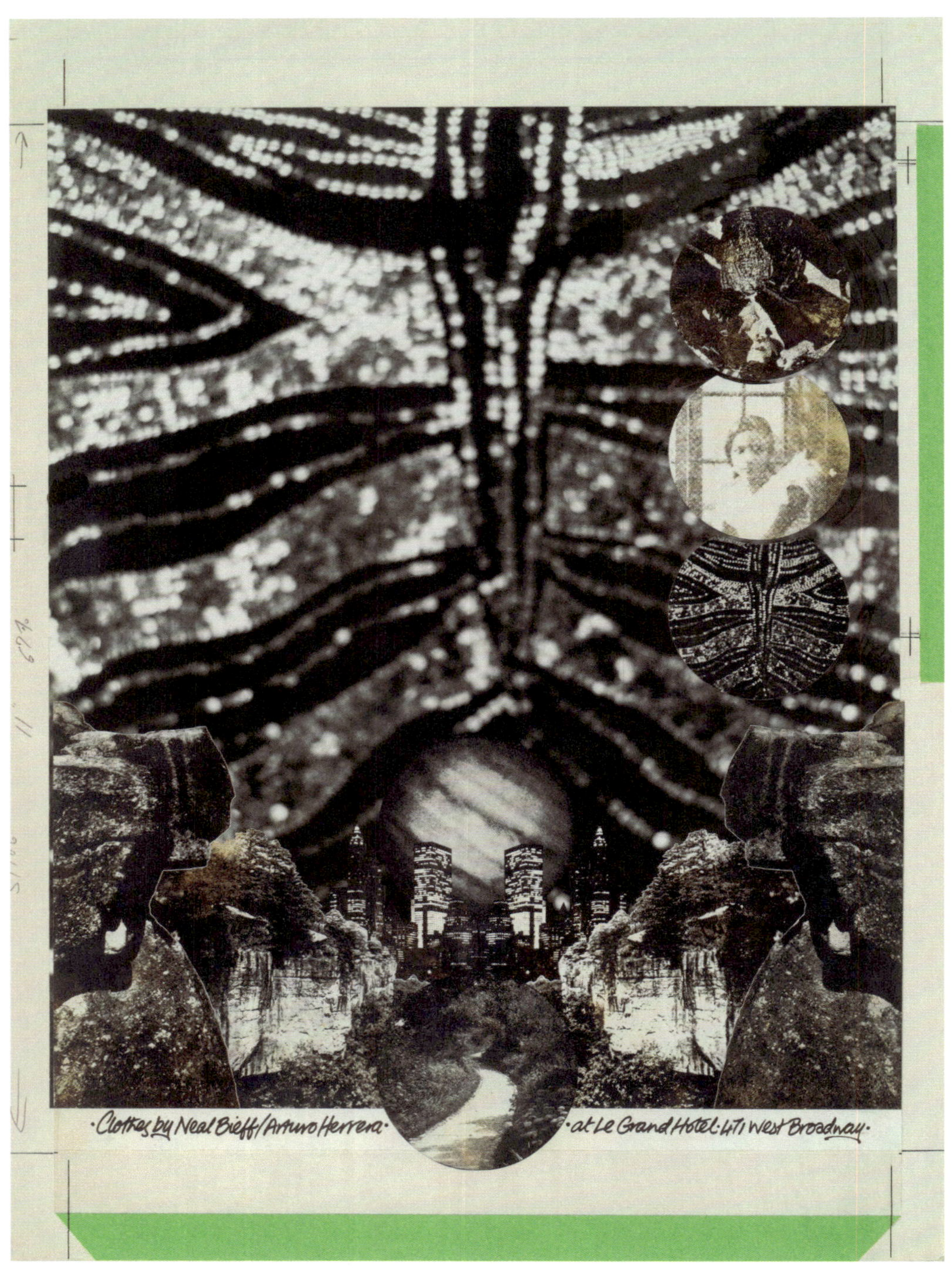

Pages 20–21: *Danceteria* poster, 1979
Photocopy, 11 x 17 in. (27.9 x 43.1 cm)

Pop Front poster, 1980
Offset, 10 x 15.25 in. (25.4 x 38.7 cm)

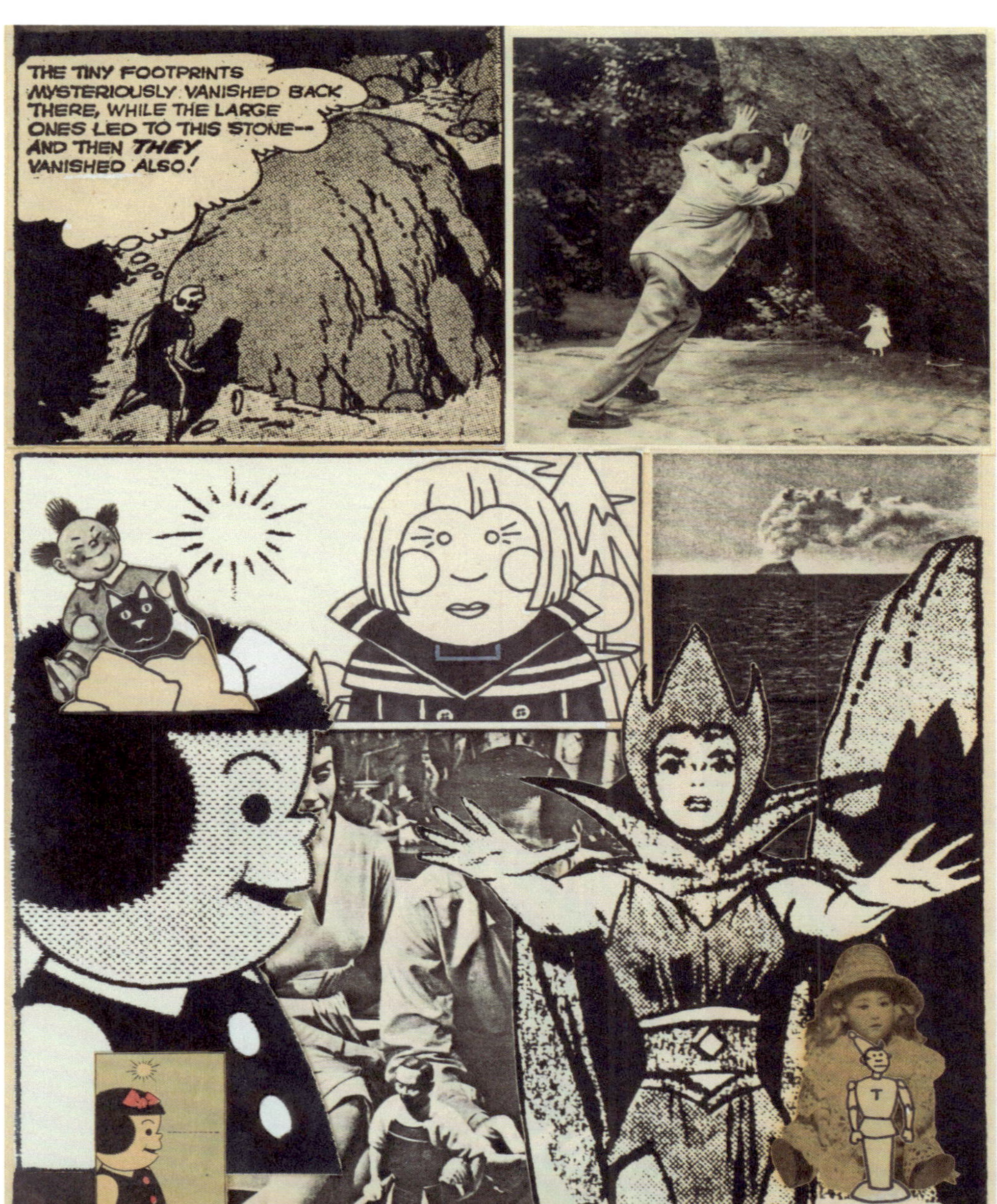

Facing page: Paste-up for
Le Grande Hotel poster, 1977/79
collage, ink, and photograph on illustration board, 18 x 24.8 in. (45.7 X 63 cm)

Untitled collage, 1977/79
Ink, comic pages, photostats on paper, 12 x 14.75 in. (30.5 x 37.5 cm)

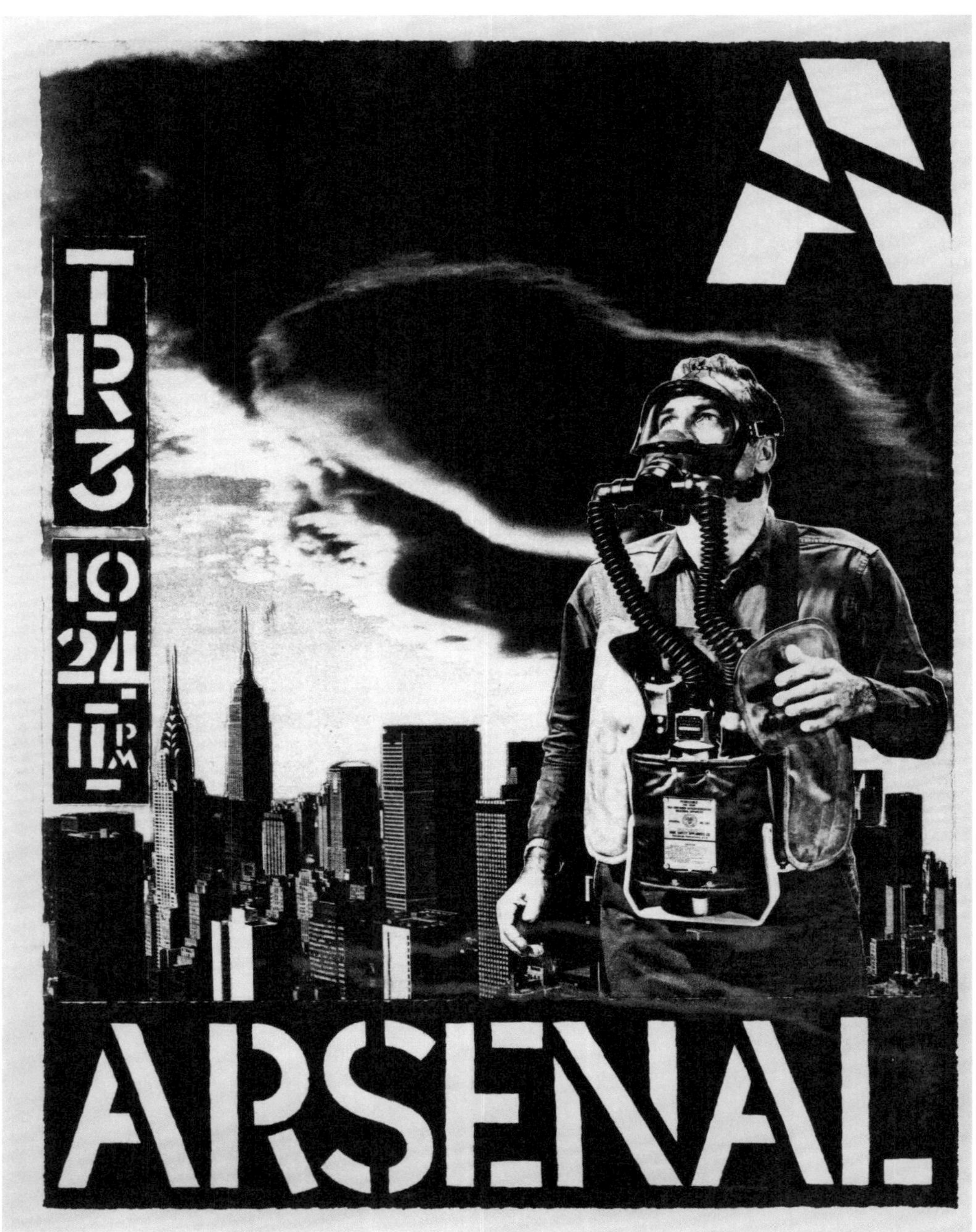

Flyer for *Arsenal at Tier 3*, New York, October 24, 1979
Photocopy, 8.5 x 11 in. (21.6 x 27.9 cm)

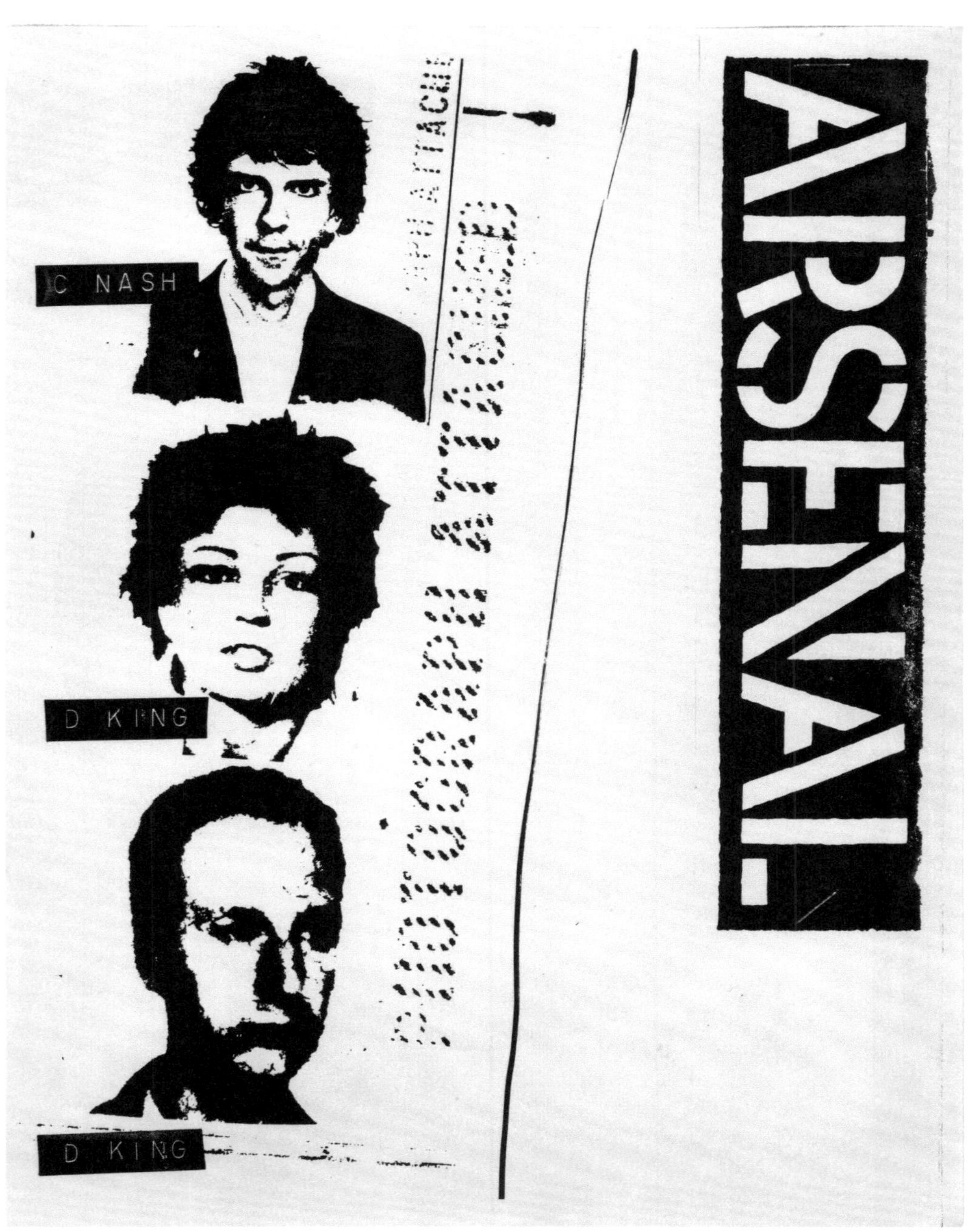

Arsenal flyer, 1977/79
Photocopy, 8.5 x 11 in. (21.6 x 27.9 cm)

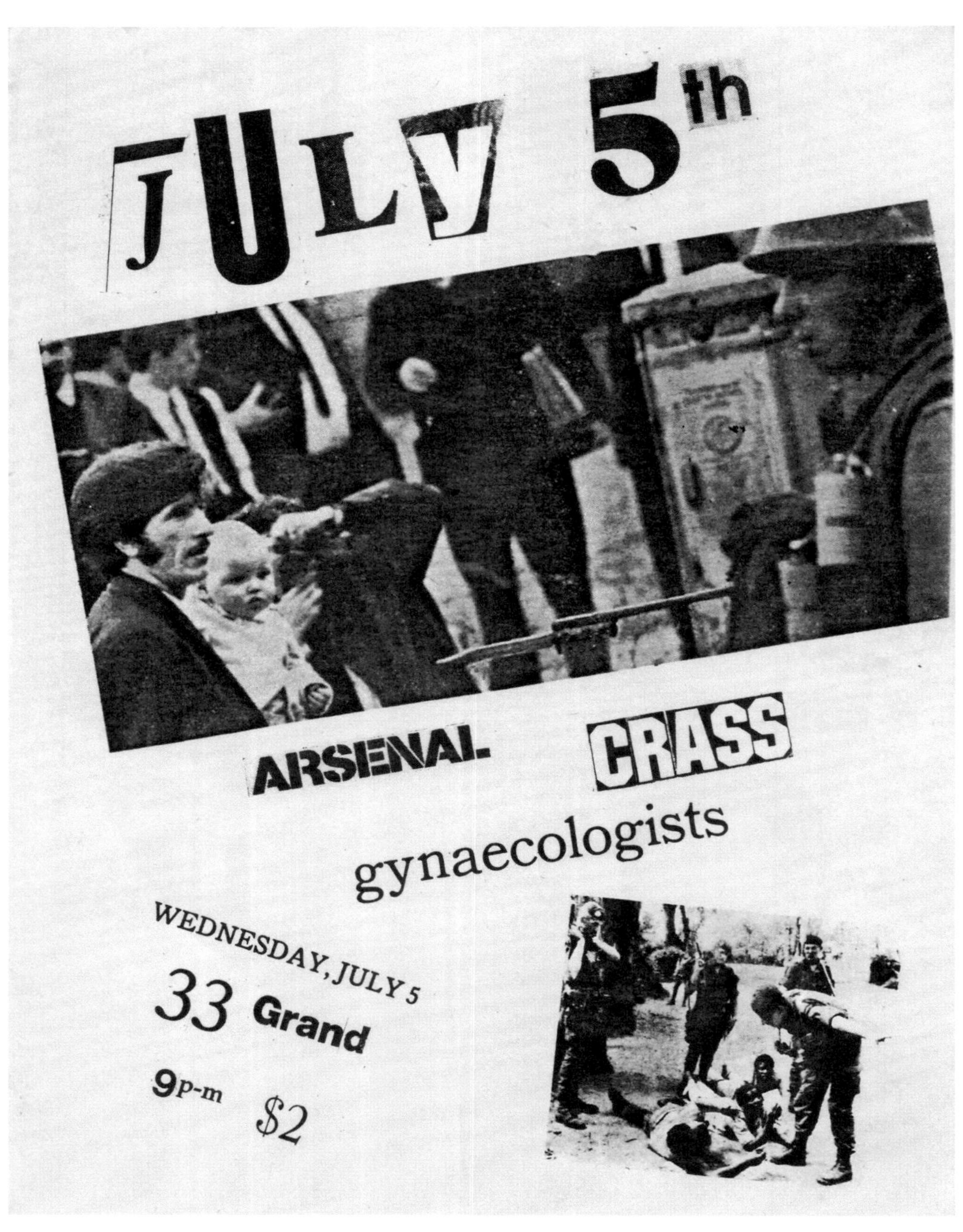

Flyer for *Arsenal with Crass and The Gynaecologists at 33 Grand*, New York, July 5, 1978
Photocopy, 8.5 x 11 in. (21.6 x 27.9 cm)

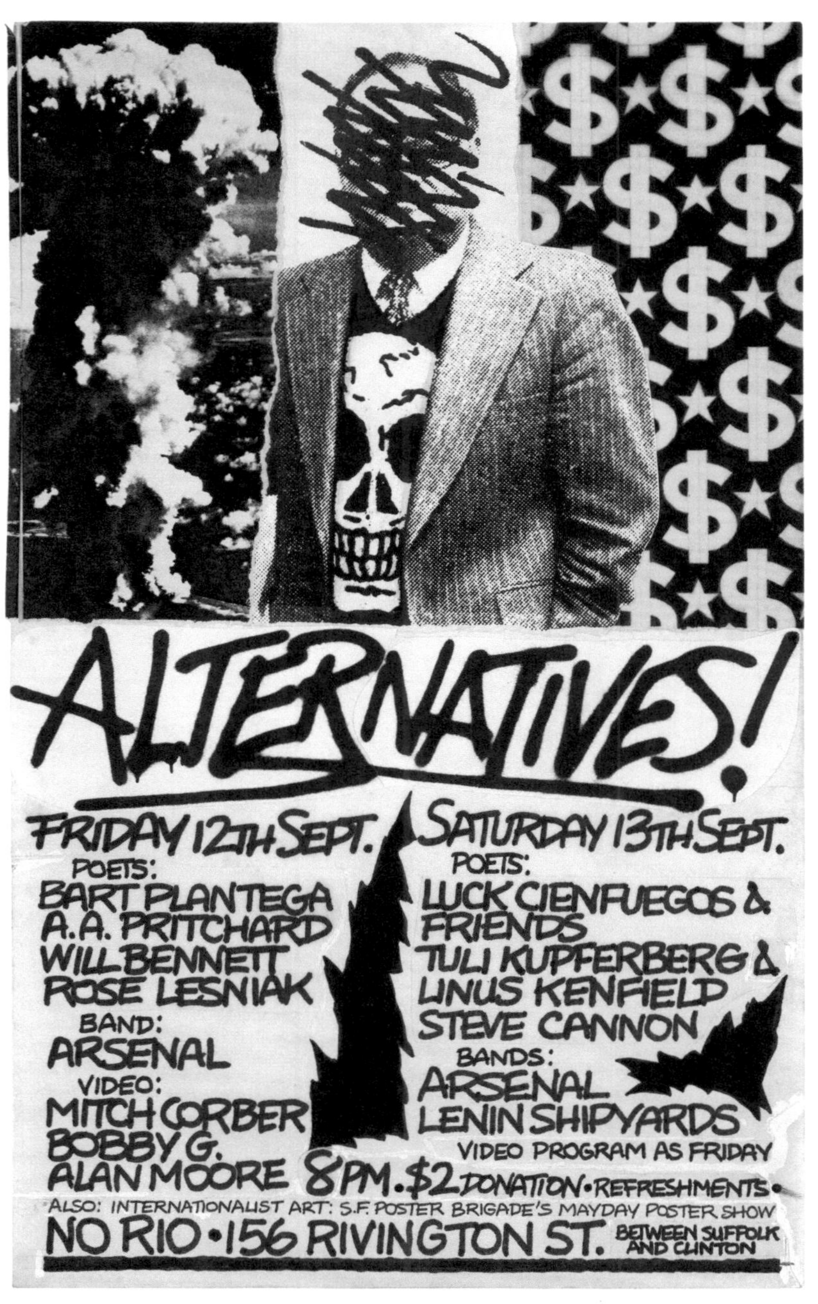

Flyer for *Arsenal at ABC No Rio*,
New York, September 12 and 13, 1980
Photocopy, 8.5 x 14 in. (21.6 x 35.6 cm)

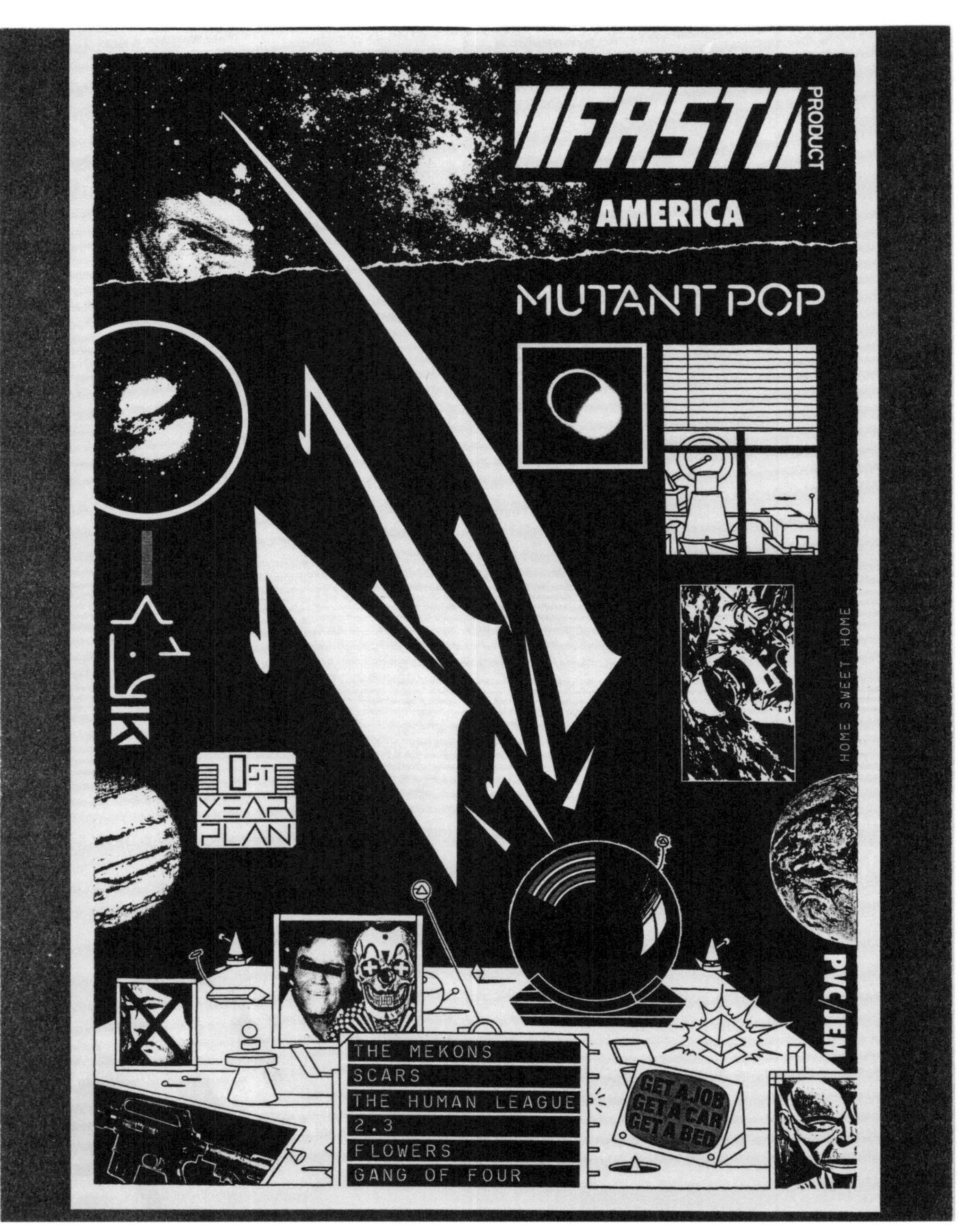

Flyer for *Mutant Pop*, 1978
Photocopy, 8.5 x 11 in. (21.6 x 27.9 cm)

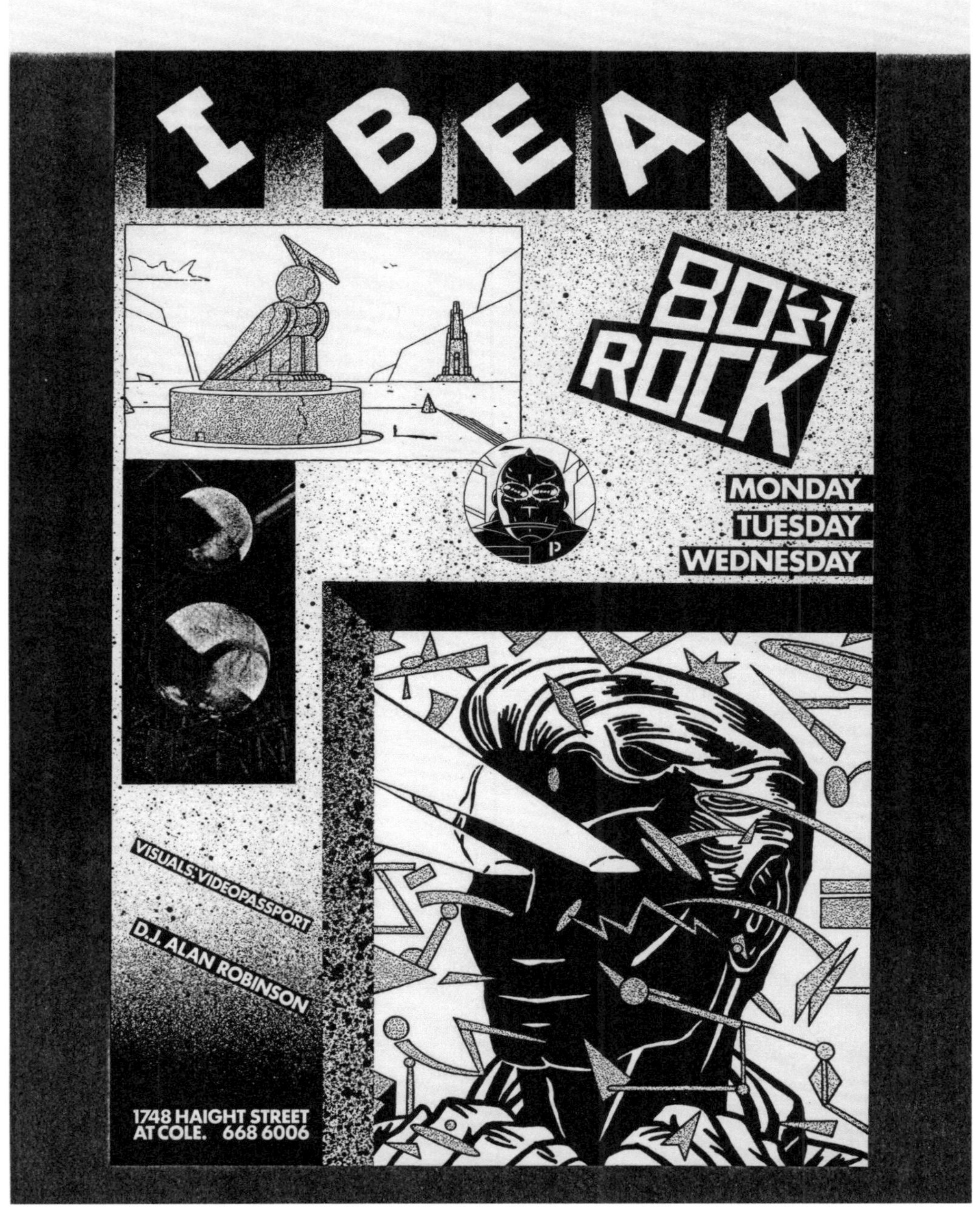

Flyer for *I Beam*, 1980s
Photocopy, 8.5 x 11 in. (21.6 x 27.9 cm)

Zines—mostly from the 1980s

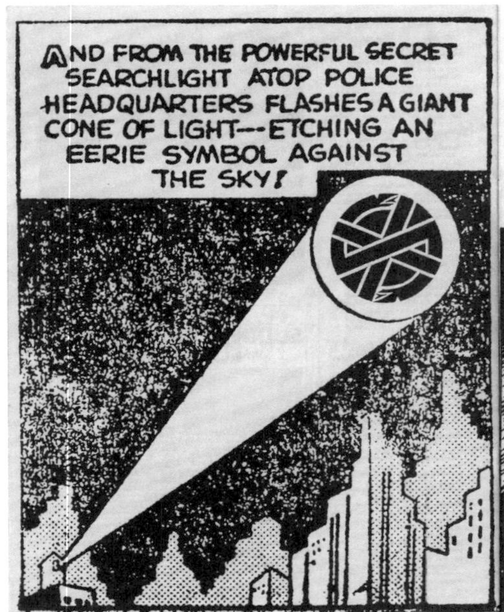

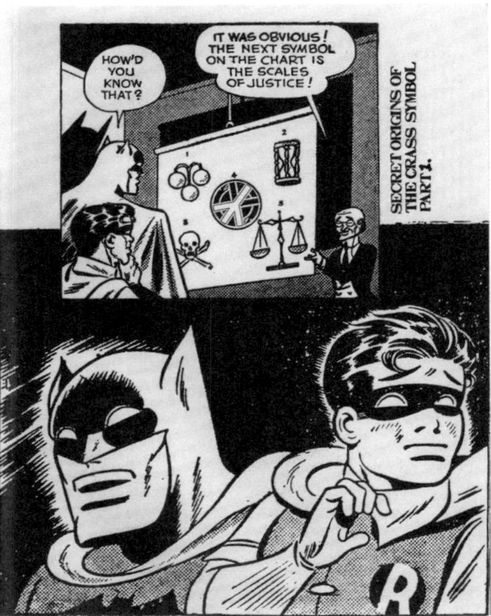

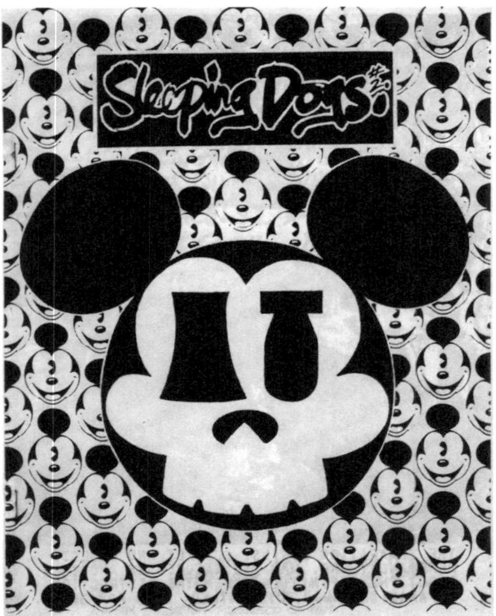

Above: *Sleeping Dogs #1*, interior spread, 1983
Offset, staple bound, 24 pages, 8.5 x 11 in.
(21.6 x 27.9 cm)

Left: Alternate cover for *Sleeping Dogs #2*, 1983
Photocopy, single sheet, 8.5 x 11 in.
(21.6 x 27.9 cm)

Facing page: *Sleeping Dogs #1*, 1983
Offset, staple bound, 24 pages, 8.5 x 11 in.
(21.6 x 27.9 cm)

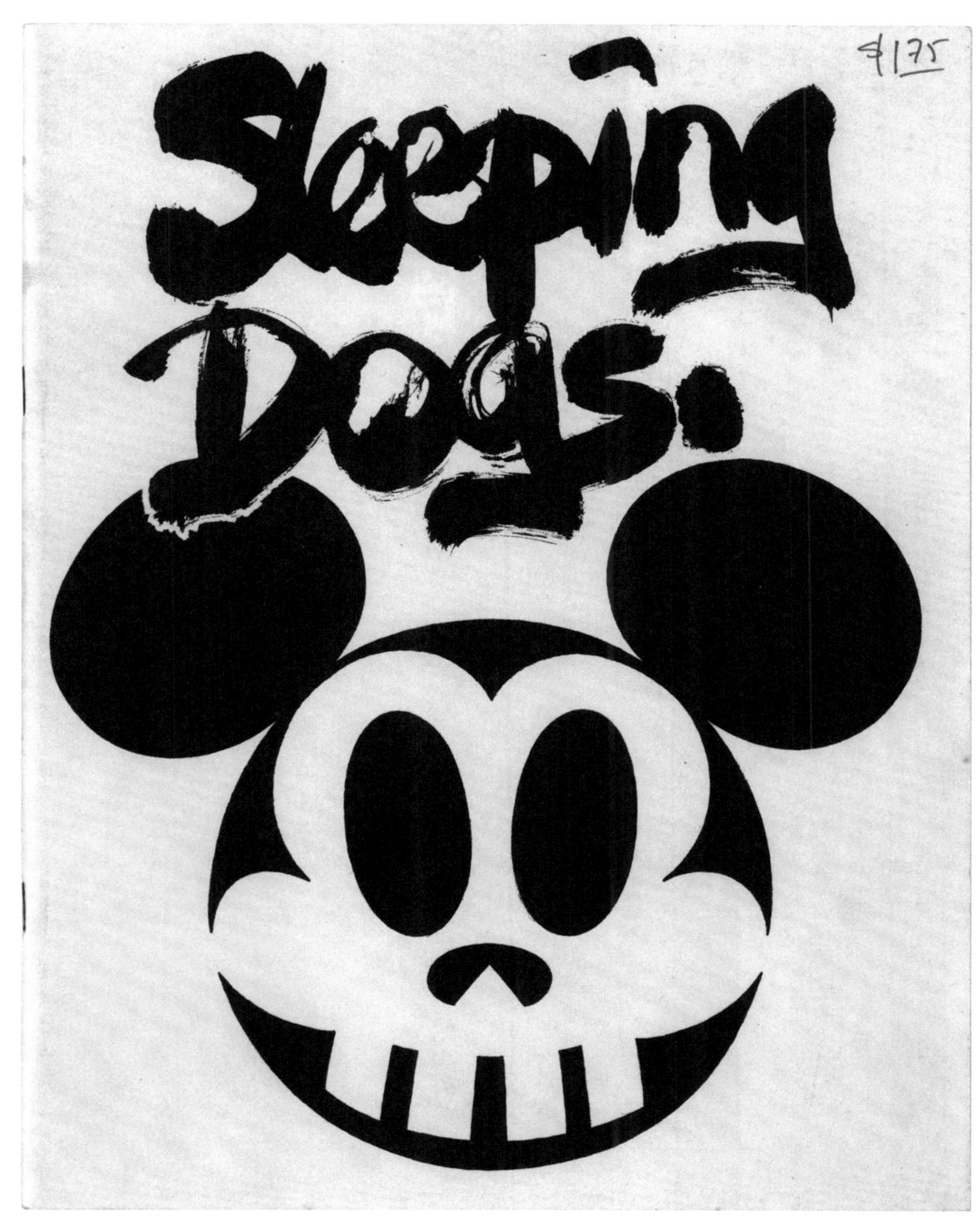
$1.75
Sleeping Dogs.

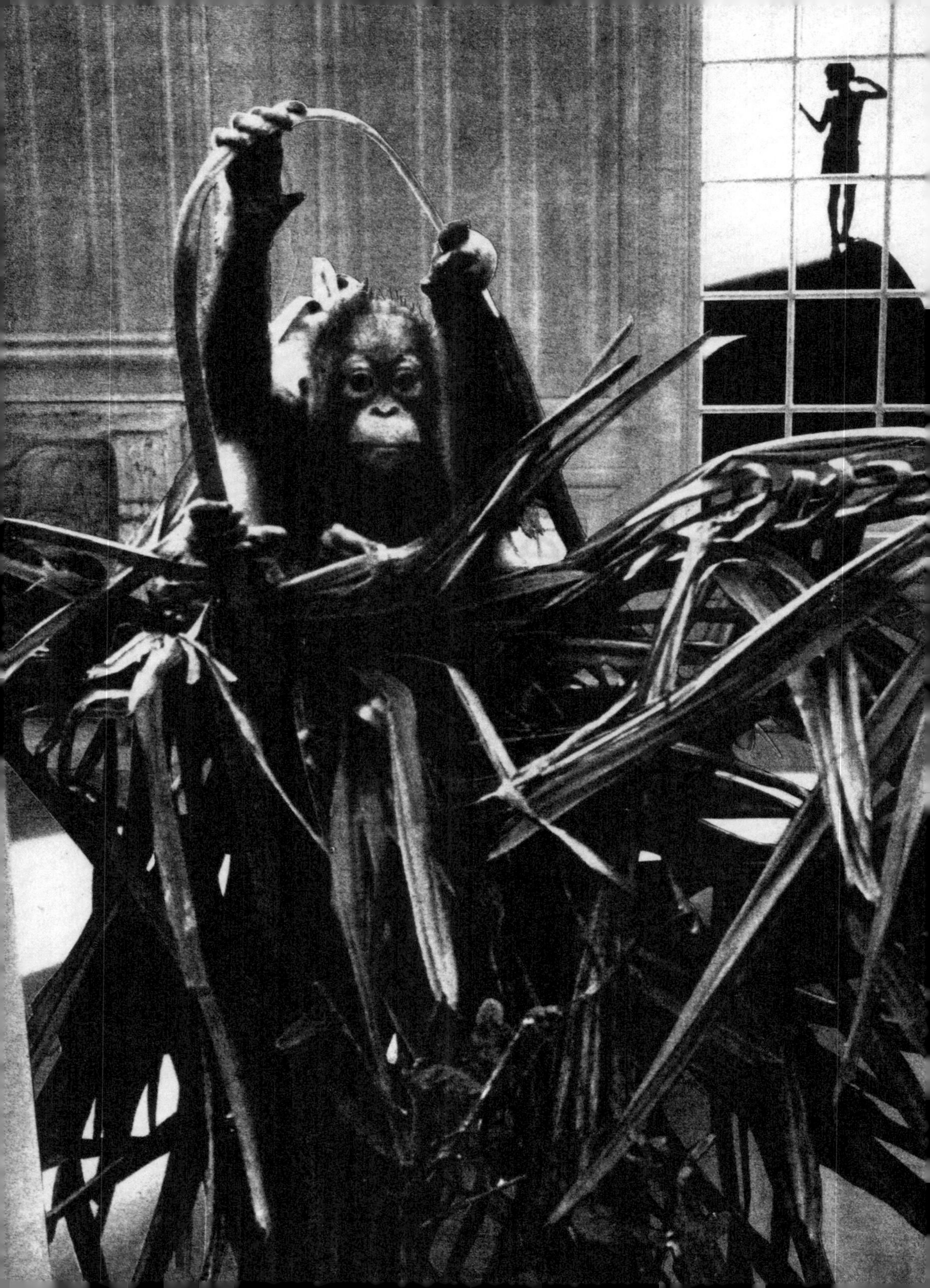

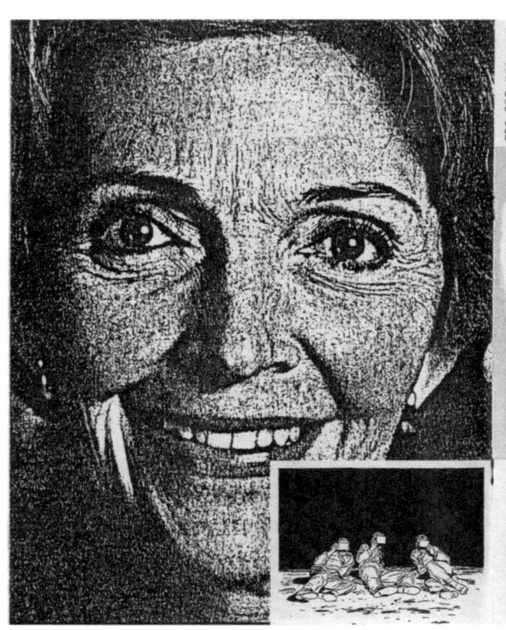

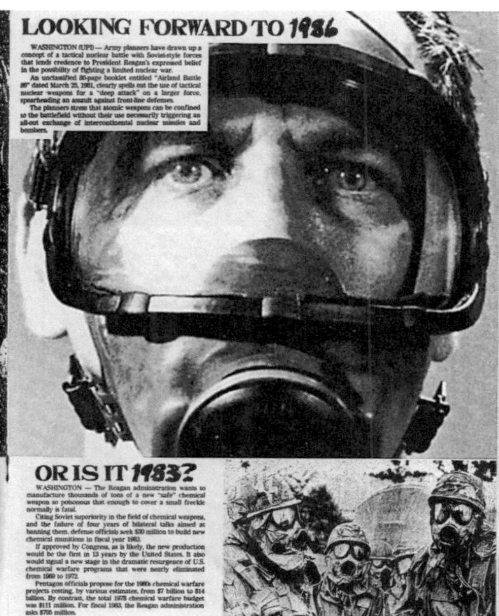

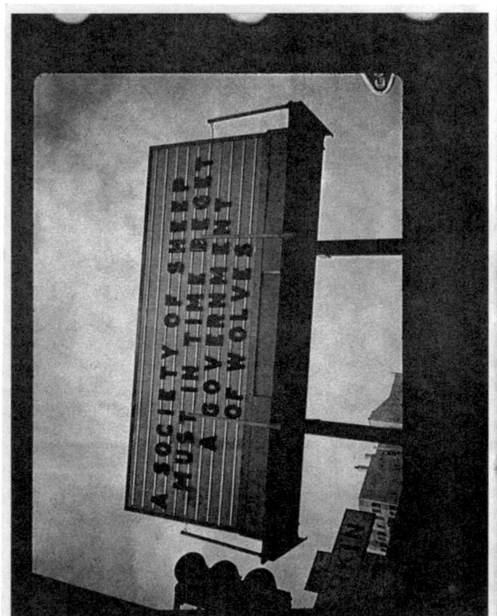

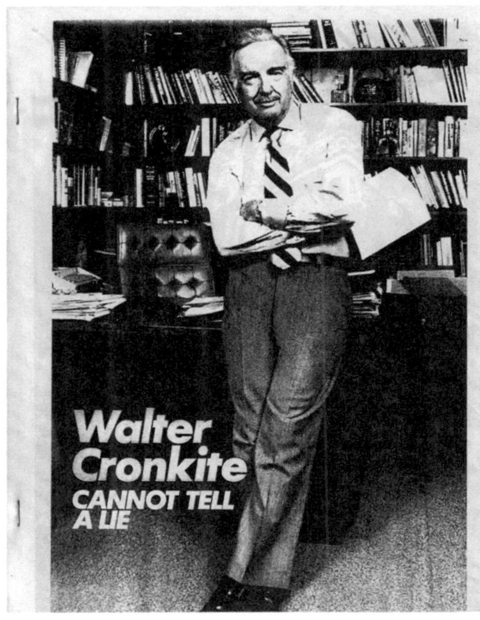

Facing page: Back cover detail, *Final Morning Extra 6: Free Poetry*, Contributors: Gatsby, Caroliner, KR, Chris/ Altamont, 1984, Photocopy, side stapled, 16 pages, 8.5 x 11 in. (21.6 x 27.9 cm)

Top: Interior spread, *Sleeping Dogs #1*, 1983, Offset, staple bound, 24 pages, 8.5 x 11 in. (21.6 x 27.9 cm)

Left: Back cover, *Sleeping Dogs #1*, 1983, Offset, staple bound, 24 pages, 8.5 x 11 in. (21.6 x 27.9 cm)

Right: Back cover, *Too Many Zombies #2*, Contributors: David King, Charlie Nash, 1984/85 Photocopy, side stapled, 6 pages, 8.5 x 11 in. (21.6 x 27.9 cm)

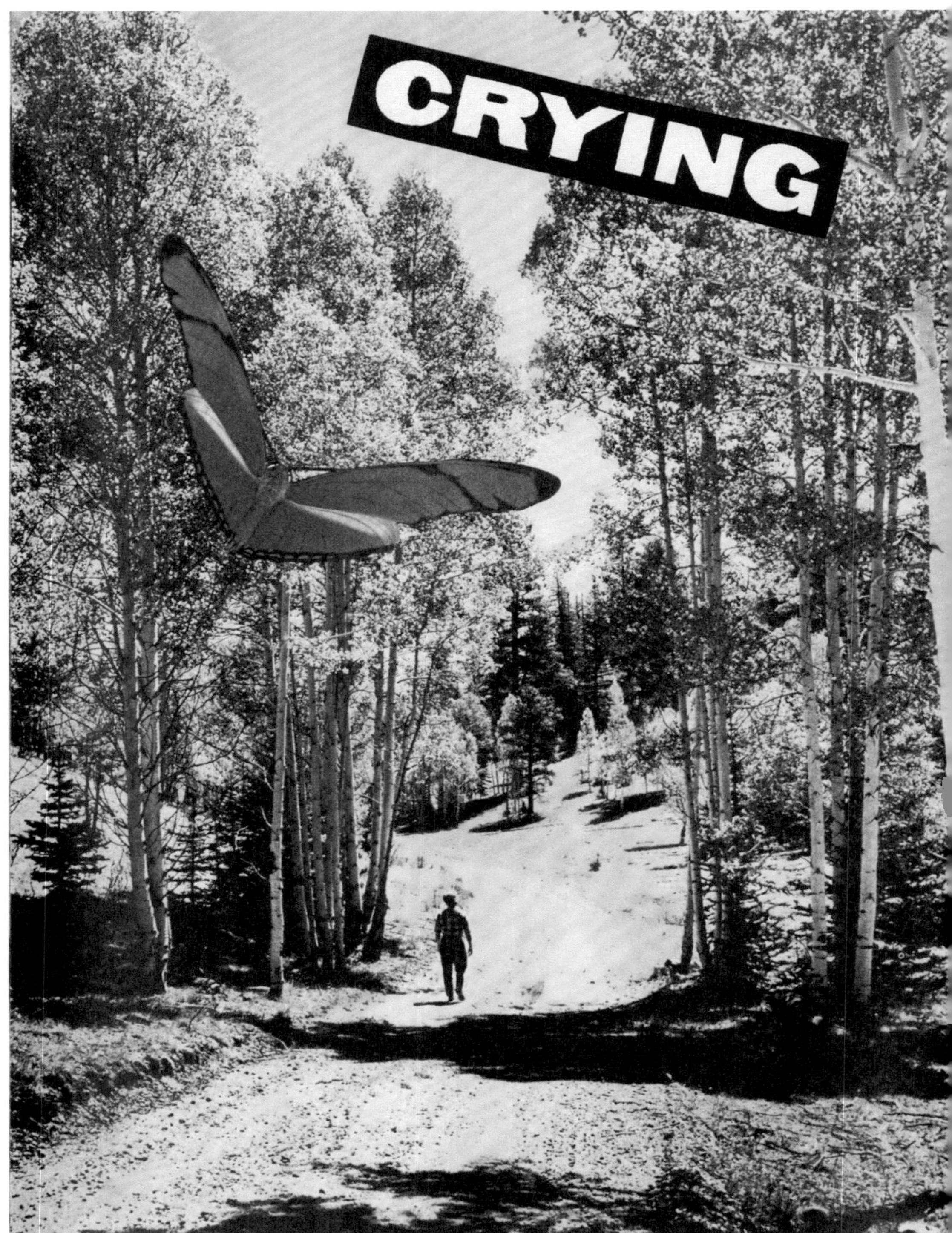
CRYING

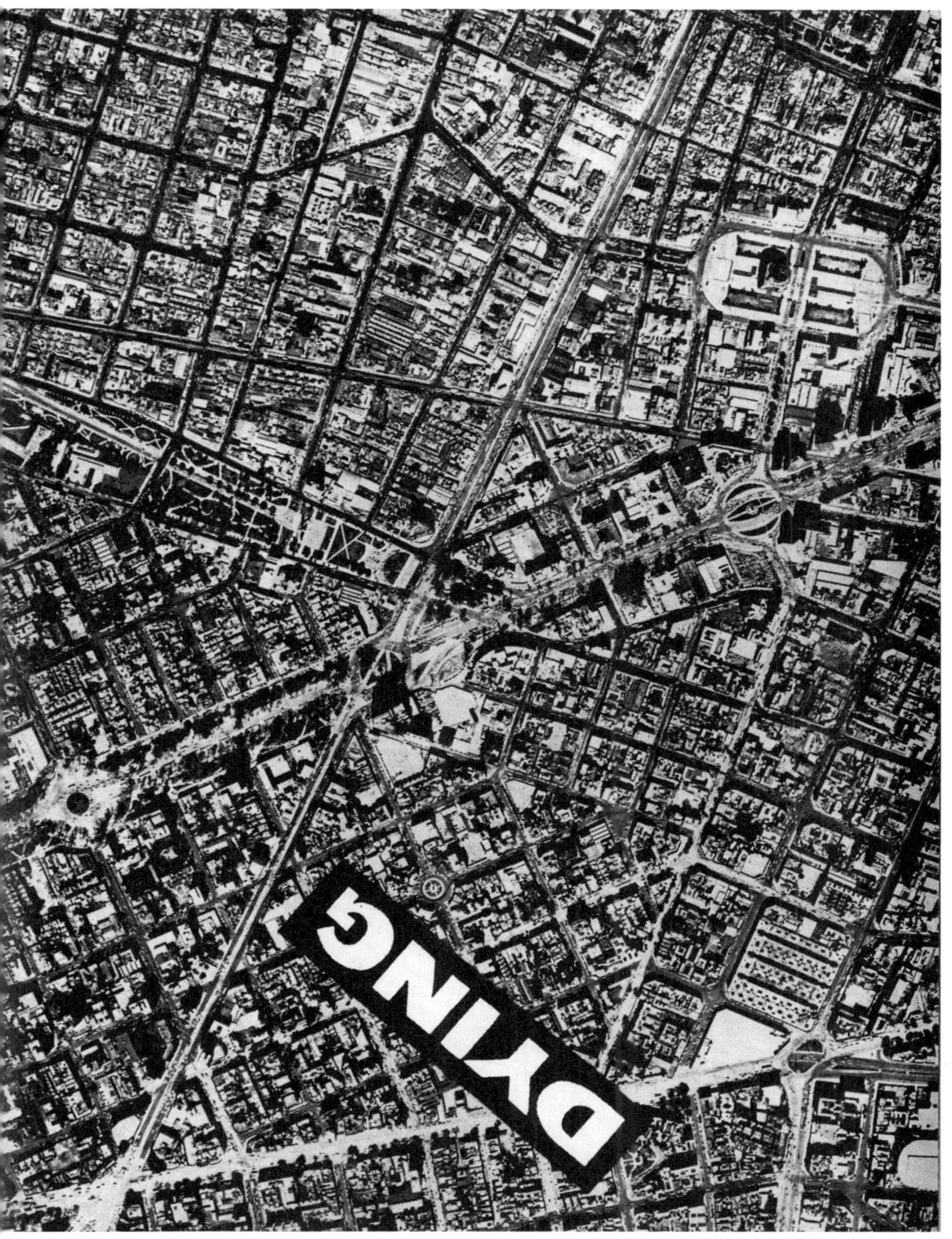
DYING

Pages 36–37: Interior spread,
Sleeping Dogs #2, 1983
Offset, staple bound, 28 pages, 8.5 x 11 in.
(21.6 x 27.9 cm)

Below: Interior spreads,
Suburbs of Hell, 1980s
Photocopy, slide bound, 38 pages, 8.5 x 11 in.
(21.6 x 27.9 cm)

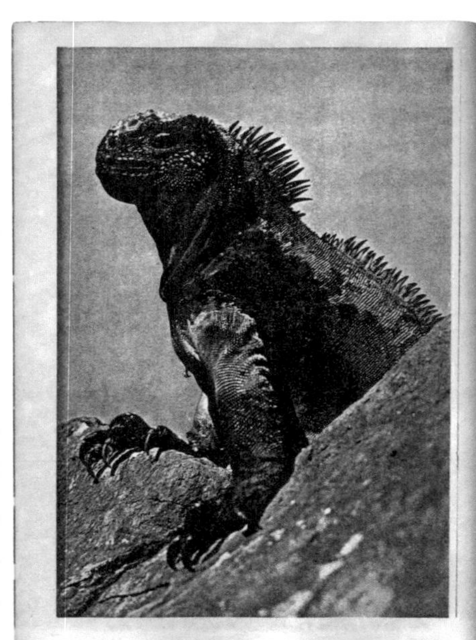

THE SOUND OF FEET WALKING ON A CRUNCHING GRAVEL PATH CAN BE REASSURING.

IT OFFERS SOME CONFIRMATION OF THIS REALITY.

THE PAVEMENT FELT SOLID BENEATH HIS FEET, BUT STILL HE WAS AFRAID OF FALLING THROUGH IT.

THE PLANE FLYING PAST HIS WINDOW CEASED TO MOVE AND HUNG MOTIONLESS IN THE SKY. THE HOUSE IN WHICH HE SAT BORROWED THE PLANES MOVEMENT AND DIRECTION. AS THE AIR RUSHED PAST THE HOUSE, OR AS THE HOUSE RUSHED PAST THE AIR, HE BEGAN TO RELAX, AND WENT BACK TO READING THE PAPER.

A CHILD WITH A DUMMY IN ITS MOUTH REGARDED HIM WITH WIDE-EYED ALARM, BUT PRESENTLY LAPSED INTO SLEEP.

THE CHILDS MOTHER, WHO WAS WEARING A DRESS PRINTED WITH LARGE SUNFLOWERS, (EACH BLOOM MEASURING ABOUT FIFTEEN INCHES ACROSS), LAID HER CHARGE OUT ROUGHLY ON THE DOUBLE SEAT LIKE AN UNWANTED BUNDLE.

AS SHE DID SO, HER FOOT NUDGED A USED COKE CAN, LYING HALF FLATTENED ON THE FLOOR.

THE LAST DREGS OF THE AMBER LIQUID SPILLED FROM IT LIKE TRICKLING BLOOD.

HE GLANCED UP SUDDENLY AND, OUT OF THE CORNER OF HIS EYE, SAW SOMETHING FLY BY (DARK, LEATHERY, FLAPPING) THAT LOOKED LIKE A PTERODACTYL.

AS HE RAN, HIS RIGHT FOOT HIT A TRIP WIRE.

THERE WAS A ROAR, A CRACKLE LIKE THAT OF FRYING BACON, NO AUDIBLE SCREAM, AND AN AFTERMATH OF HALF CLOTHED PORTIONS OF HIS BLOODIED FLESH.

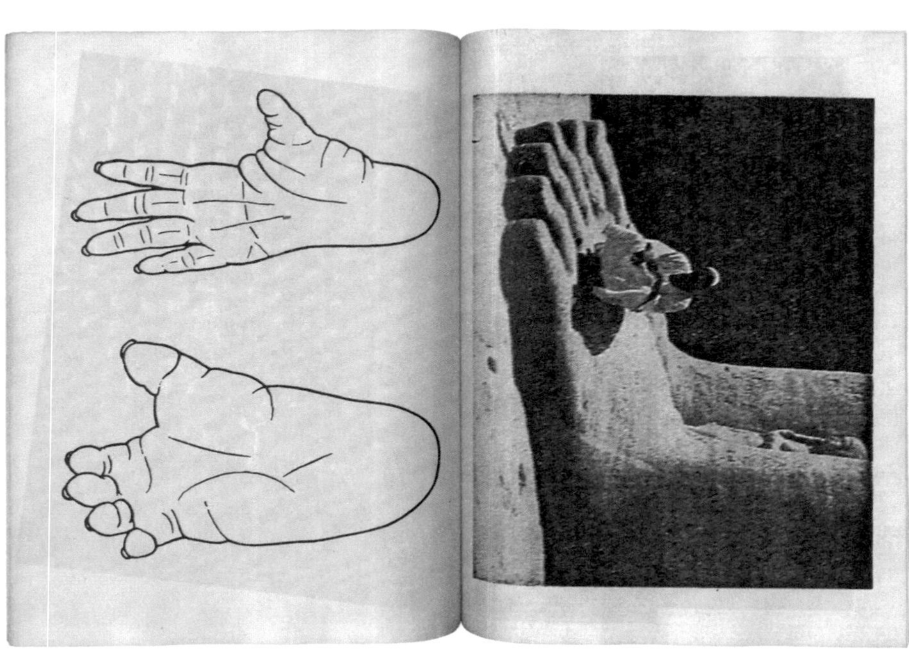

Suburbs of Hell, 1980s
Photocopy, slide bound, 38 pages, 8.5 x 11 in. (21.6 x 27.9 cm)

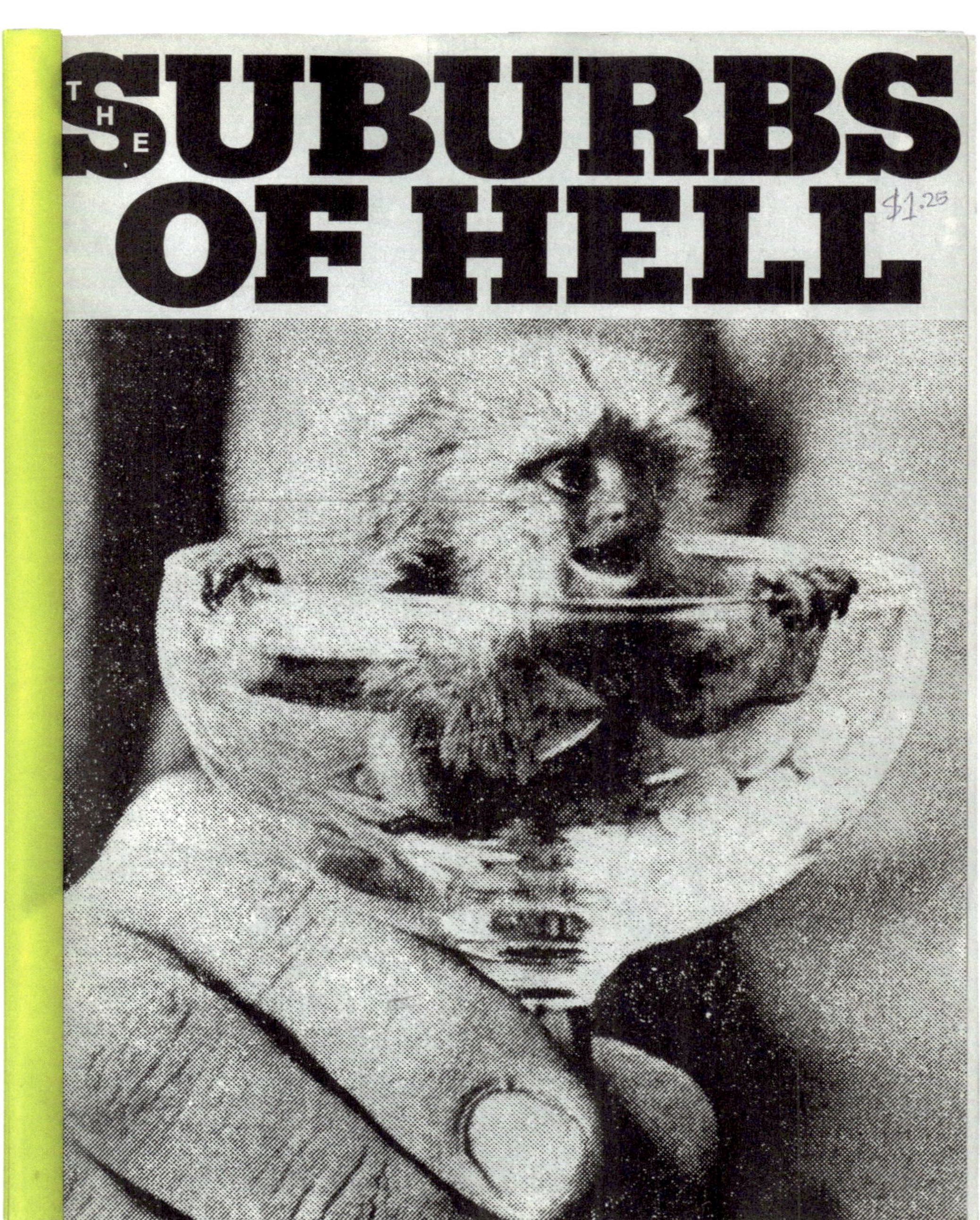

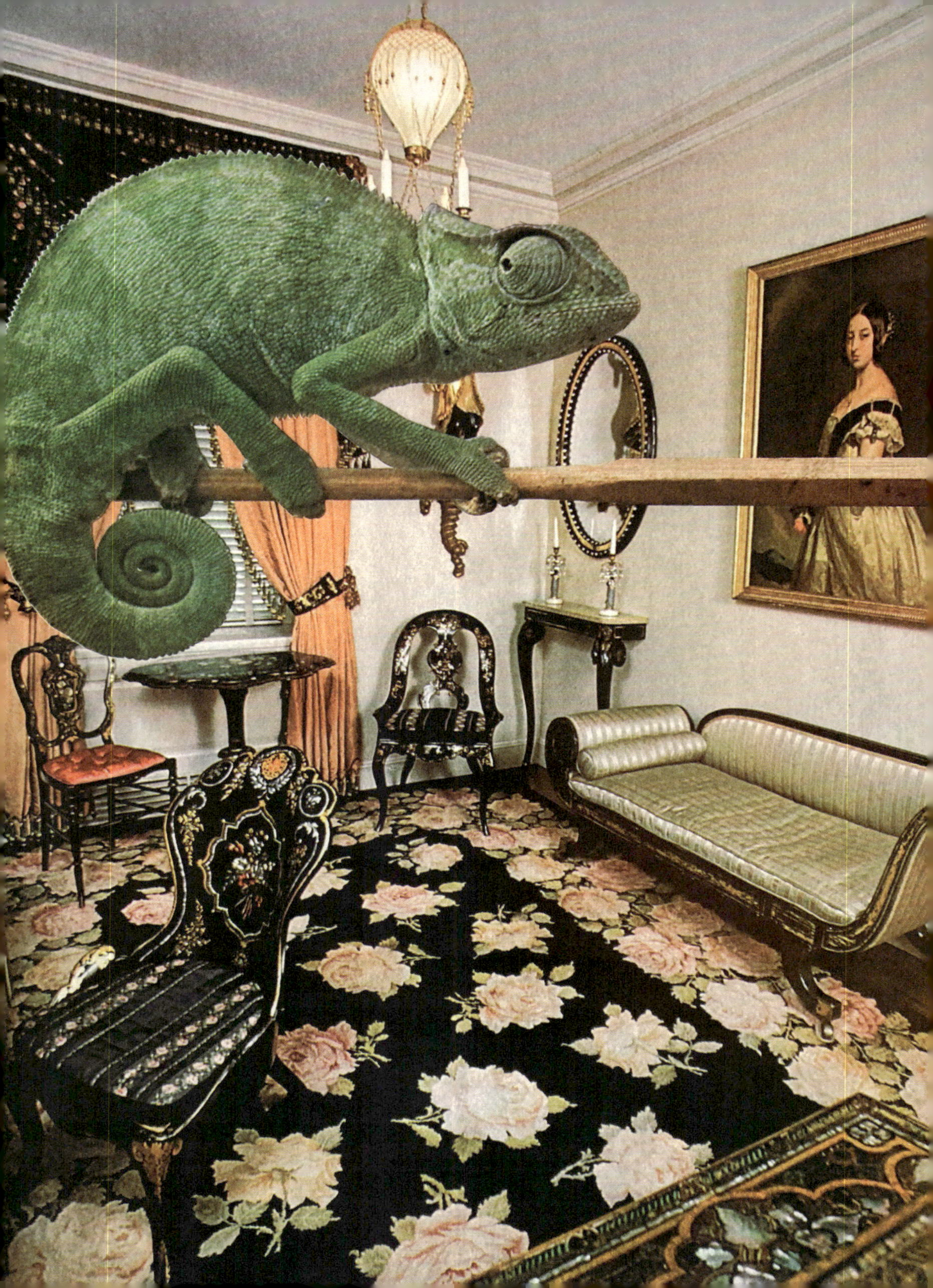

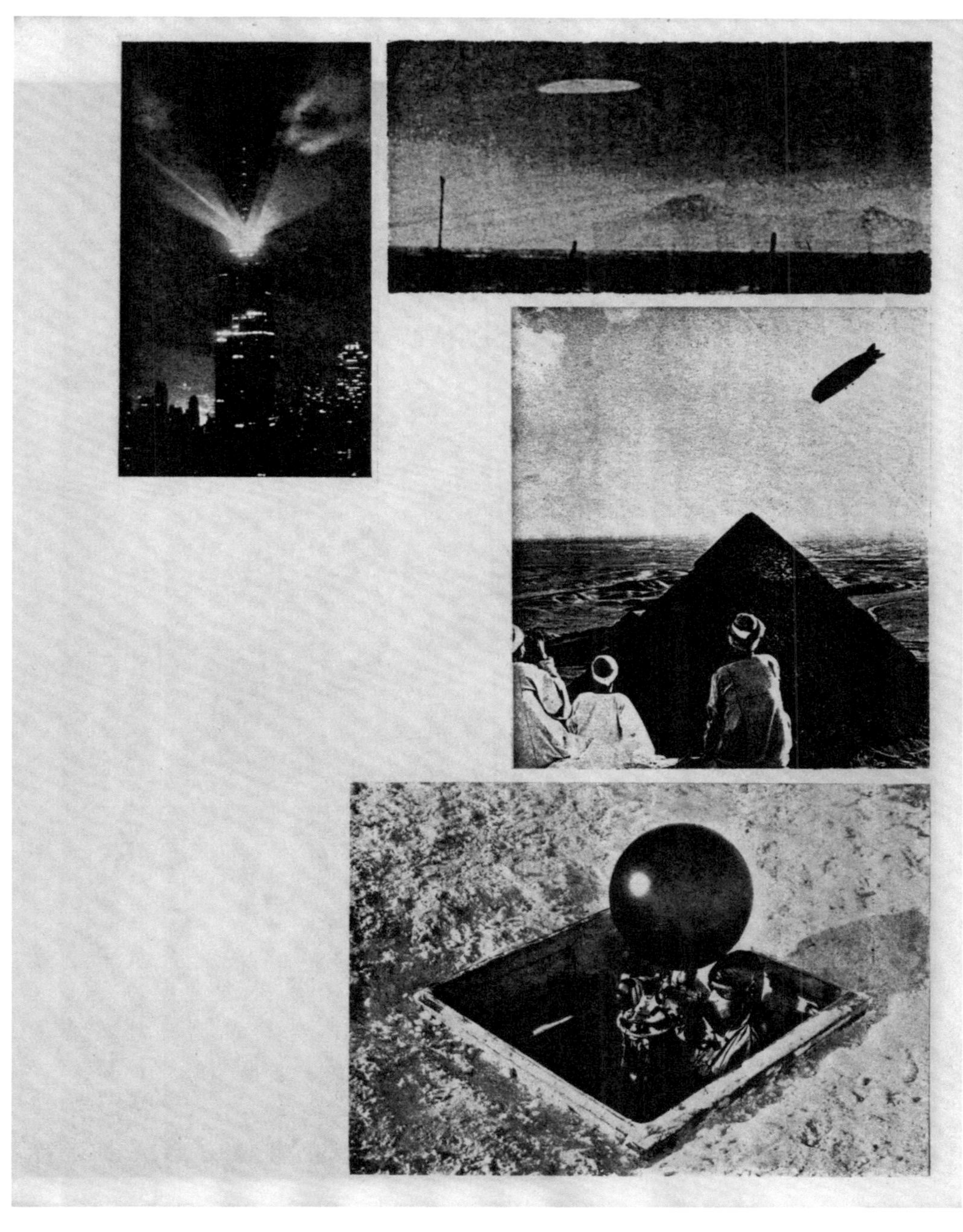

Facing page: Collage paste-up for *Beware #2*, 1981/82
Photocopy, side stapled, 12 pages, 8.5 x 11 in.
(21.6 x 27.9 cm)

Above: Interior page, *Suburbs of Hell*, 1980s
Photocopy, slide bound, 38 pages, 8.5 x 11 in.
(21.6 x 27.9 cm)

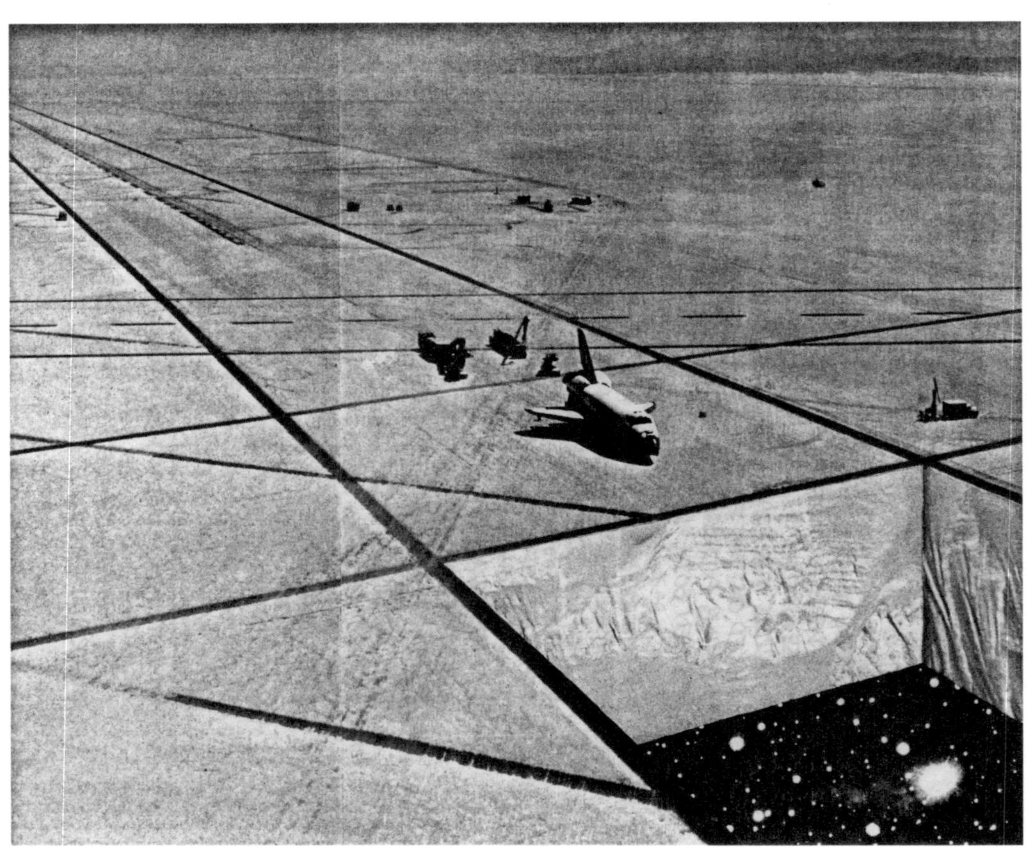

Above: Interior page, *Suburbs of Hell*, 1980s
Photocopy, slide bound, 38 pages, 8.5 x 11 in.
(21.6 x 27.9 cm)

Facing page: *Untitled altered image*, 1980s
Found image with pencil and ink, 9 x 11″ in.
(22.9 x 27.9 cm)

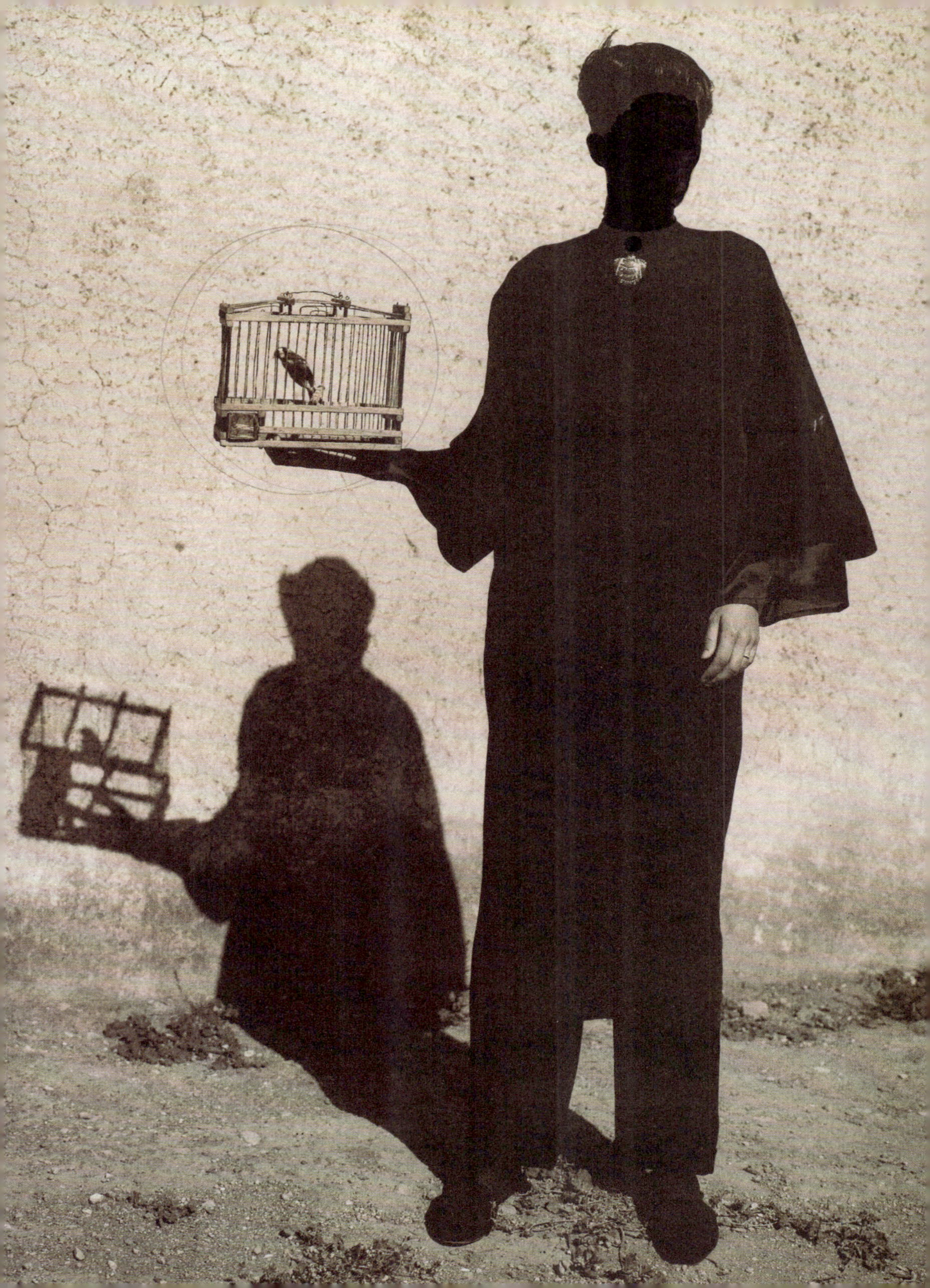

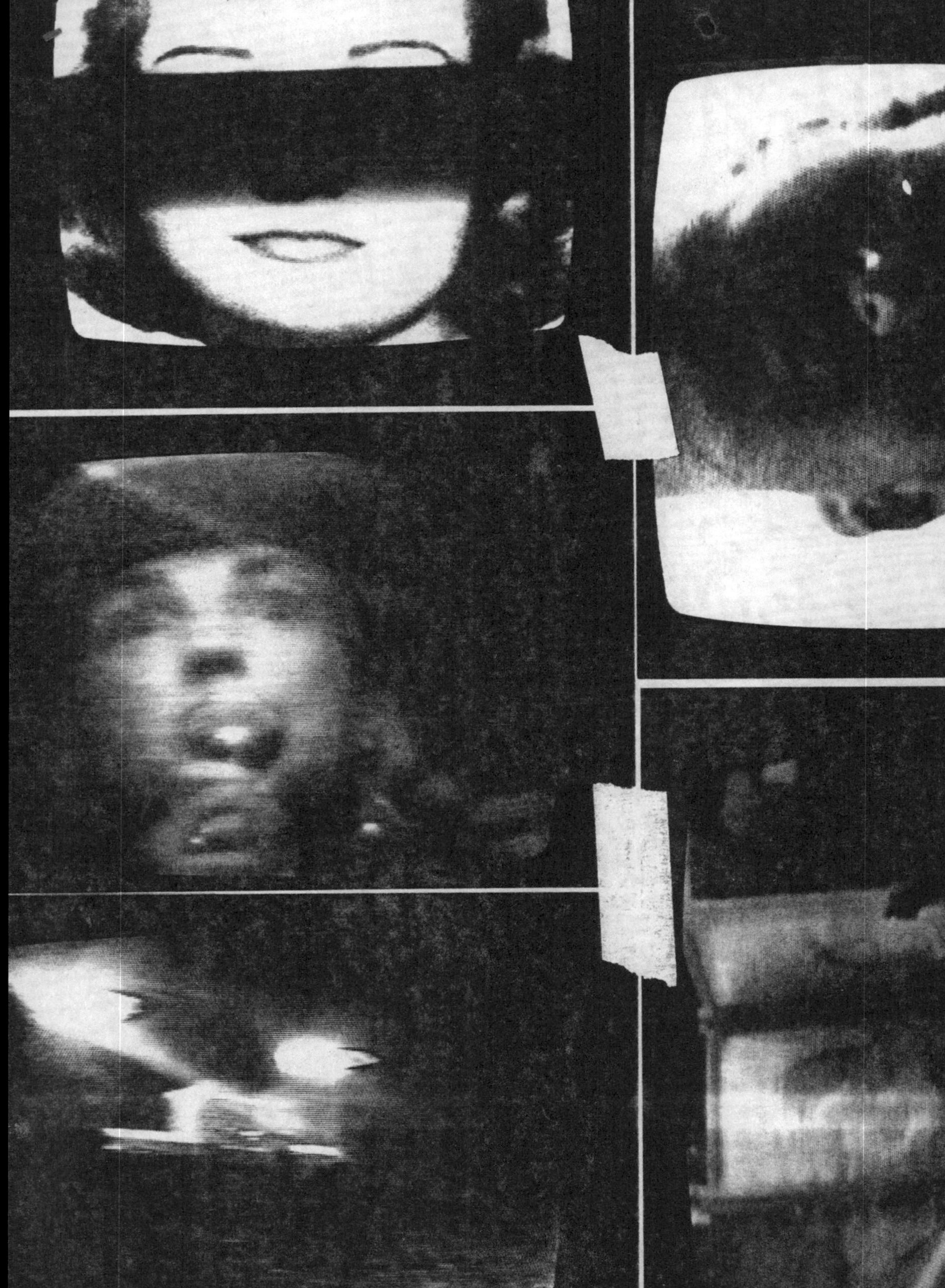

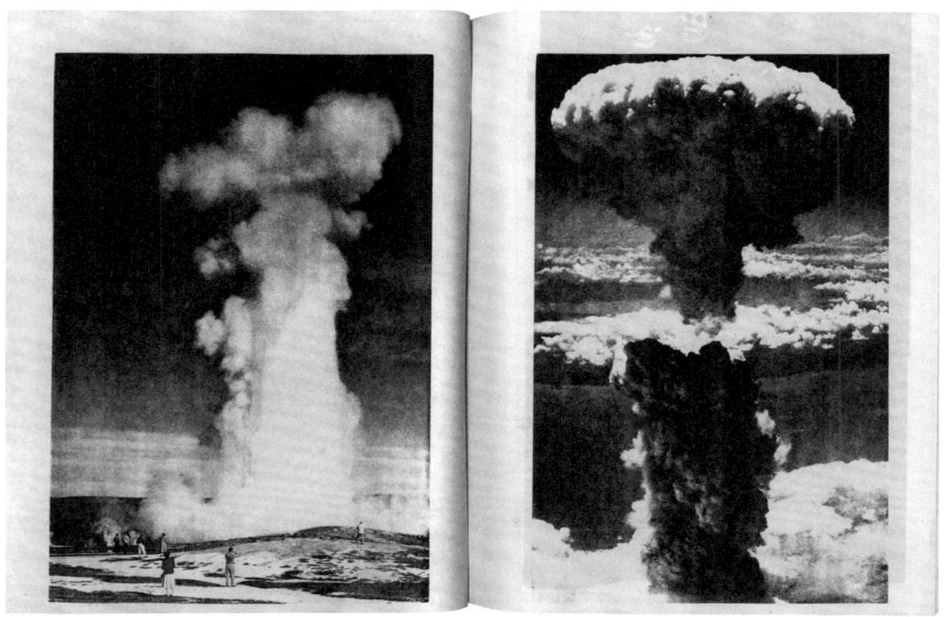

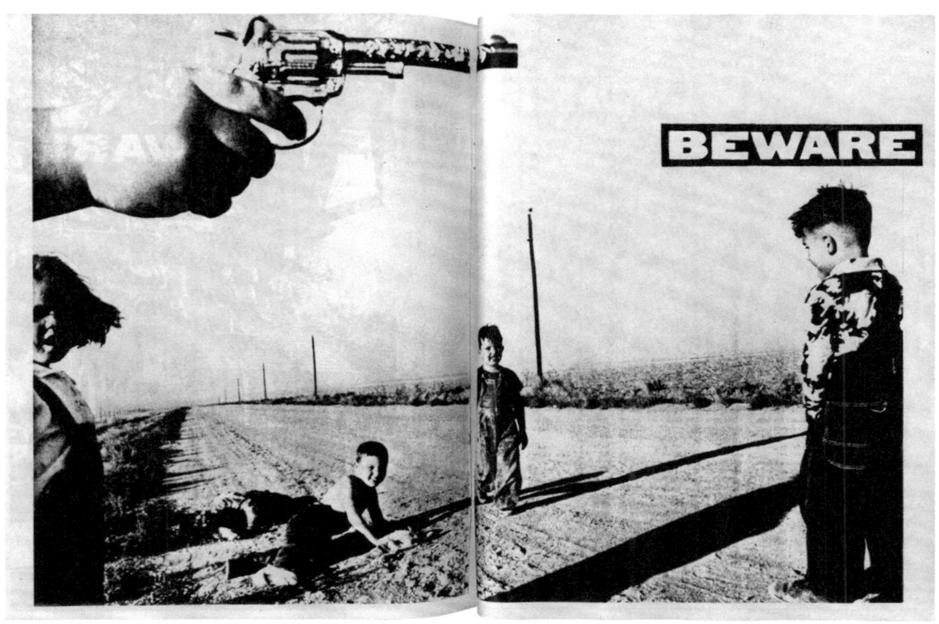

Facing page: *Don't Believe Them*, promo zine for *Sleeping Dogs: Don't Believe Them*, a video by Steve Bull, 1984
Photocopy, side stapled, 6 pages, 8.5 x 11 in. (21.6 x 27.9 cm)

Top: *Dead Men's Clothes as Too Many Zombies*, 1984/85
Photocopy, side stapled, 14 pages,
8.5 x 11 in. (21.6 x 27.9 cm)

Bottom: *Beware #1*, 1981/82
Photocopy, side stapled, 8 pages, 8.5 x 11 in. (21.6 x 27.9 cm)

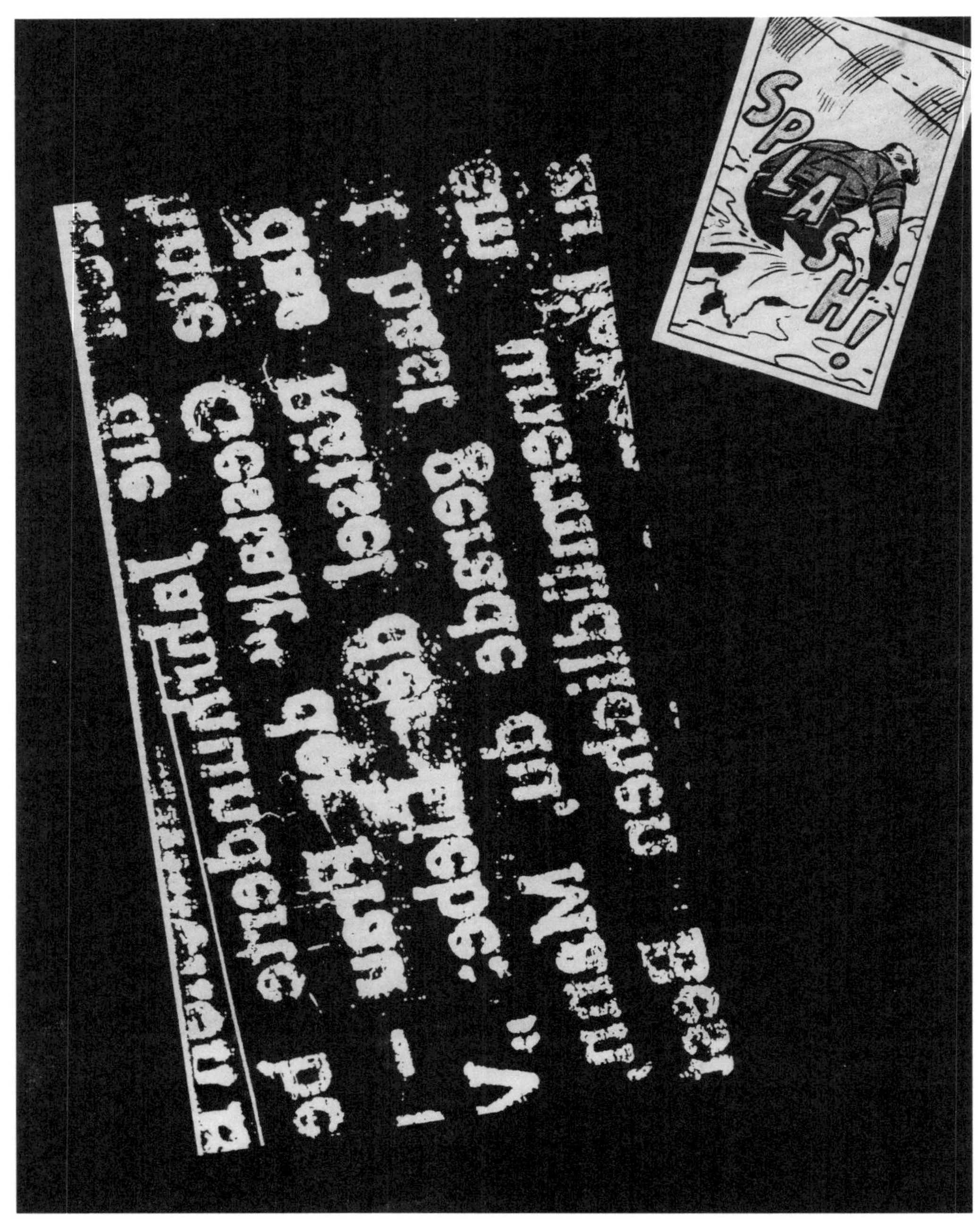

Interior page, *No 1 #1*, Contributors: Beate Prido, Margot Koch, Dirty Dog (David King), 1987
Photocopy, side stapled, 10 pages,
8.5 x 11 in. (21.6 x 27.9 cm)

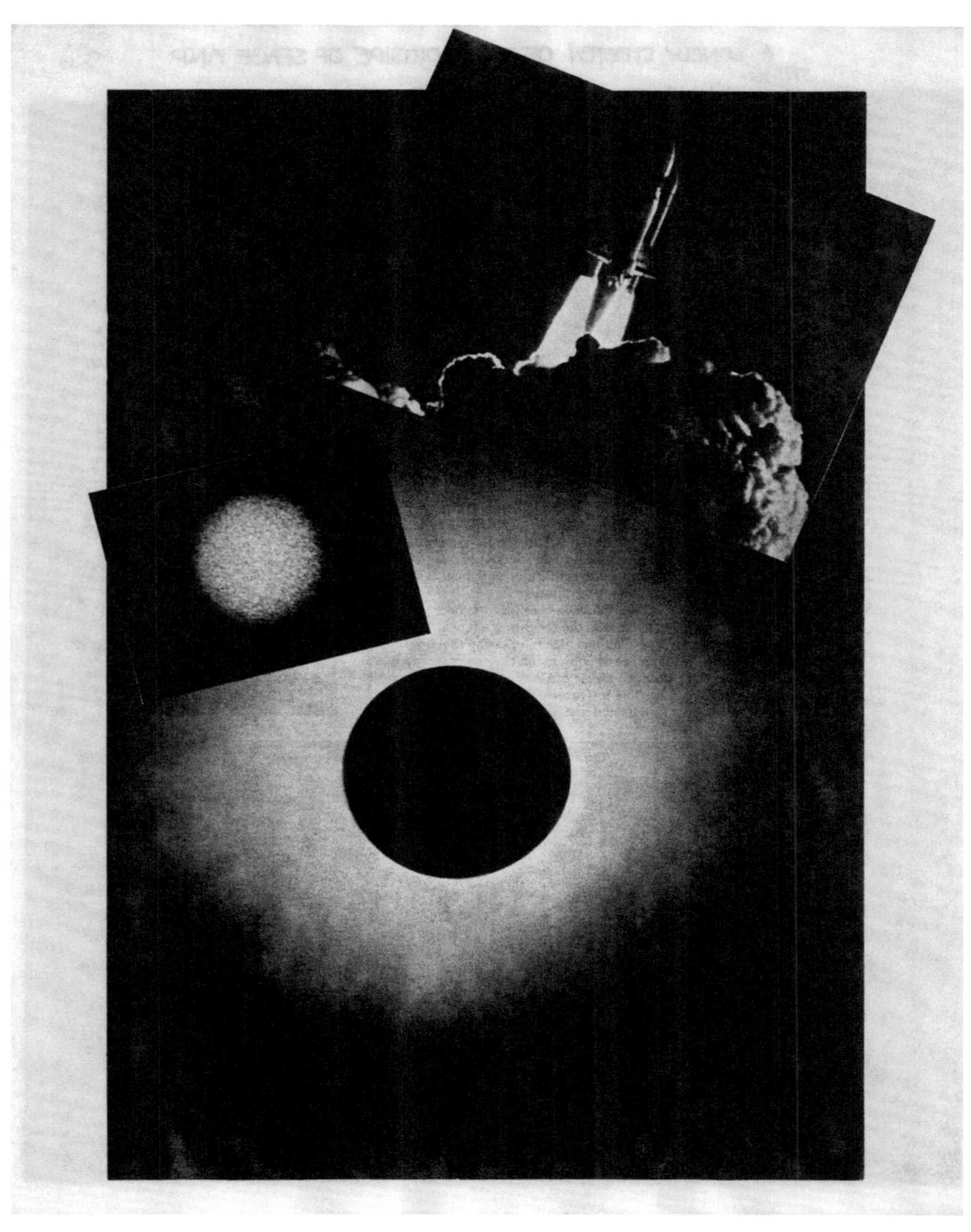

Interior page, *Suburbs of Hell*, 1980s
Photocopy, slide bound, 38 pages,
8.5 x 11 in. (21.6 x 27.9 cm)

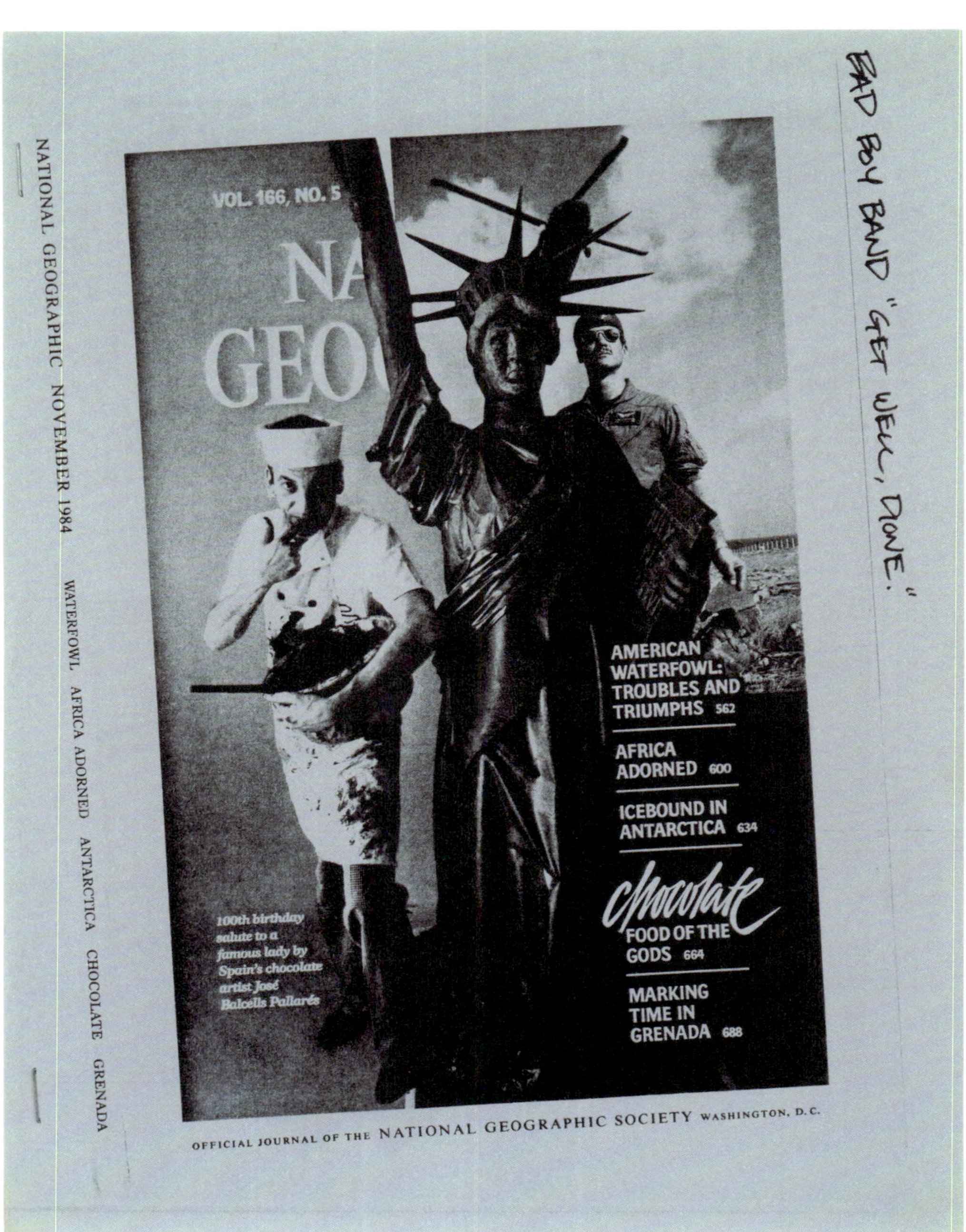

Brain Rust Zine #1, 1984
Photocopy, side stapled, 4 pages,
8.5 x 11 in. (21.6 x 27.9 cm)

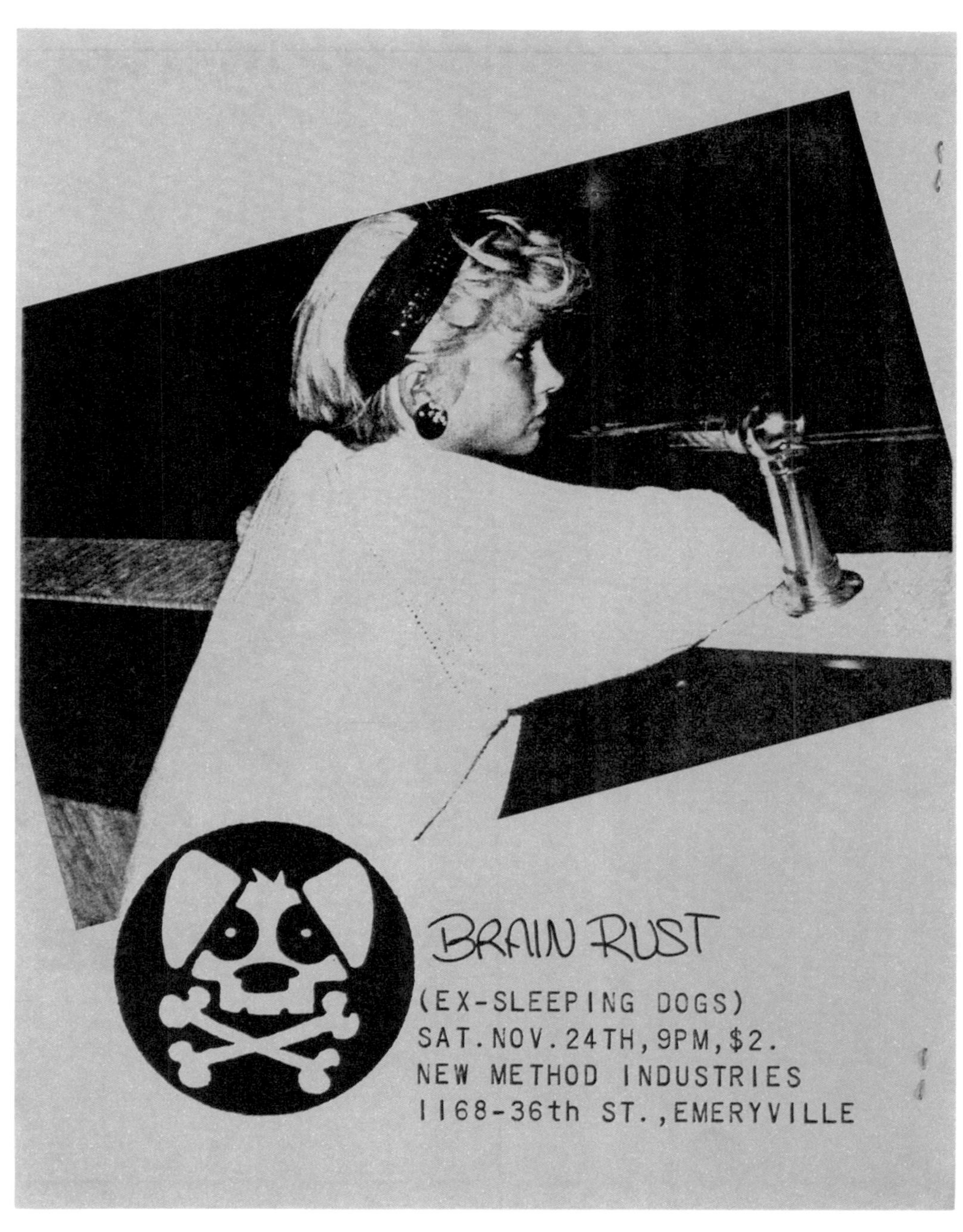

Back cover, *Brain Rust Zine #1*, 1984
Photocopy, side stapled, 4 pages,
8.5 x 11 in. (21.6 x 27.9 cm)

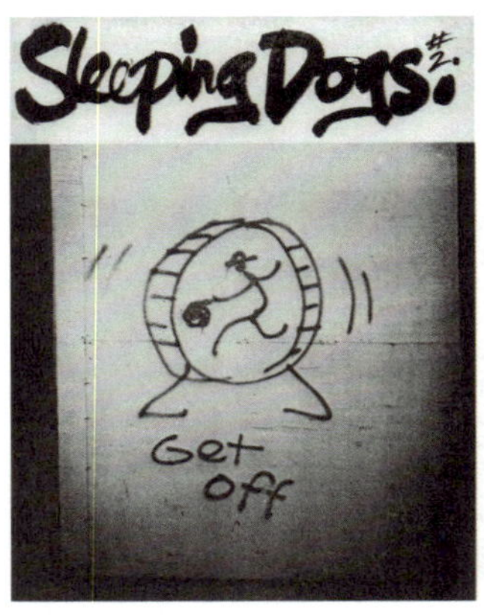

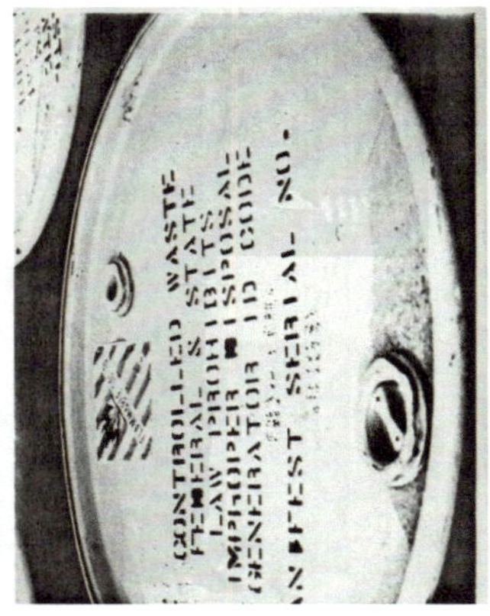

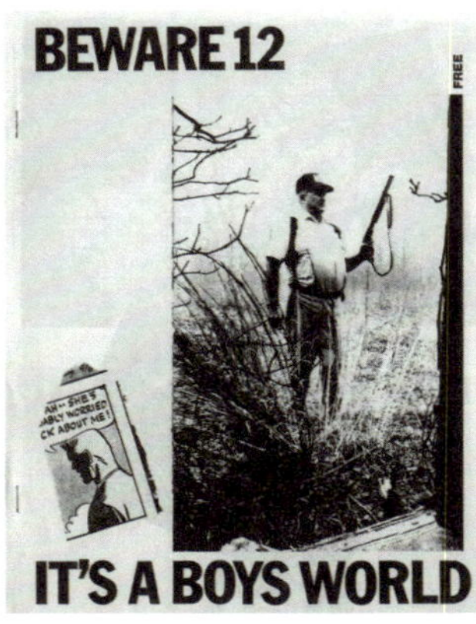

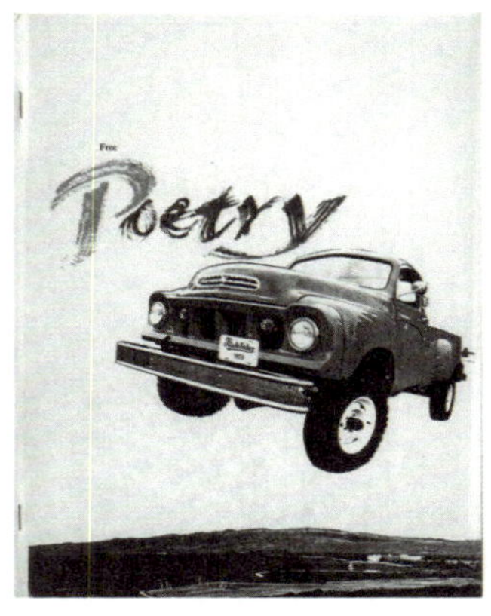

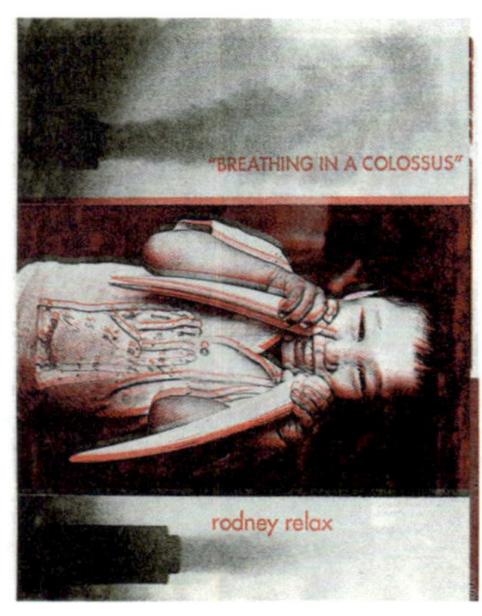

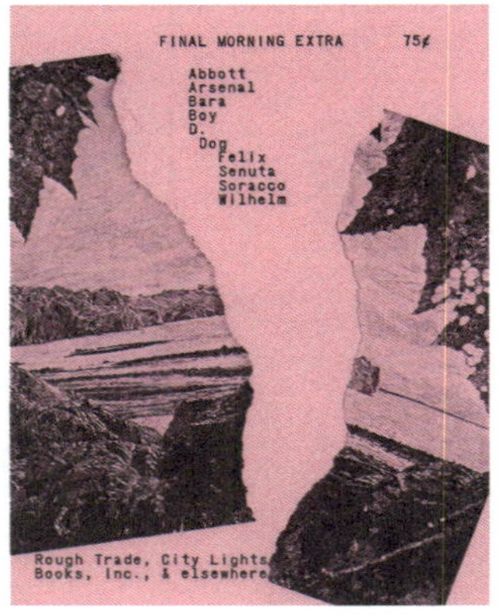

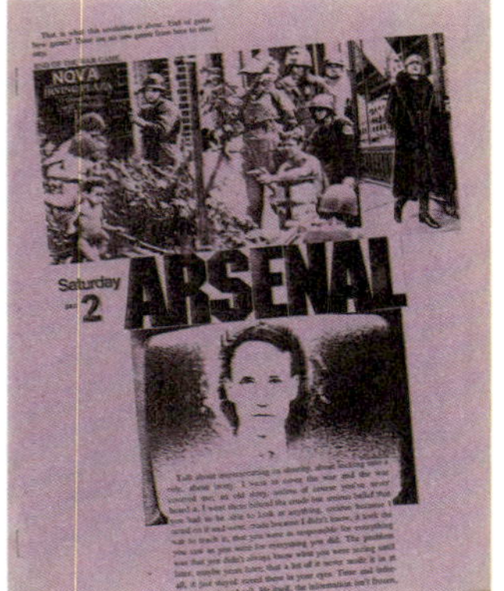

Left to right, top to bottom:
Sleeping Dogs #2, 1983
Offset, staple bound, 28 pages,
8.5 x 11 in. (21.6 x 27.9 cm)

Too Many Zombies Mailer,
Contributors: David King,
Charlie Nash, 1984/85
Photocopy, side stapled, 4 pages,
7 x 8.5 in. (17.8 x 21.6 cm)

Beware #12, 1981/82
Photocopy, side stapled, 6 pages,
8.5 x 11 in. (21.6 x 27.9 cm)

Final Morning Extra 6: Free Poetry,
Contributors: Gatsby, Caroliner,
KR and Chris/ Altamont, 1984
Photocopy, side stapled, 16 pages,
8.5 x 11 in. (21.6 x 27.9 cm)

Dreaming in a Colossus by Rodney
Relax, Published by .xtrasensual.
Press, Type: Freddie Baer,
Graphics: Skazoo & Dirty Dog
(David King), 1990
Two color Xerox, staple bound,
6 pages with foldout, 8.5 x 11 in.
(21.6 x 27.9 cm)

Flyer for *Final Morning
Extra*, 1980s
Photocopy, 8.5 x 11 in.
(21.6 x 27.9 cm)

Too Many Zombies #11,
Contributors: David King,
Charlie Nash, 1984/85
Photocopy, side stapled, 4 pages,
8.5 x 11 in. (21.6 x 27.9 cm)

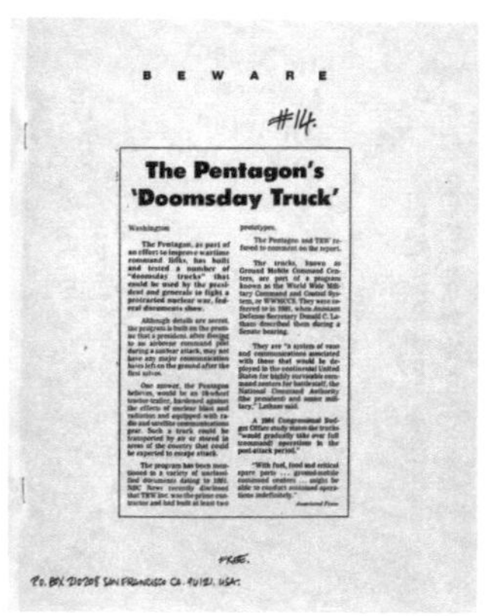

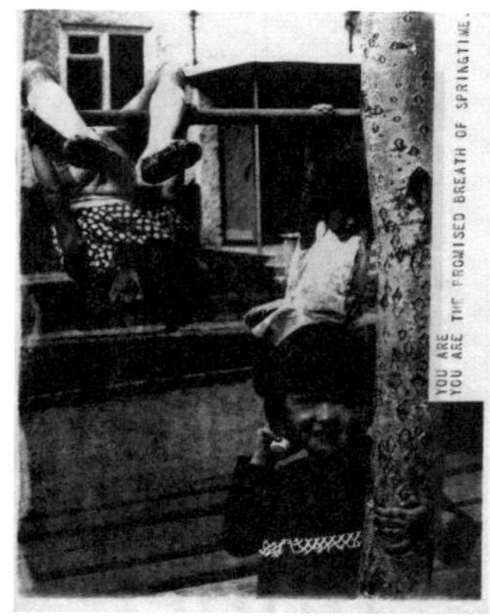

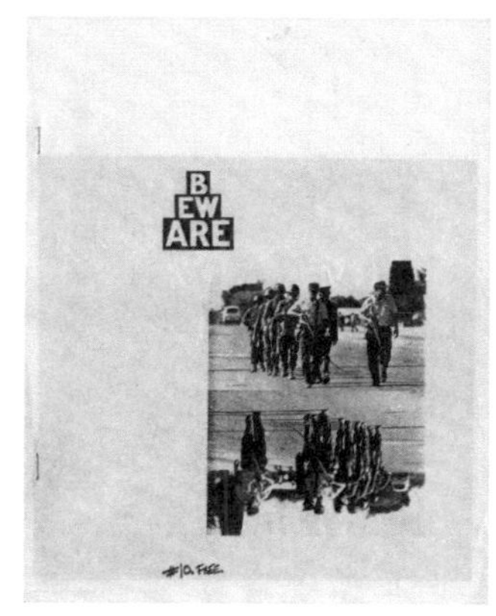

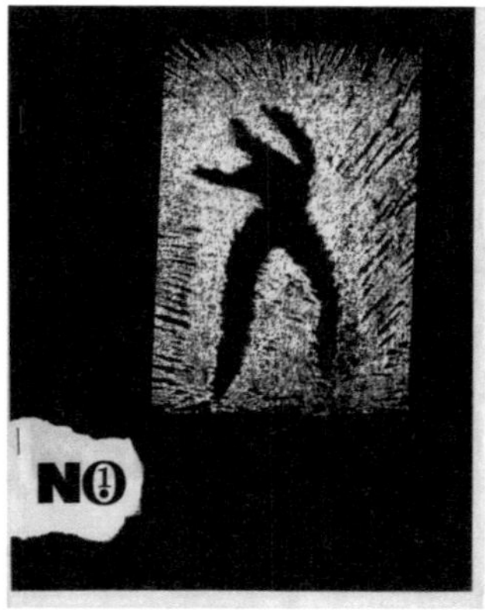

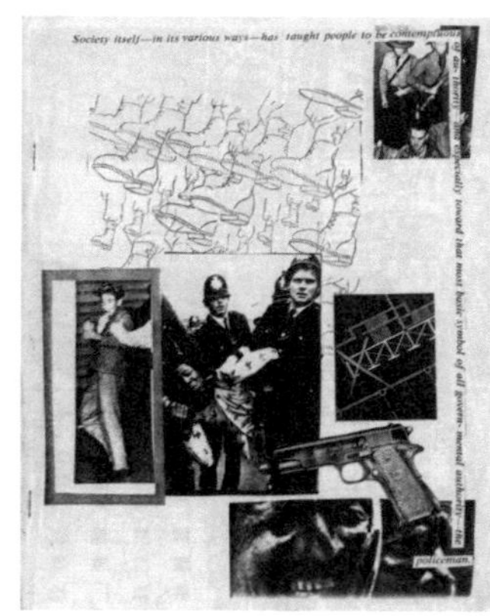

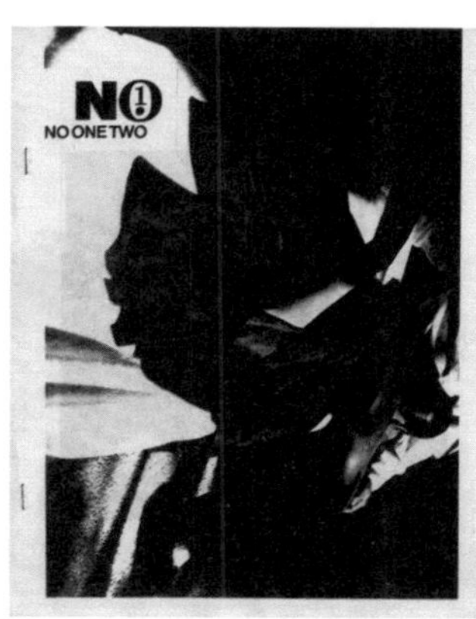

Left to right, top to bottom:
Beware #14, 1981/82
Photocopy, side stapled, 6 pages,
8.5 x 11 in. (21.6 x 27.9 cm)

Beware #11, 1981/82
Photocopy, side stapled, 8 pages,
8.5 x 11 in. (21.6 x 27.9 cm)

Beware #10, 1981/82
Photocopy, side stapled, 8 pages,
8.5 x 11 in. (21.6 x 27.9 cm)

No 1 #1, Contributors: Beate Prido, Margot Koch, Dirty Dog (David King) 1987
Photocopy, side stapled, 10 pages,
8.5 x 11 in. (21.6 x 27.9 cm)

Final Morning Extra 3 (Final 3), Contributors: Michael X. King, Terese Svoboda, Peter Mumford, Kurt Flansborg, G.X. Jupiter Larson, Tony Anthony, Megan Jasper, Jacob Reinstein, Willy Idle, Phlegm Pets, Alice Guberman-Carin, Burnt Raisins, Felix Svoboda-Bull 1983/84
Photocopy, side stapled, 14 pages,
8.5 x 11 in. (21.6 x 27.9 cm)

No 1 #2, Contributors: Beate Priolo, Dirty Dog (David King), 1987
Photocopy, side stapled, 10 pages,
8.5 x 11 in. (21.6 x 27.9 cm)

Too Many Zombies #22, Contributors: David King, Charlie Nash, 1984/85
Photocopy, 2 pages,
8.5 x 11 in. (21.6 x 27.9 cm)

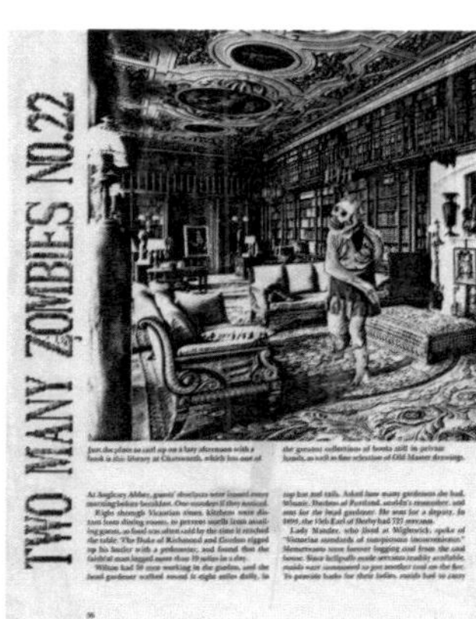

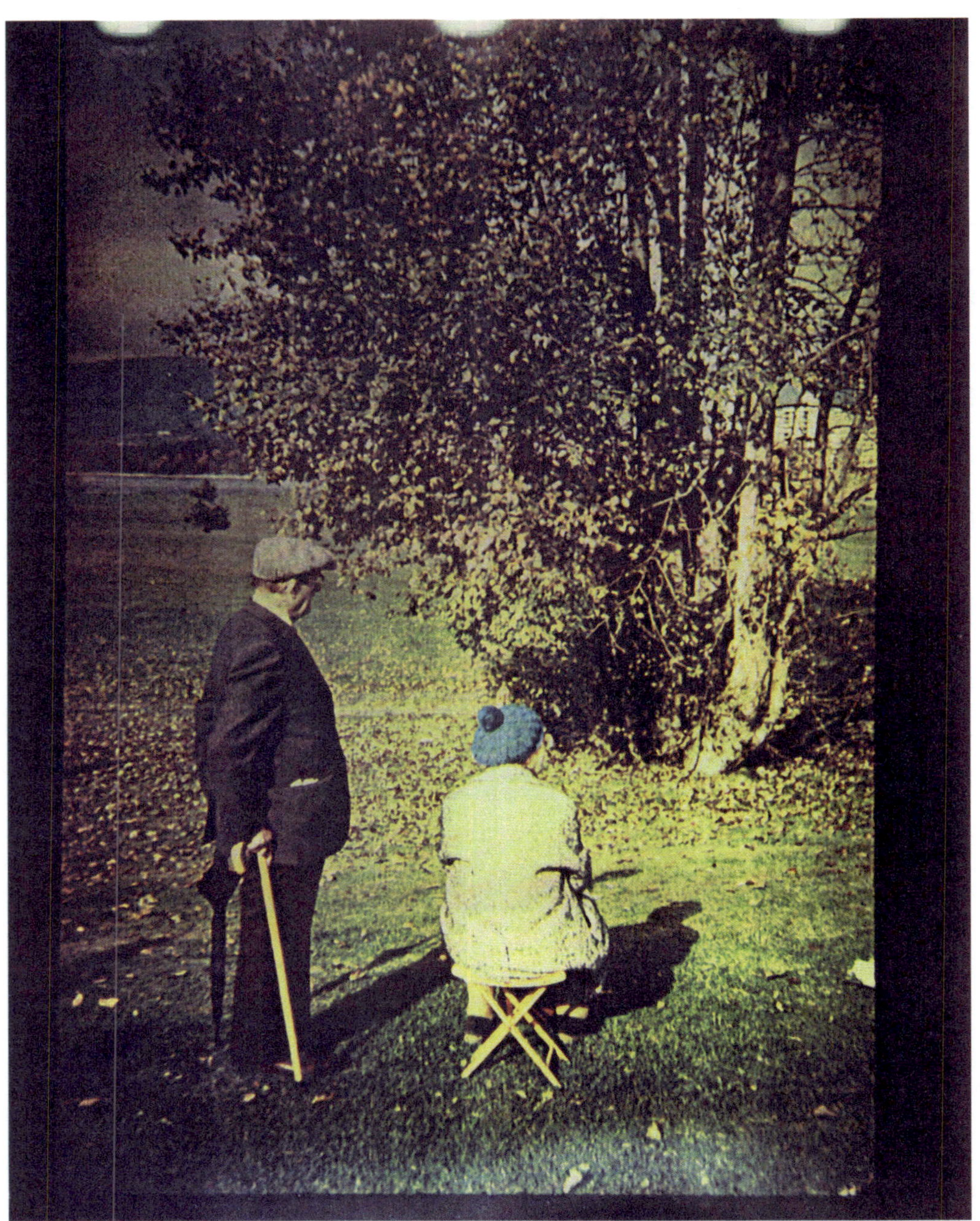

Original art, *Beware #8*, 1981/82
Color Xerox, 8.5 x 11 in. (21.6 x 27.9 cm)

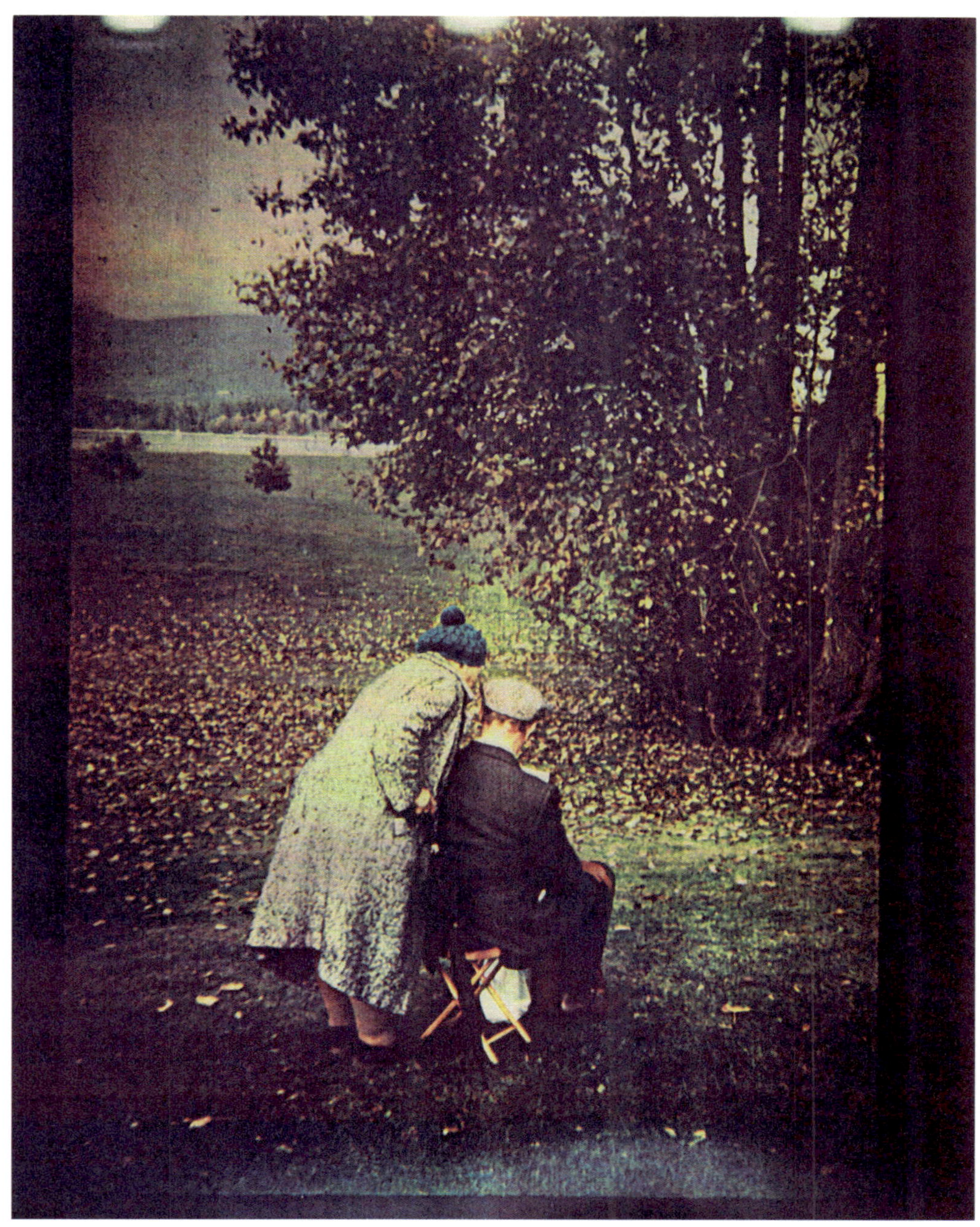

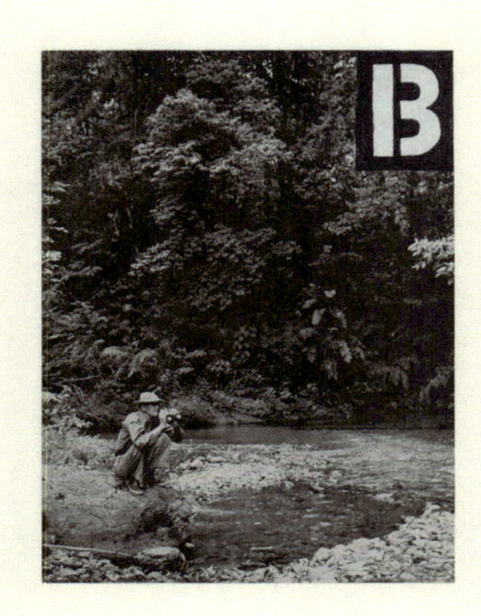
B

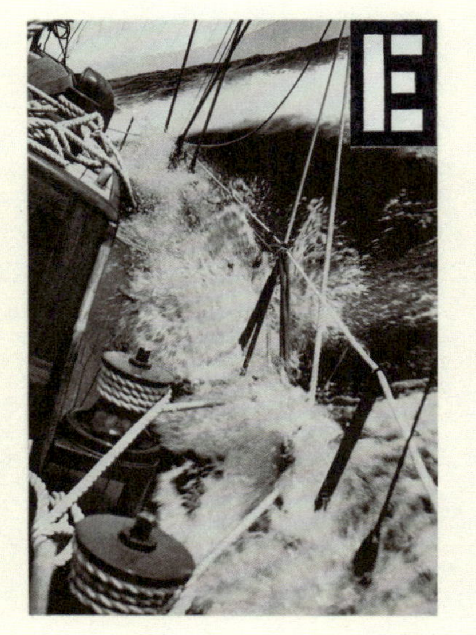
E

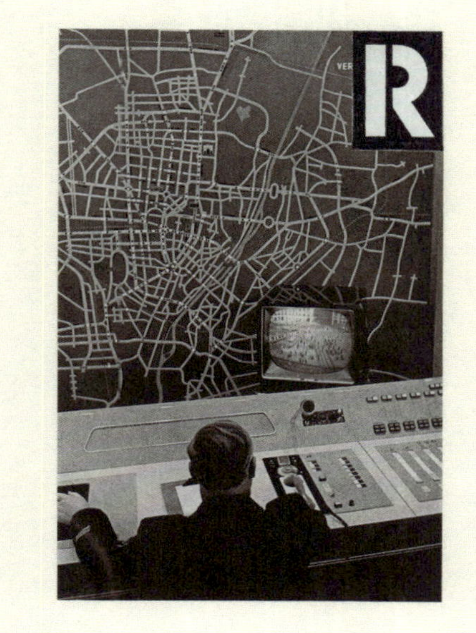
R

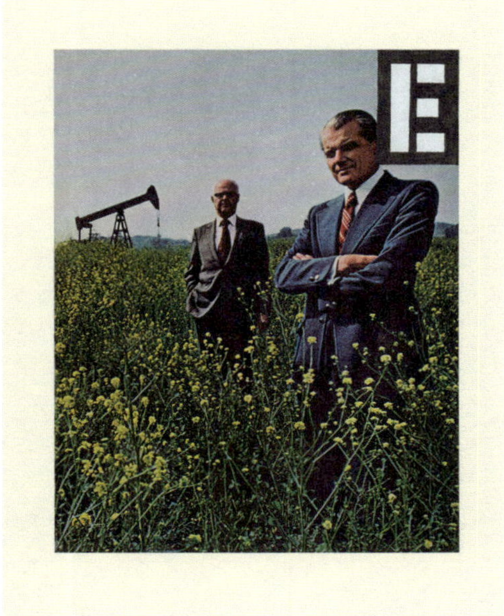
E

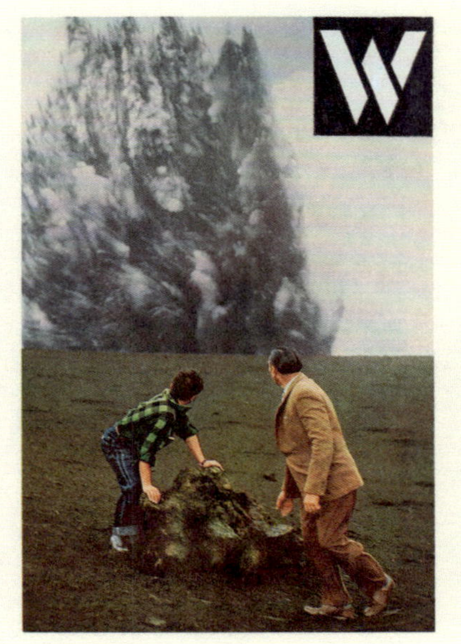

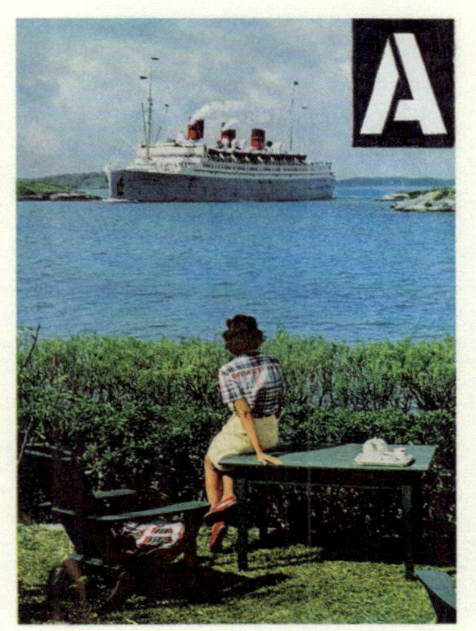

Paste-ups for *Beware #11*, 1980s
Collage with pen and ink, each
8.5 x 11 in. (21.6 x 27.9 cm)

Pages 56–57: Interior spread,
Beware #10, 1981/82
Photocopy, side stapled, 8 pages,
8.5 x 11 in. (21.6 x 27.9 cm)

He likes
hardware.

She's into
ftwear.

He likes
hardware.

She's into
ftwear.

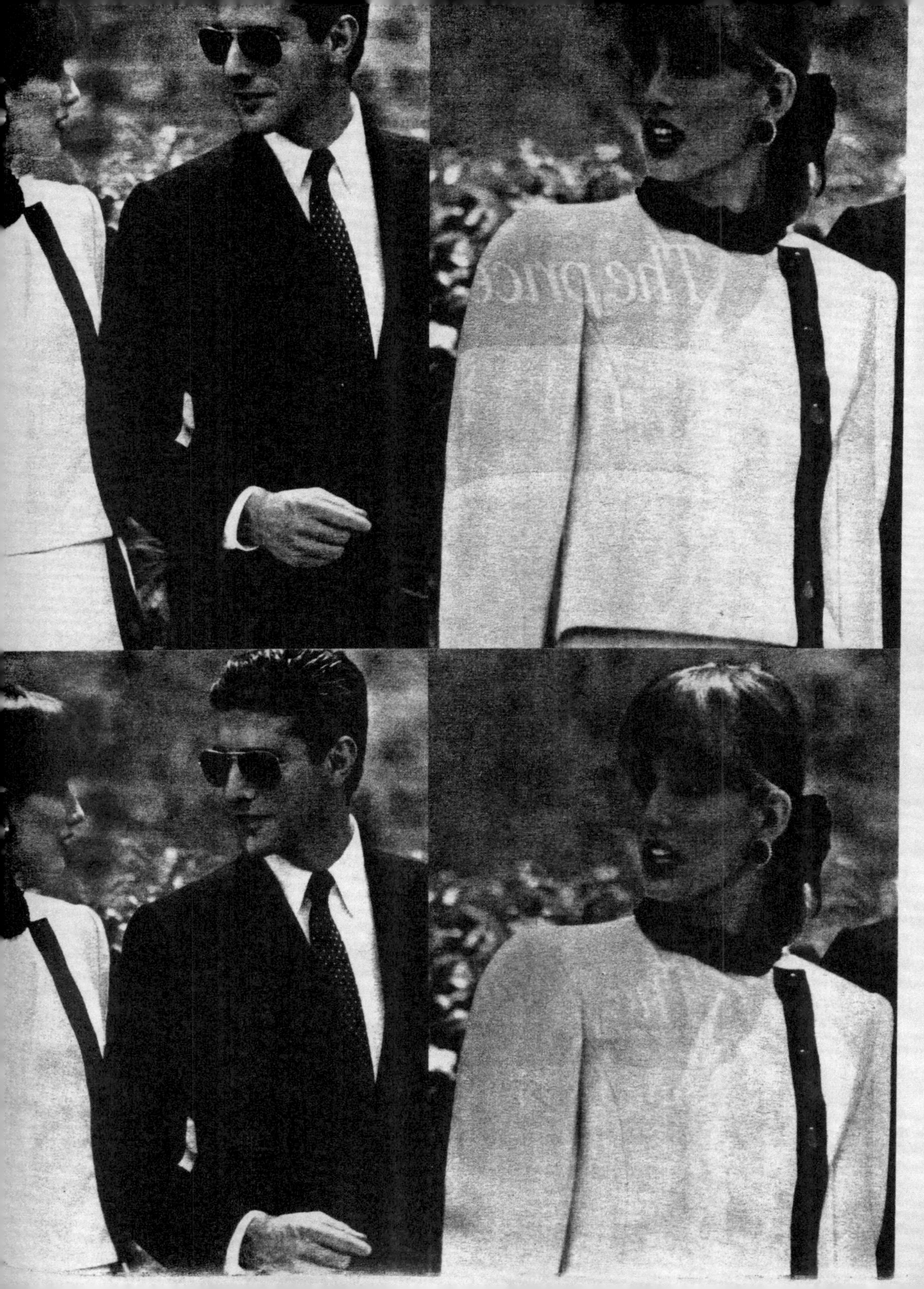

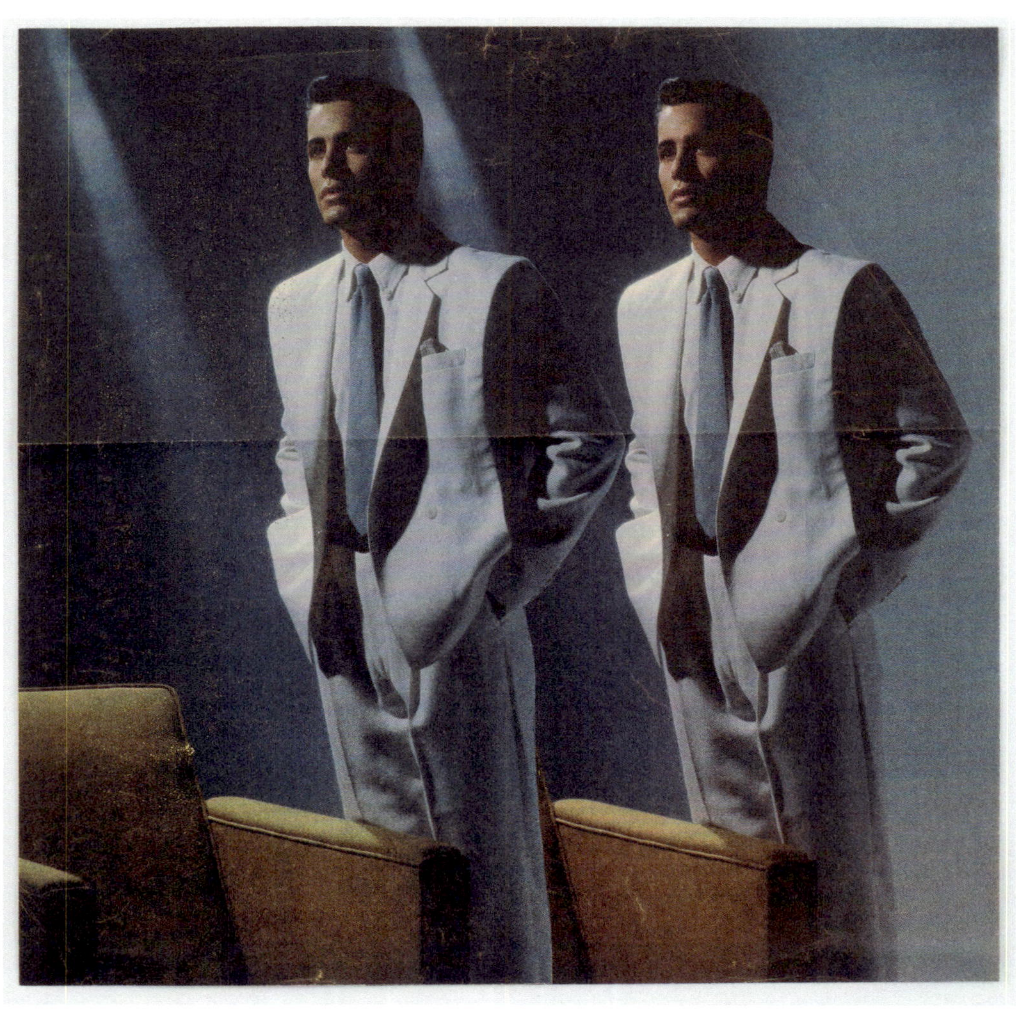

Collage for *Beware #10*, 1981/82
Magazine pages, 10.75 x 10.75 in. (27.3 X 27.3 cm)

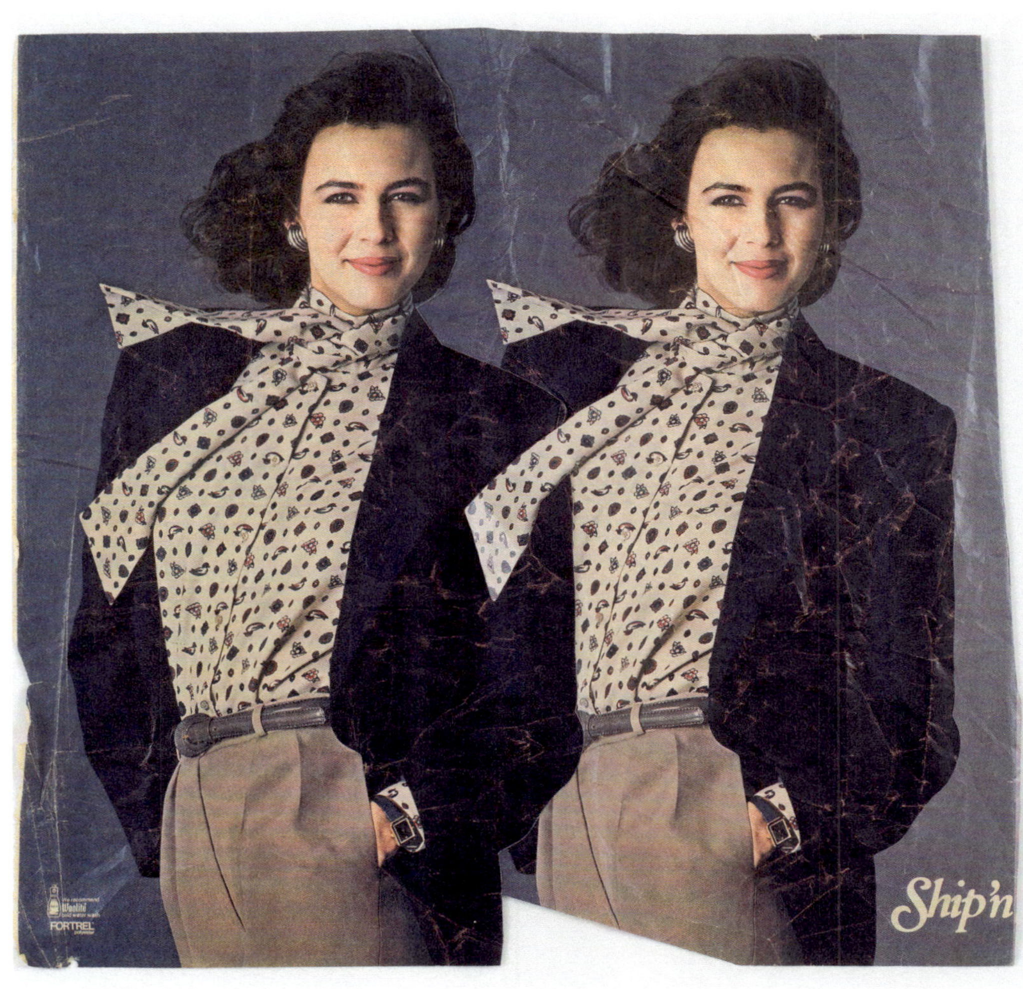

Collage for *Beware #10*, 1981/82
Magazine pages, 11.75 x 12.5 in. (29.9 X 31.8 cm)

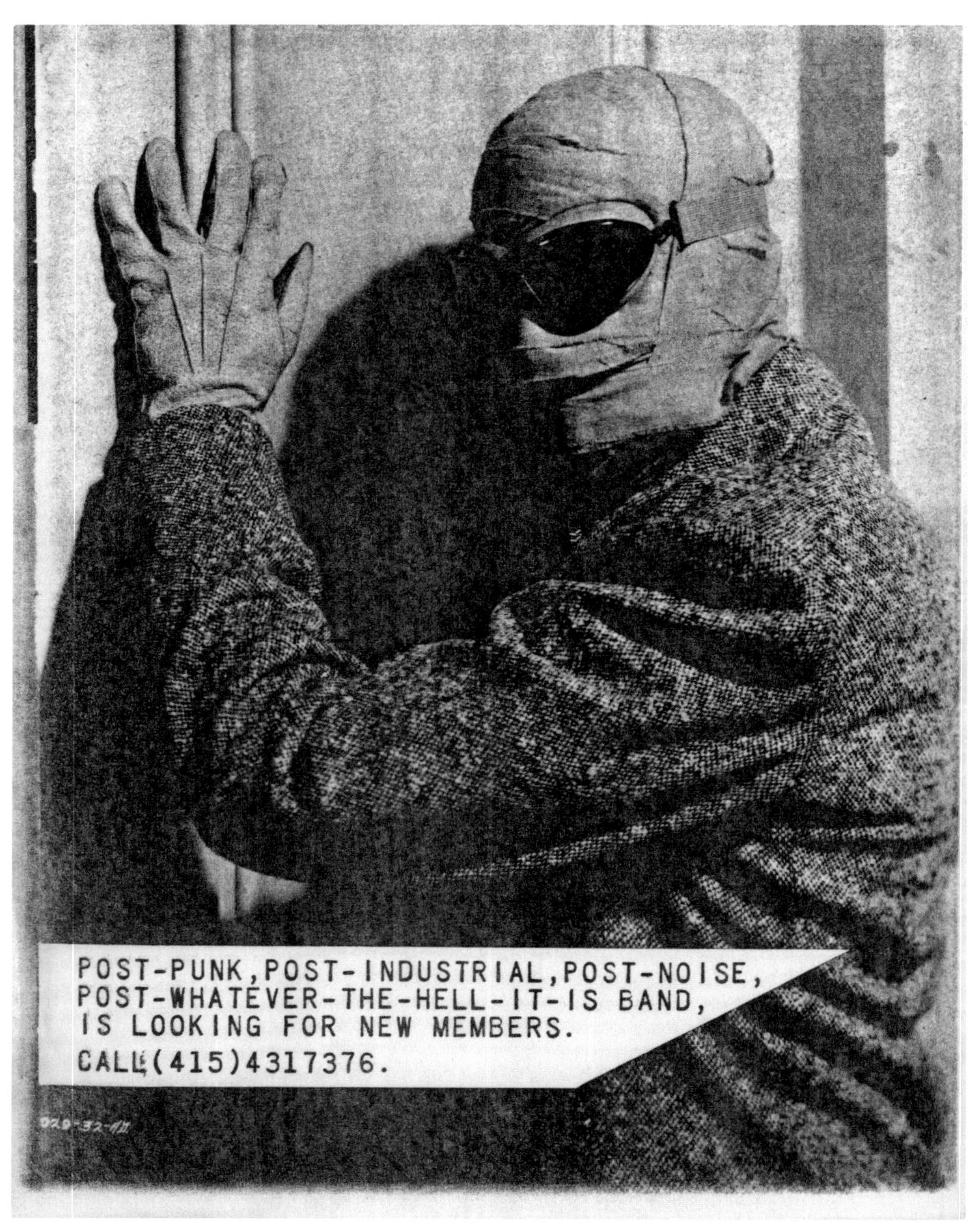

Brain Rust flyer, 1980s
Photocopy, 8.5 x 11 in. (21.6 x 27.9 cm)

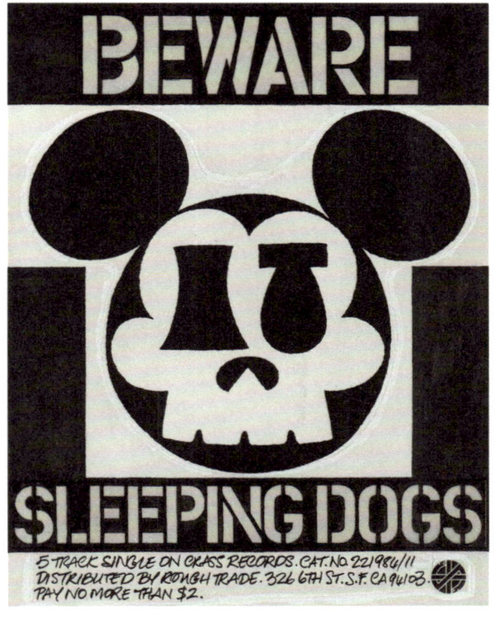

Clockwise from top left: Flyer paste-up for *Sleeping Dogs Beware* single, 1982
Photocopy, ink, and white-out, 8.5 x 11 in. (21.6 x 27.9 cm)

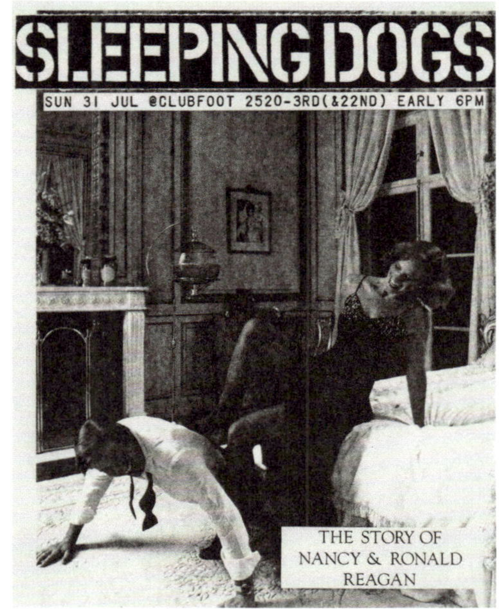

Flyer for *Sleeping Dogs at Club Foot*, San Francisco, July 31, 1983
Photocopy, 8.5 x 11 in. (21.6 x 27.9 cm)

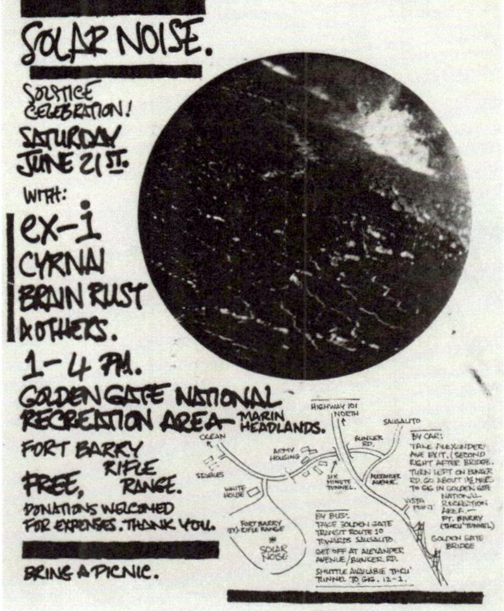

Flyer for *Solar Noise at the Marin Headlands*, June 21, 1986
Photocopy, 8.5 x 11 in. (21.6 x 27.9 cm)

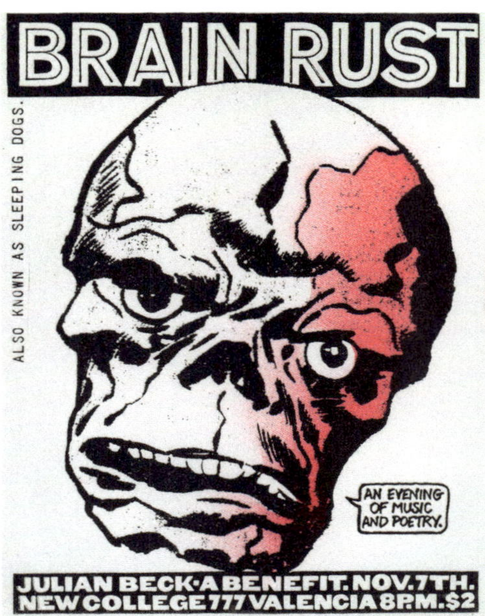

Flyer for *Brain Rust at the New College*, San Francisco, November 7, 1985
Photocopy with spray paint, 8.5 x 11 in. (21.6 x 27.9 cm)

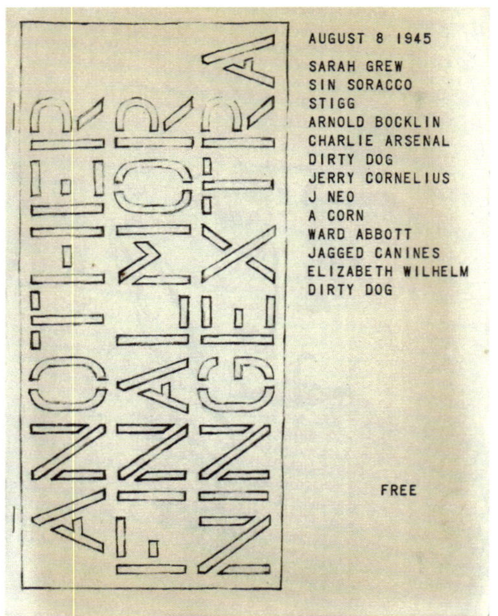

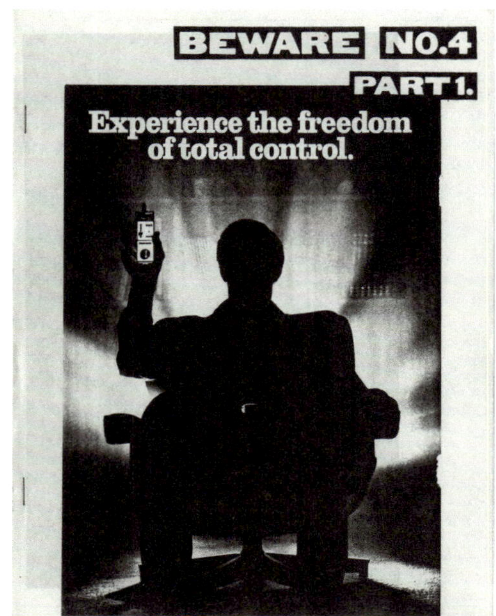

Another Final Morning Extra, Contributors: Sarah Grew, Sin Soracco, Stigg, Arnold Bocklin, Charlie Arsenal, Dirty Dog (David King), Jerry Cornelius, J Neo, A Corn, Ward Abbott, Jagged Canines, Elizabeth Wilhelm, 1983
Photocopy, side stapled, 14 pages, 8.5 x 11 in. (21.6 x 27.9 cm)

Beware #4, 1981/82
Photocopy, side stapled, 14 pages, 8.5 x 11 in. (21.6 x 27.9 cm)

Facing page: *Beware #17*, 1981/82
Photocopy, side stapled, 18 pages, 8.5 x 11 in. (21.6 x 27.9 cm)

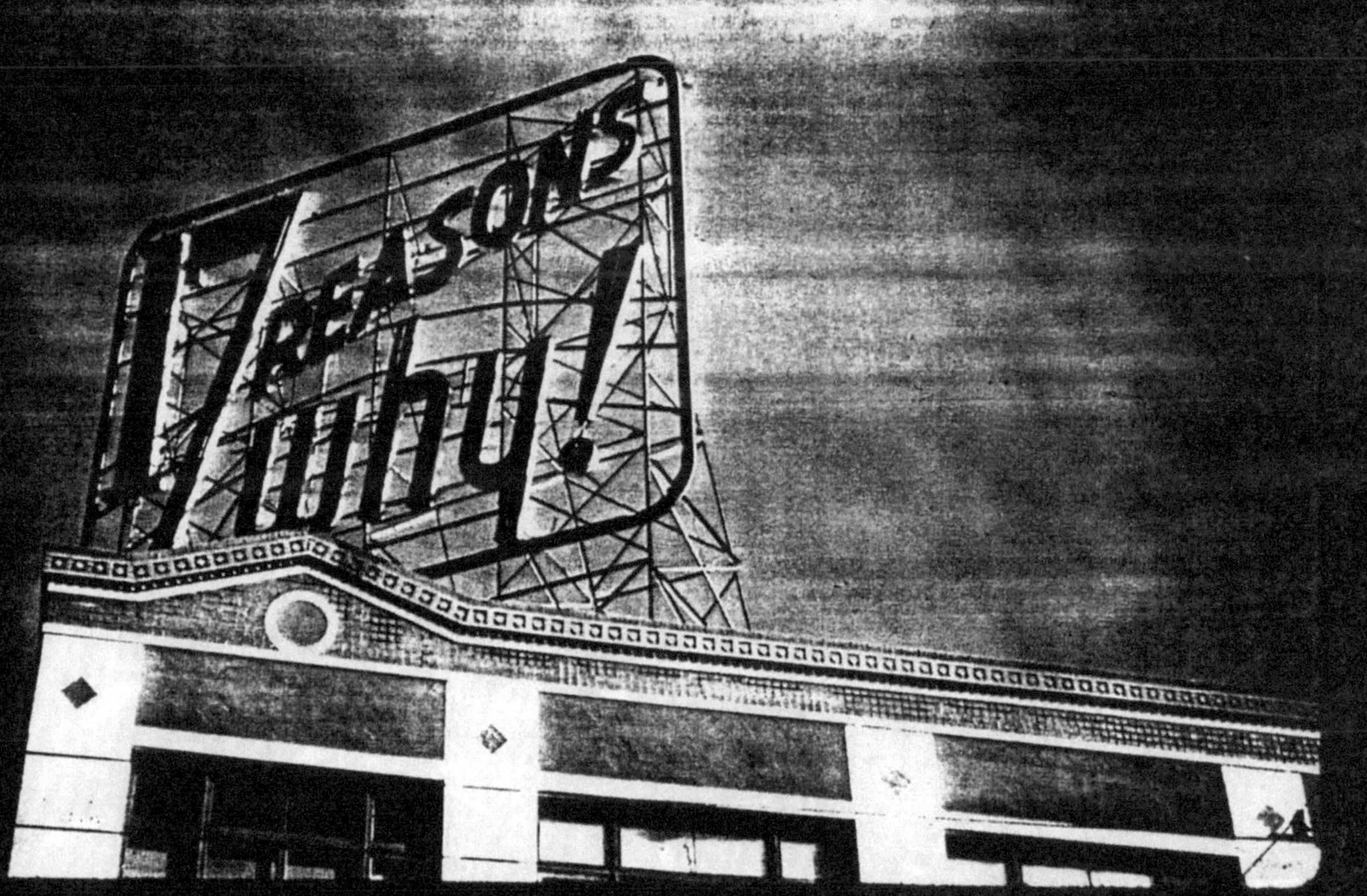
7
REASONS
Why!

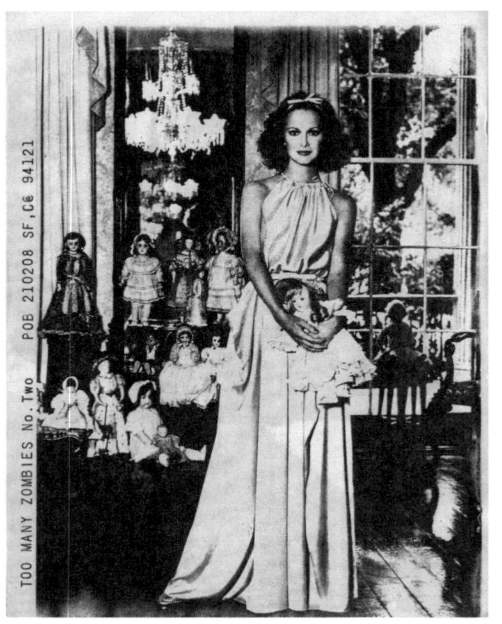
TOO MANY ZOMBIES No.Two
POB 210208 SF,CA 94121

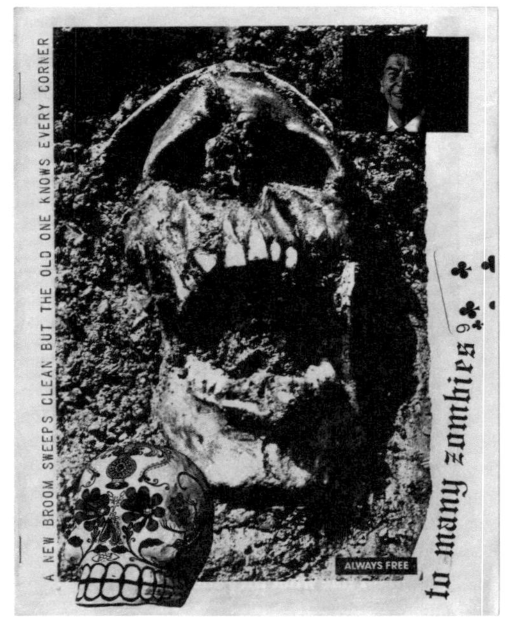
A NEW BROOM SWEEPS CLEAN BUT THE OLD ONE KNOWS EVERY CORNER
ALWAYS FREE
to many zombies 9

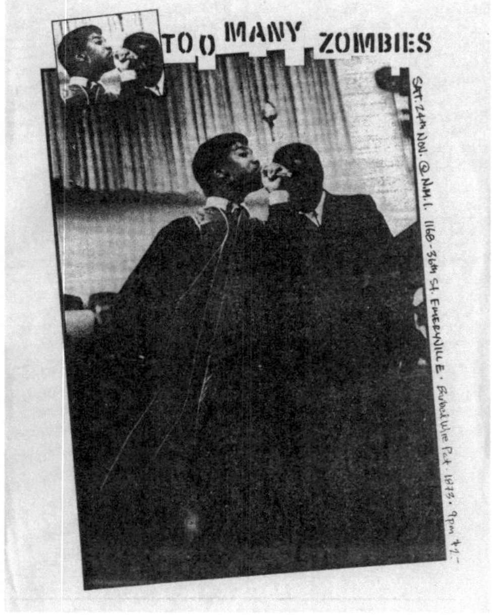
TOO MANY ZOMBIES
SAT 24th NOV. @ N.M.I. 1160-36th St. EMERYVILLE

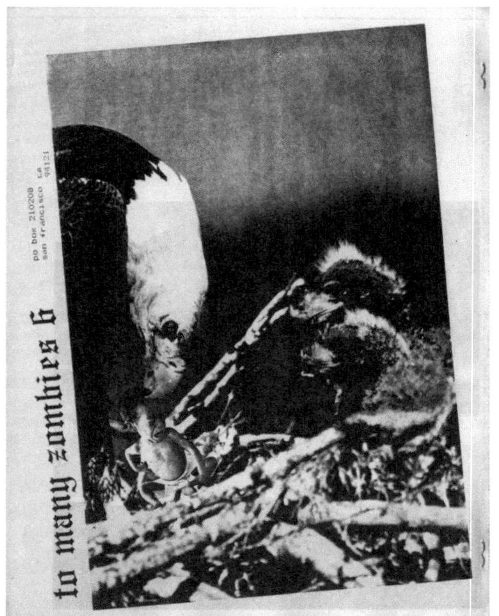
to many zombies 6
po box 210208 ca
san francisco 94121

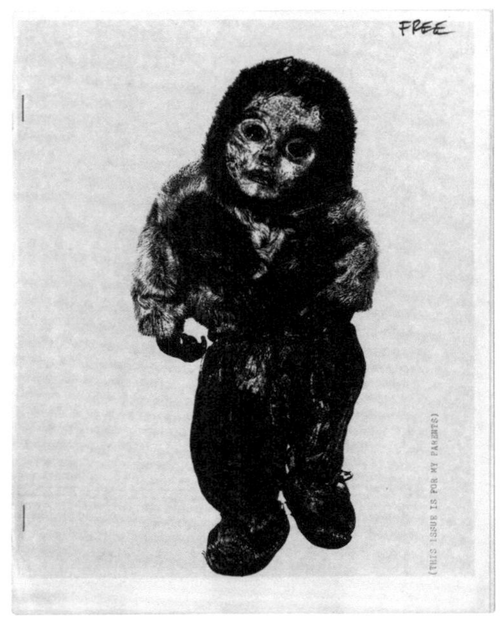

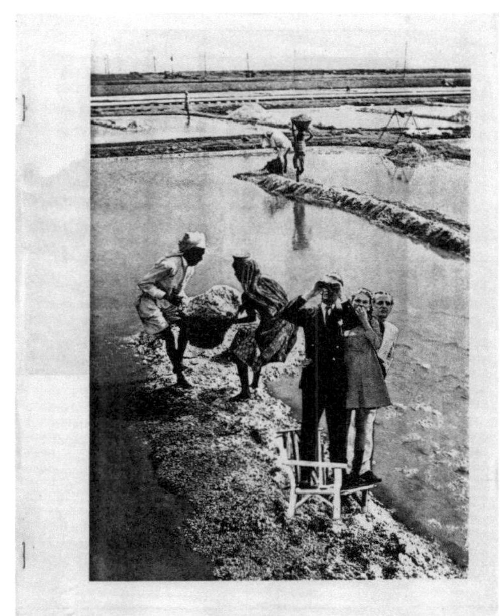

Facing page, clockwise from top left: Back cover, *Too Many Zombies #2*, Contributors: David King, Charlie Nash, 1984/85, Photocopy, side stapled, 6 pages, 8.5 x 11 in. (21.6 x 27.9 cm)

Too Many Zombies #9, Contributors: David King, Charlie Nash, 1984/85, Photocopy, side stapled, 10 pages, 8.5 x 11 in. (21.6 x 27.9 cm)

Back cover, *Too Many Zombies #6*, Contributors: David King, Charlie Nash, 1984/85, Photocopy, side stapled, 12 pages, 8.5 x 11 in. (21.6 x 27.9 cm)

Flyer for *Too Many Zombies at New Method Industries Warehouse*, Emeryville, CA. Nov. 24, 1984 Photocopy, 8.5 x 11 in. (21.6 x 27.9 cm)

Above, clockwise from top left: *Too Many Final Morning Zombies Extra 107*, Contributors: David King, Charlie Nash, Shagnasty, Barrington Bailey, Denver Tucson, Stigs, assorted anonymous, 1985 Photocopy, side stapled, 28 pages, 8.5 x 11 in. (21.6 x 27.9 cm)

Too Many Zombies #4, Contributors: David King, Charlie Nash, 1984/85, Photocopy, side stapled, 10 pages, 8.5 x 11 in. (21.6 x 27.9 cm)

Too Many Zombies #6, Contributors: David King, Charlie Nash, 1984/85 Photocopy, side stapled, 12 pages, 8.5 x 11 in. (21.6 x 27.9 cm)

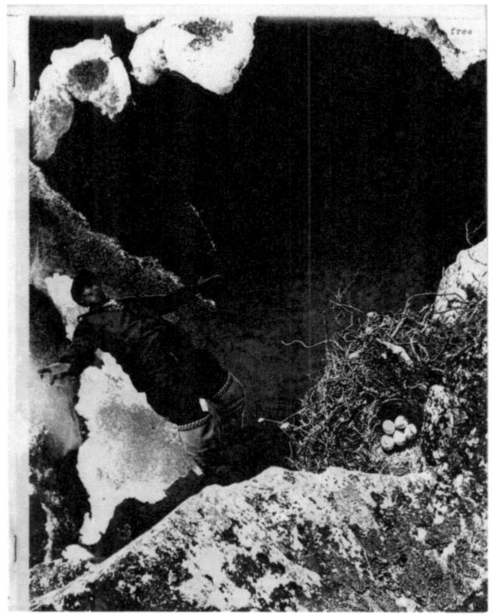

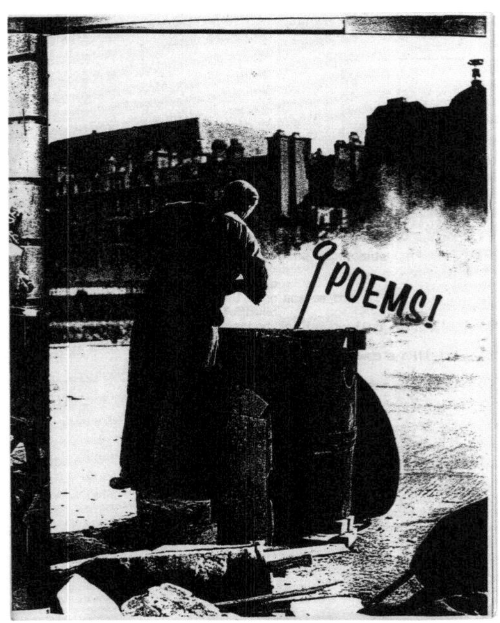

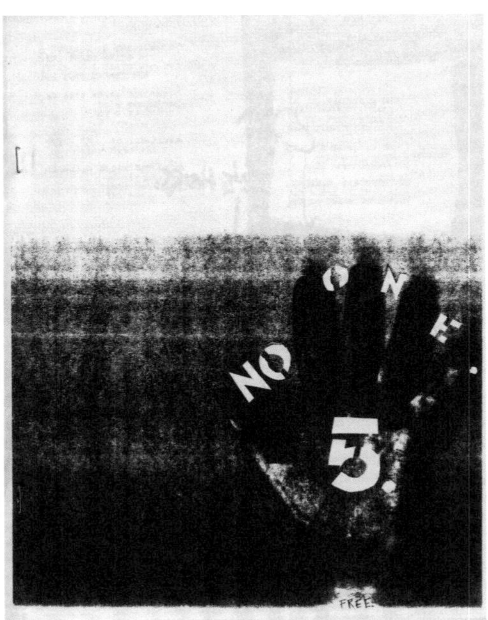

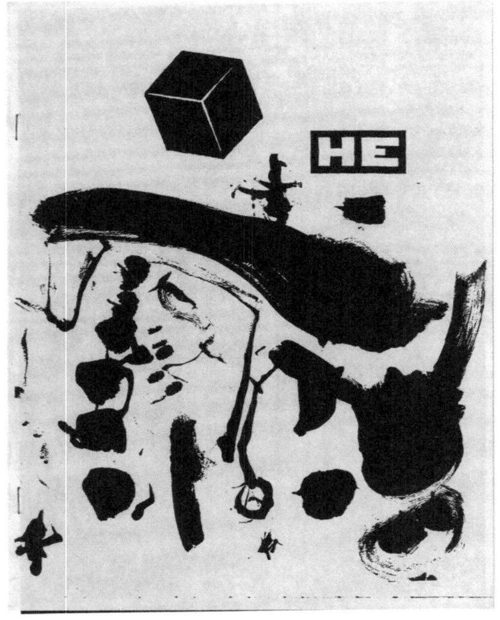

Clockwise from top left: *Poems!*, Poetry zine made for Diane DiPrima's poetry class at the San Francisco Art Institute. Contributors: George Andrews, Cameron Bamberger, Gregory Cruikshank, Django Golden, Rebekah Horne, Ron W. Ibon, David King, Leah Korican, Philip McGaughy, Asako Sumii, Quillon Swane, Dave Warnke, Spring 1992
Photocopy, side stapled, 40 pages, 8.5 x 11 in. (21.6 x 27.9 cm)

No 1 #5, Contributors: Paul Weinman and Dirty Dog (David King) 1987/88
Photocopy, side stapled, 4 pages, 8.5 x 11 in. (21.6 x 27.9 cm)

Beware #9, 1981/82
Photocopy, side stapled, 6 pages, 8.5 x 11 in. (21.6 x 27.9 cm)

Facing page: *Final Morning Extra #4*, Contributors: Bunny Hubcap, Mat Lock, Rippstirl, Nazik Malika and Bad Boy, Ward Abbott, Sean, 1984
Photocopy, side stapled, 20 pages, 8.5 x 11 in. (21.6 x 27.9 cm)

FINAL
OUR

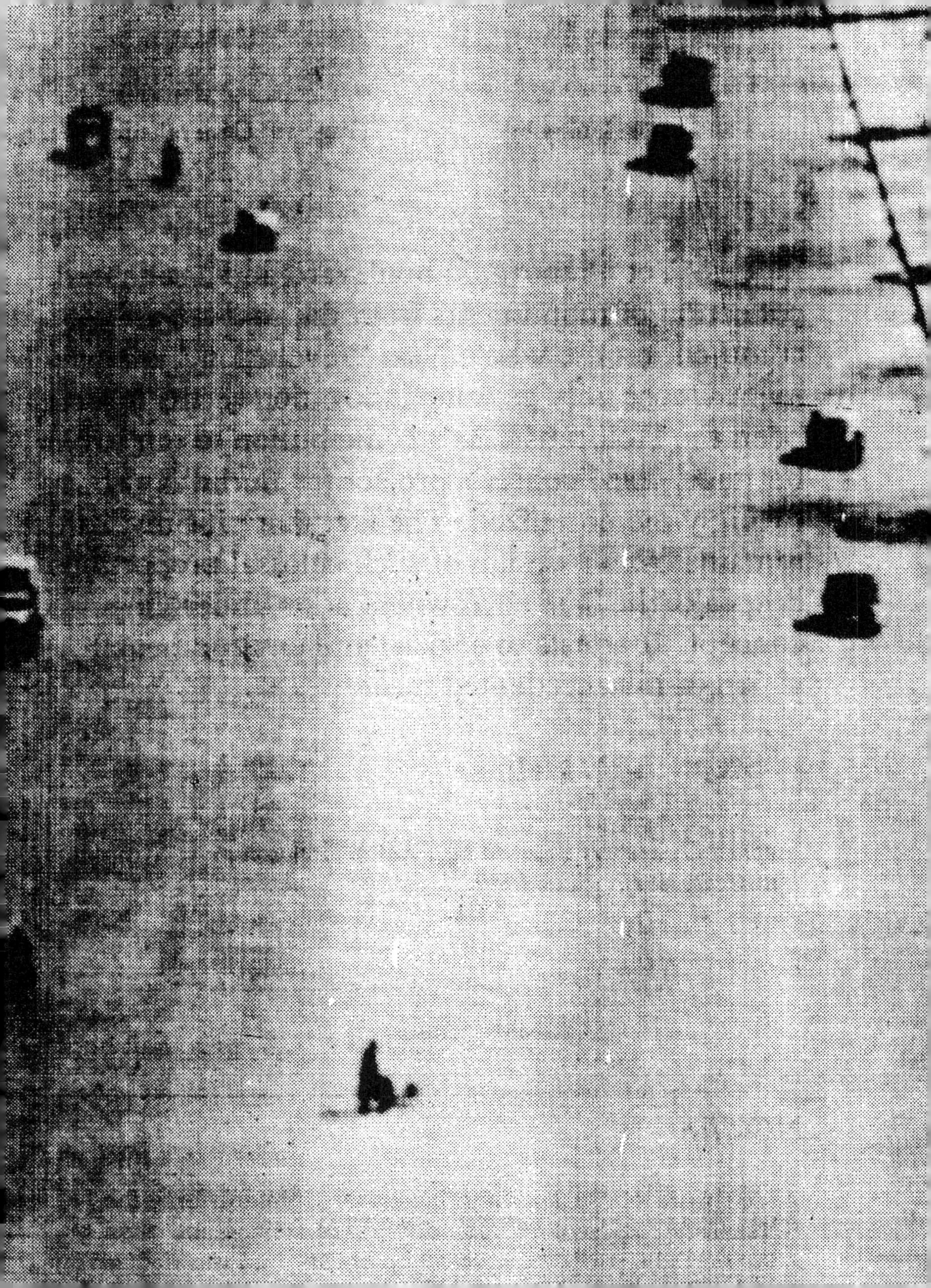

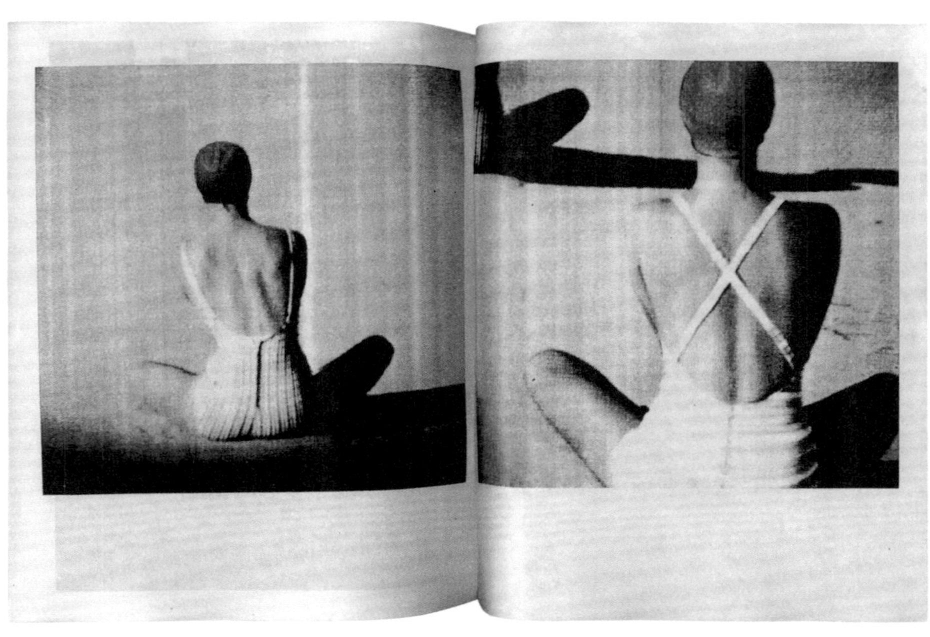

Facing page: *Brandenburg Gate*, 1980s
Photocopy, slide bound, 32 pages,
8.5 x 11 in. (21.6 x 27.9 cm)

Interior spread, *No 1 #1*, Contributors: Beate Prido, Margot Koch, Dirty Dog (David King), 1987
Photocopy, side stapled, 10 pages,
8.5 x 11 in. (21.6 x 27.9 cm)

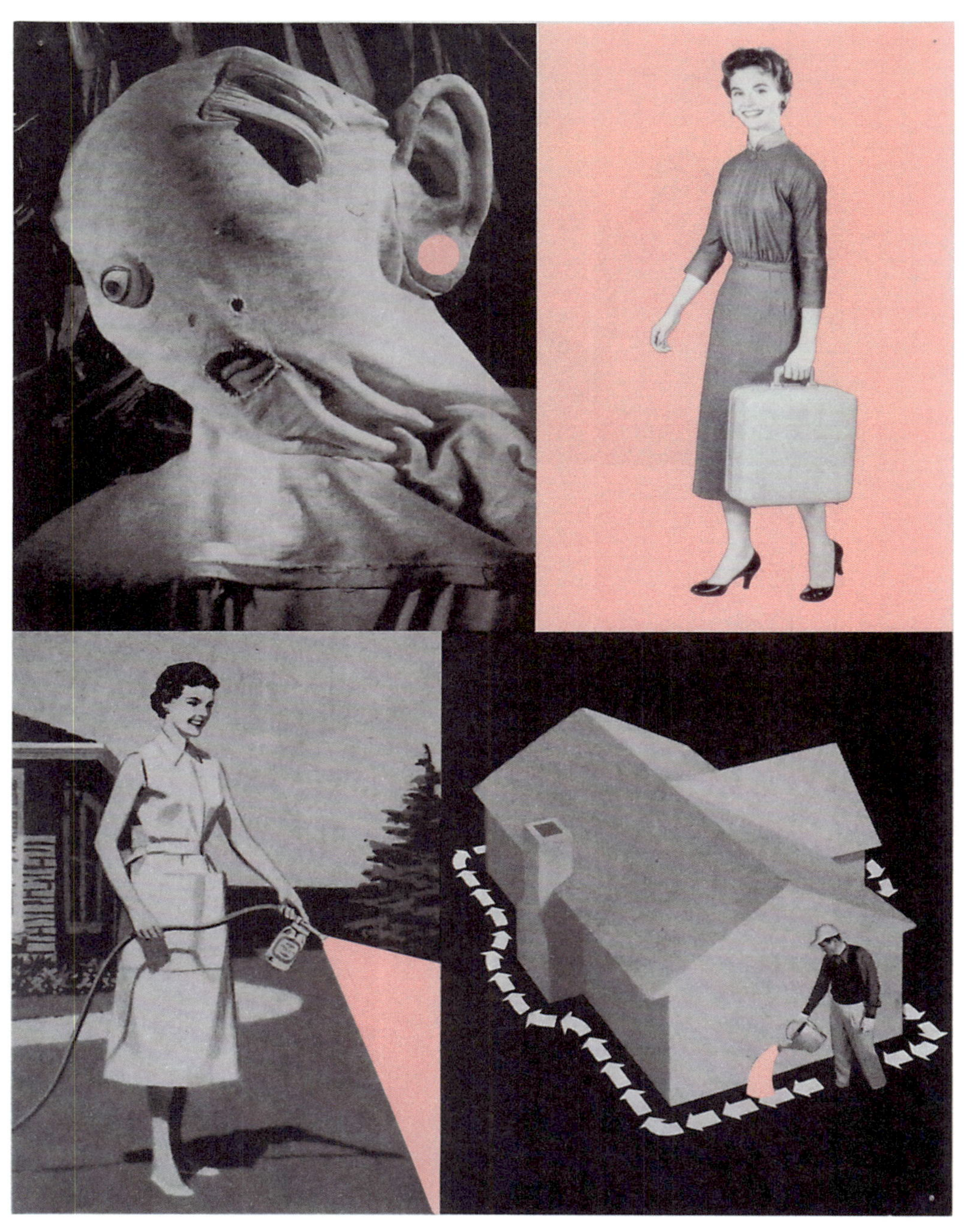

Interior page, 7 *Teen*, MoST Books, 2017
Digital press, plastic slide binding, 32 pages,
edition of 15, 8.5 x 11 in. (21.6 x 27.99 cm)

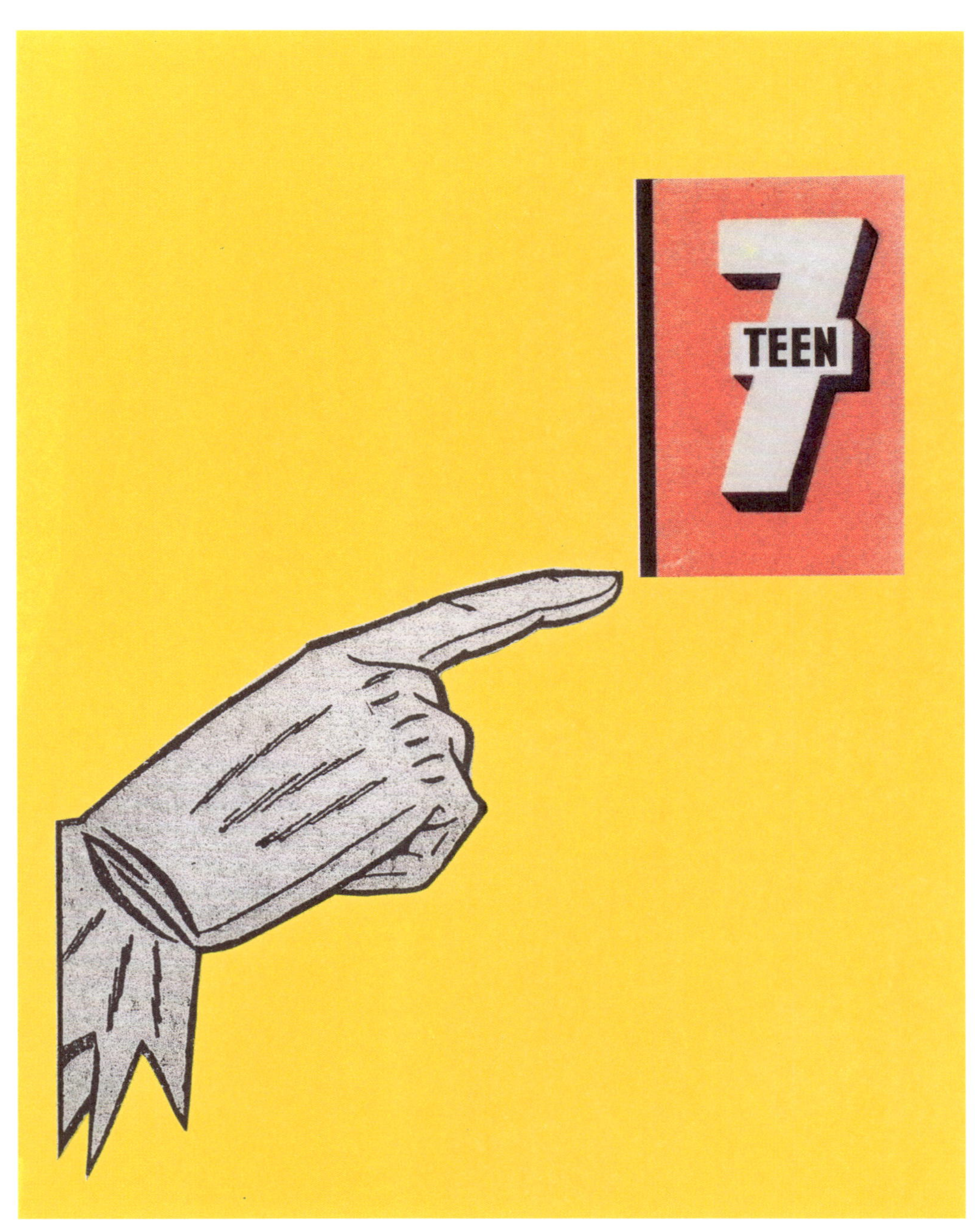

7 Teen, MoST Books, 2017
Digital press, plastic slide binding, 32 pages, edition of 15, 8.5 x 11 in. (21.6 x 27.99 cm)

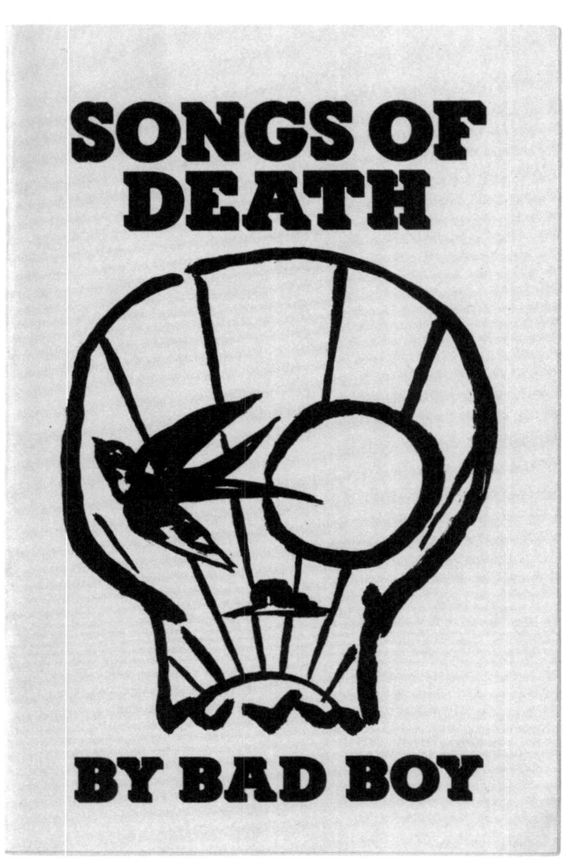

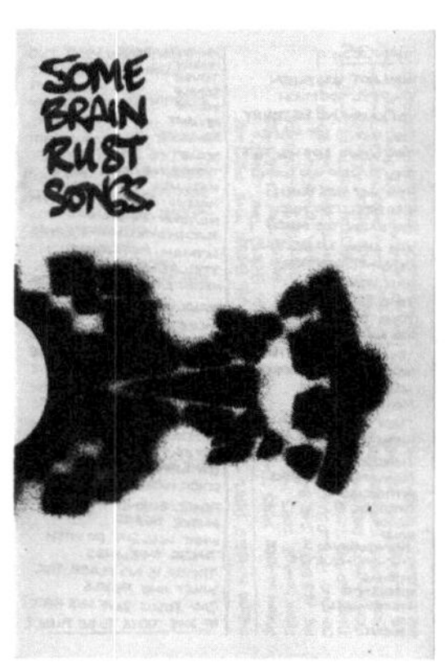

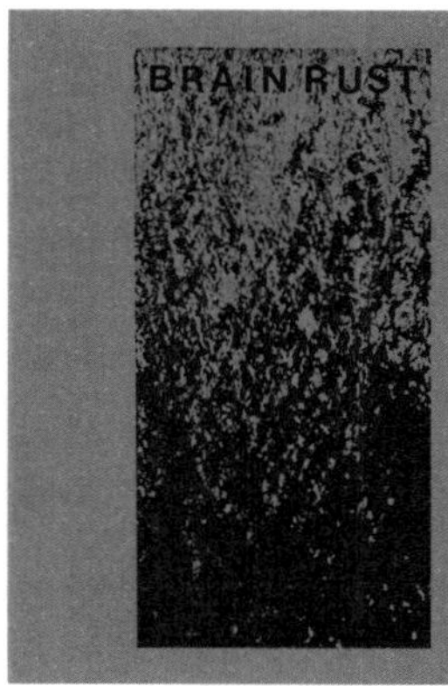

Clockwise from top: *Songs of Death* by Bad Boy, Illustrations by Kris Force, Cover and Art Direction by Dirty Dog (David King), Typesetting by Catastrophe Graphics, published by Squash Press, 1986
Photocopy, staple bound, 20 pages,
5.5 x 8.5 in. (14 x 21.6 cm)

Brain Rust Zine #2, 1984/88
Photocopy, staple bound, 12 pages,
5.5 x 8.5 in. (14 x 21.6 cm)

Some Brain Rust Songs, 1984/88
Photocopy, staple bound, 8 pages,
5.5 x 8.5 in. (14 x 21.6 cm)

Facing page: Interior page, *7 Teen*, MoST Books, 2017, Digital press, plastic slide binding, 32 pages, edition of 15,
8.5 x 11 in. (21.6 x 27.9 cm)

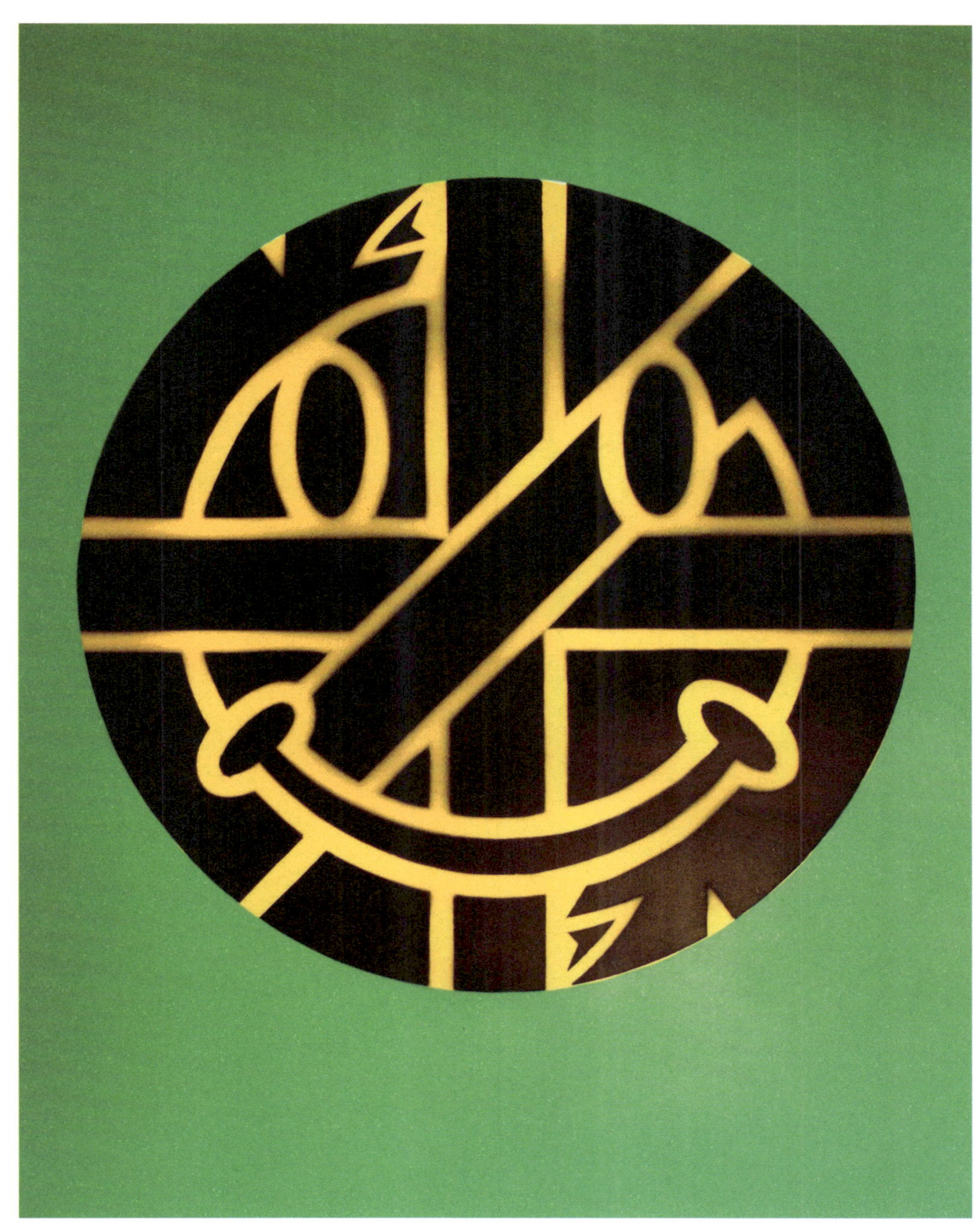

Self published, MoST Books, 1990s–2000s

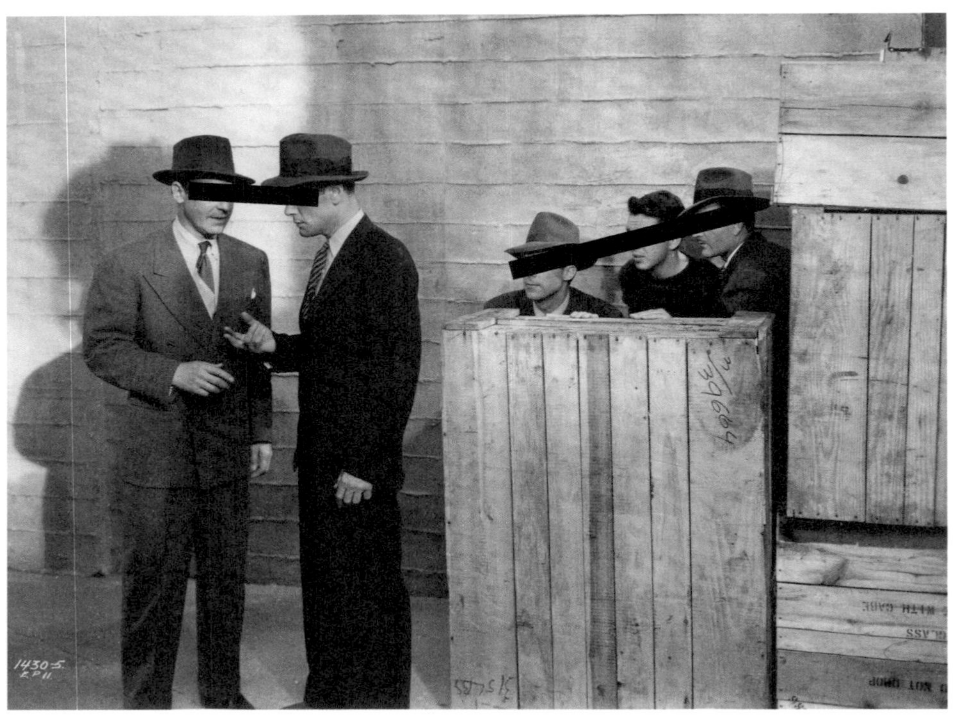

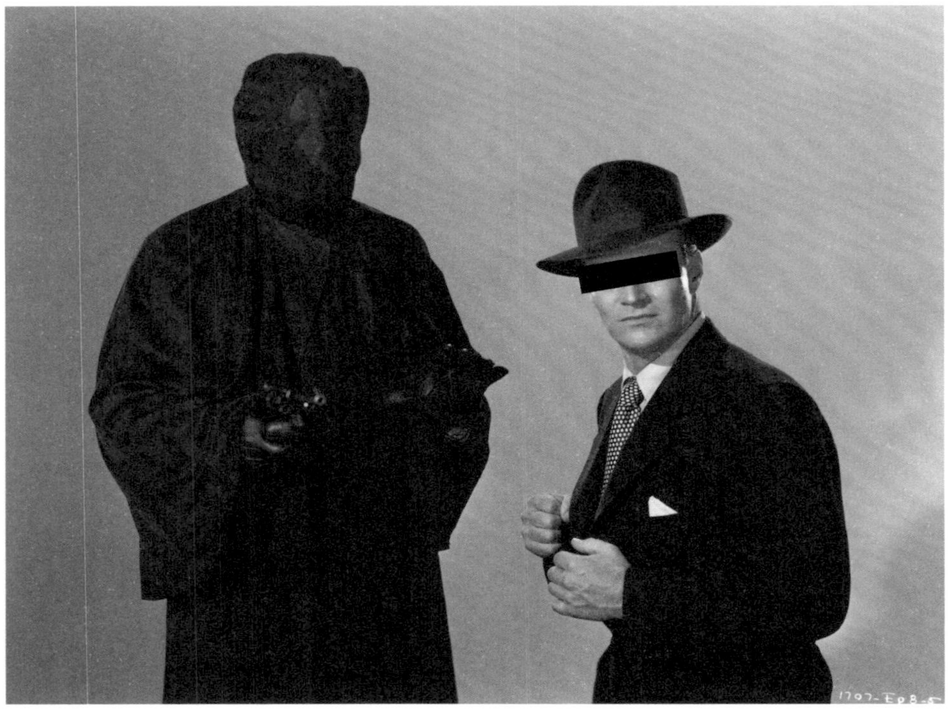

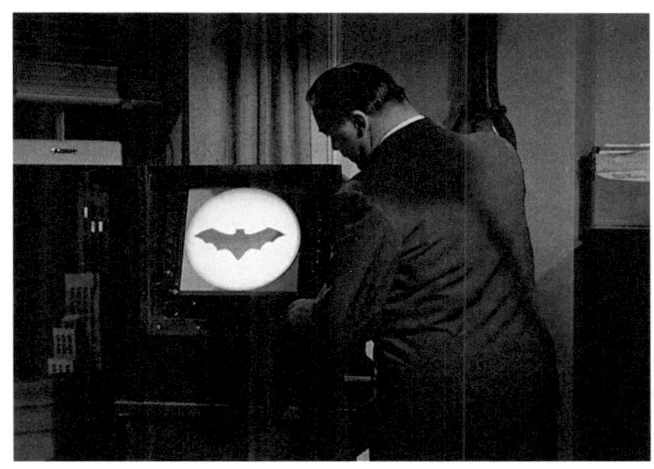

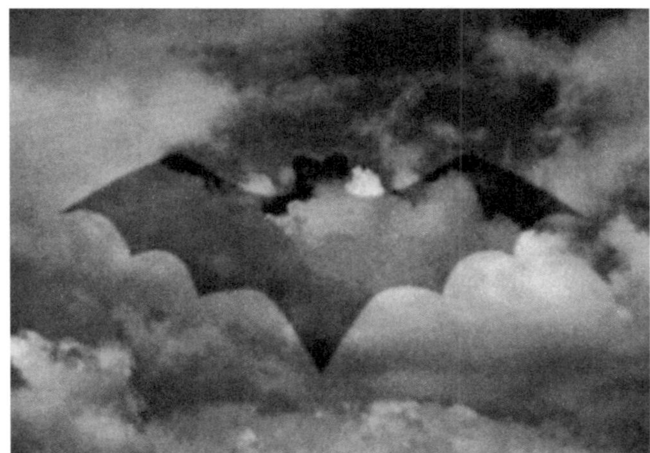

Facing page: *Who Was That Masked Man?*, davidanthonyking.com, 2012
Digital press, staple bound, 20 pages, 11 X 8.5 in. (27.9 x 21.6 cm)

Right: Outtake from *I Dreamt I Dwelt in Marble Halls*, 2012
Shutterfly digital press, perfect bound, 22 pages, hardcover, 12 x 12 in. (30.5 x 30.5 cm)

I Dreamt I Dwelt in Marble Halls, 2012
Shutterfly digital press, perfect bound, 22 pages, hardcover, 12 x 12 in. (30.5 x 30.5 cm)

Outtake from *I Dreamt I Dwelt in Marble Halls*, 2012
Shutterfly digital press, perfect bound, 22 pages, hardcover, 12 x 12 in. (30.5 x 30.5 cm)

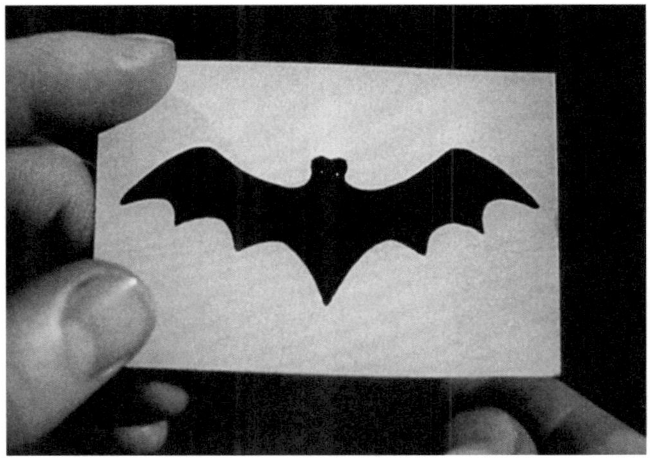

Gas Gun, MoST Books, 2019
Digital press, perfect bound, 26 pages,
hardcover, 8.25 x 10.25 in. (21 x 26 cm)

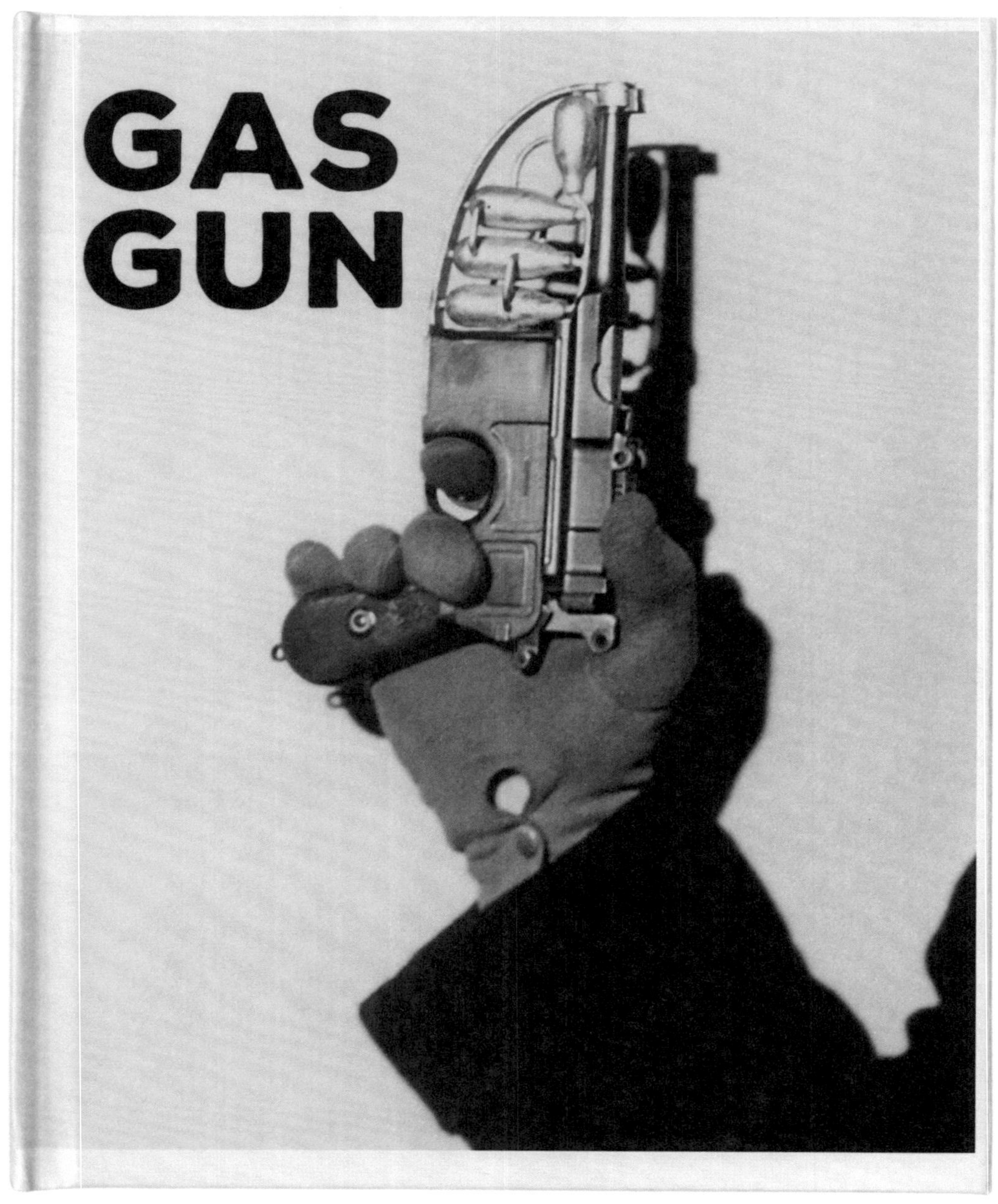

The Somnambulists, Homage to California, MOsT Books, 2008
Apple print-on-demand digital press, perfect bound, 38 pages,
11.25 x 8.75 in. (28.6 x 22.2 cm)

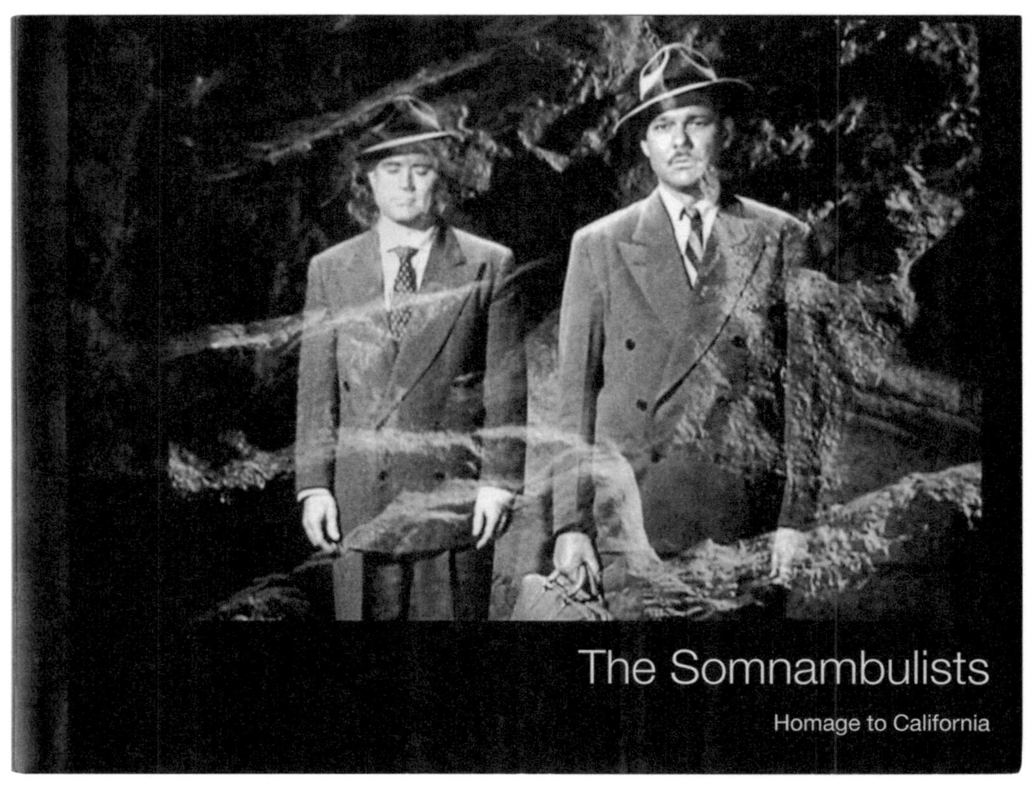

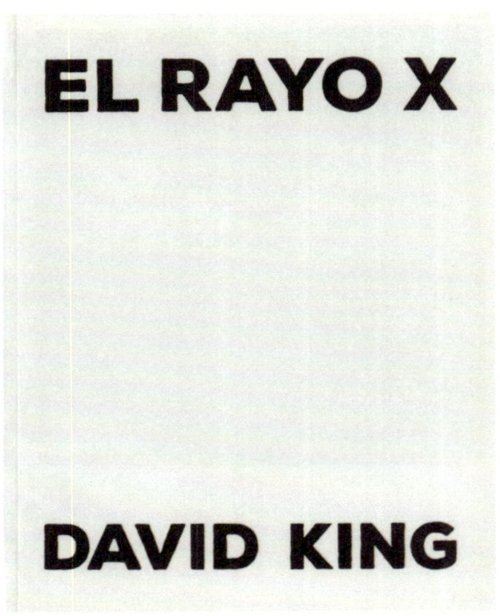

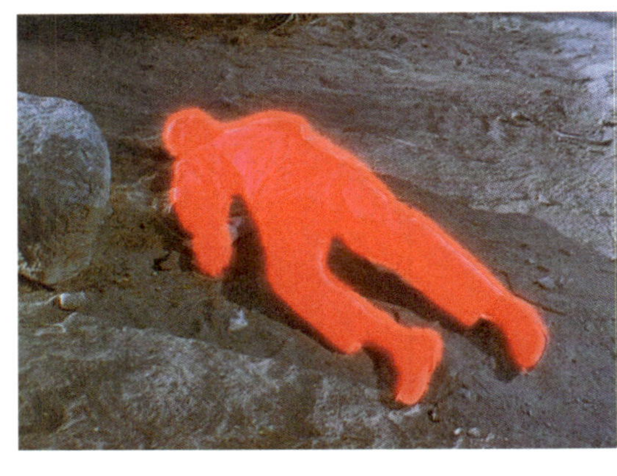

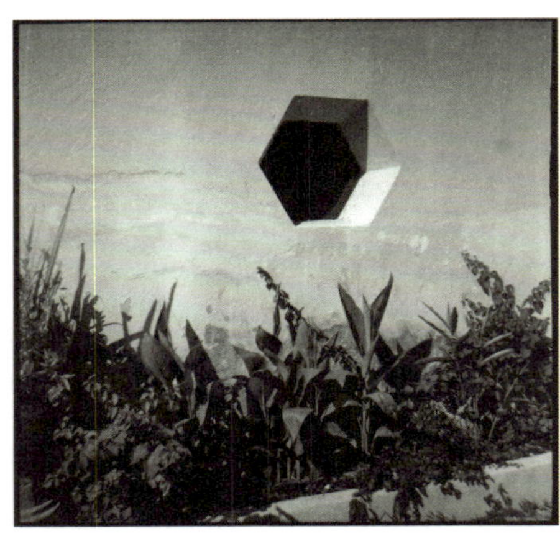

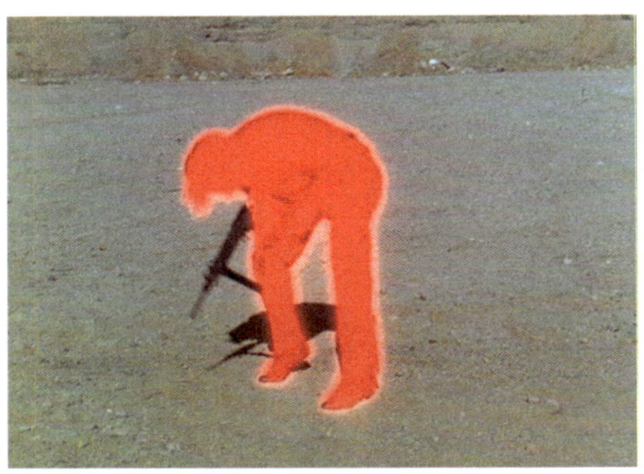

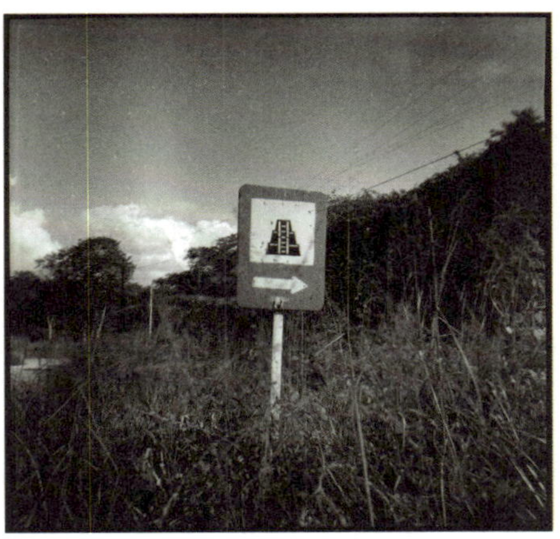

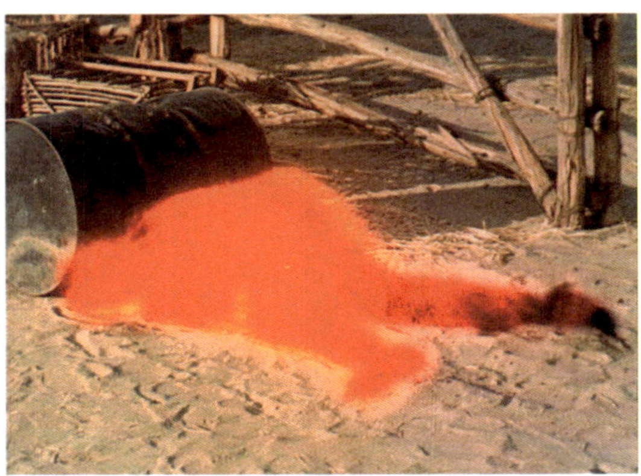

Clockwise from lower left: *El Rayo X*, MoST Books, 2019
Digital press, perfect bound, 20 pages, 8 x 10 in. (20.3 x 25.4 cm)

Every Red Death, MOsT Books, 2016
Apple print-on-demand digital press, perfect bound, 46 pages, hardcover, 11.25 x 8.75 in. (28.6 x 22.2 cm)

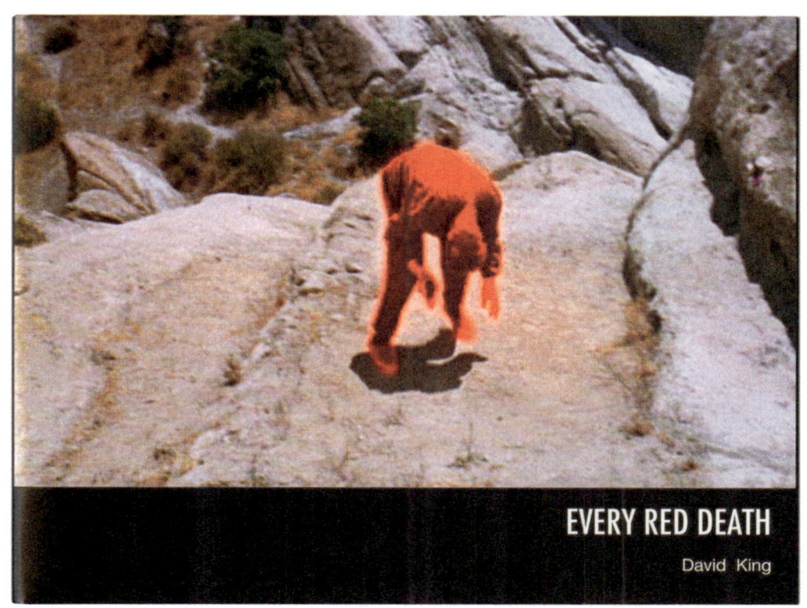

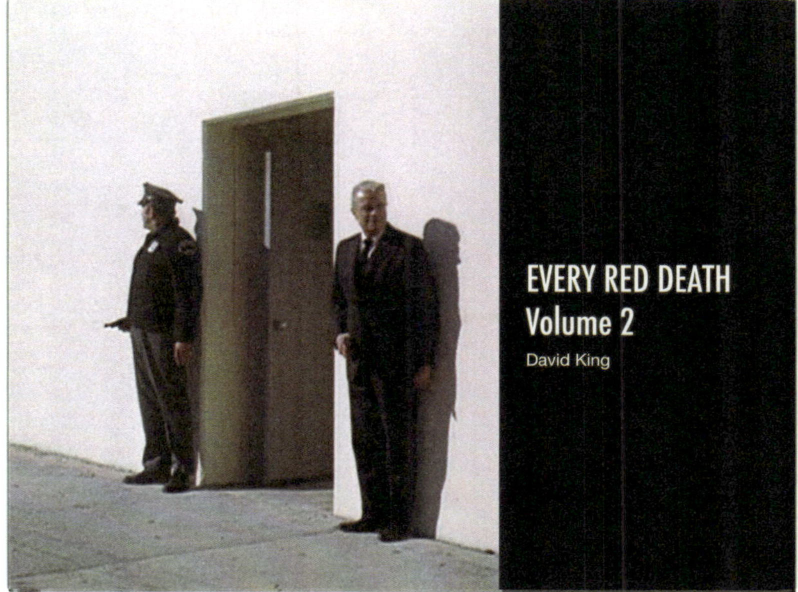

Every Red Death, MOsT Books, 2016
Apple print-on-demand digital press, perfect bound, 46 pages, hardcover, 11.25 x 8.75 in. (28.6 x 22.2 cm)

Every Red Death Volume 2, MOsT Books, 2000s
Apple print-on-demand digital press, perfect bound, 20 pages, hardcover, 11.25 x 8.75 in. (28.6 x 22.2 cm)

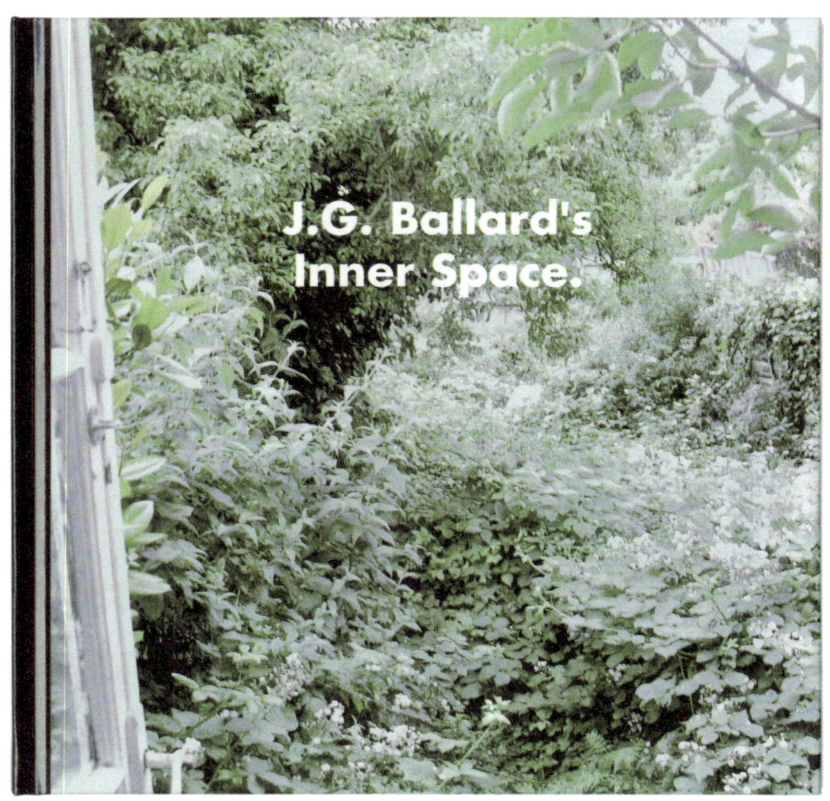
J.G. Ballard's
Inner Space.

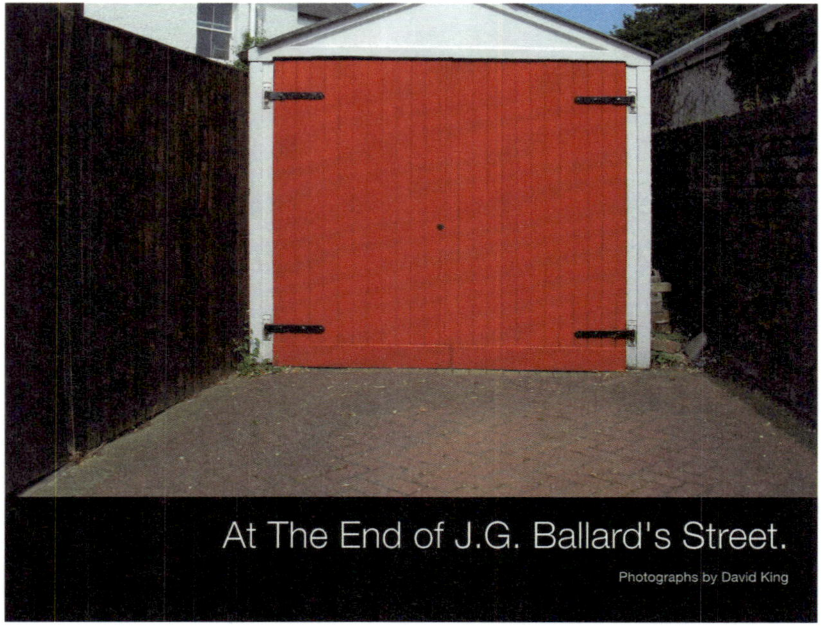
At The End of J.G. Ballard's Street.
Photographs by David King

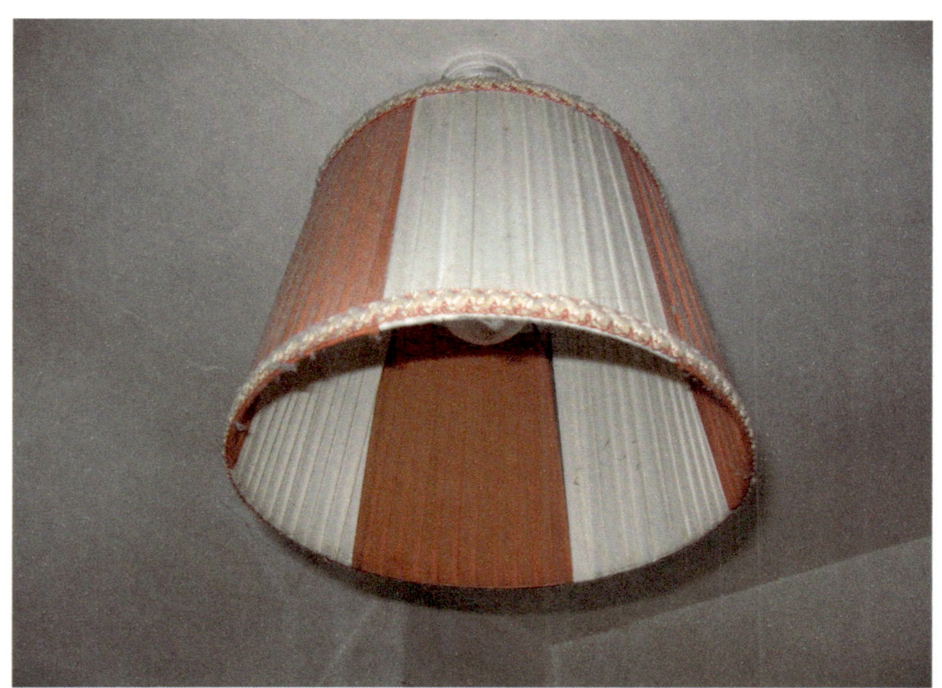

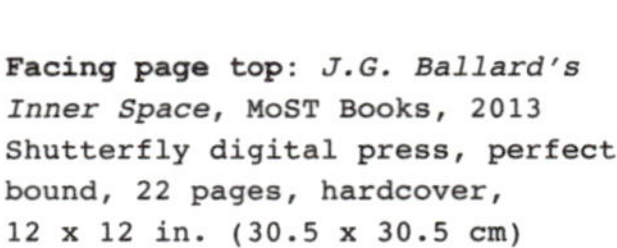

Facing page top: *J.G. Ballard's Inner Space*, MoST Books, 2013
Shutterfly digital press, perfect bound, 22 pages, hardcover,
12 x 12 in. (30.5 x 30.5 cm)

At The End of J.G Ballard's Street, 2010
Prototype, never realized,
32 pages, 11.25 x 8.75 in.
(28.6 x 22.2 cm)

Top and right: *J.G. Ballard's Inner Space*, MoST Books, 2013
Shutterfly digital press, perfect bound, 22 pages, hardcover,
12 x 12 in. (30.5 x 30.5 cm)

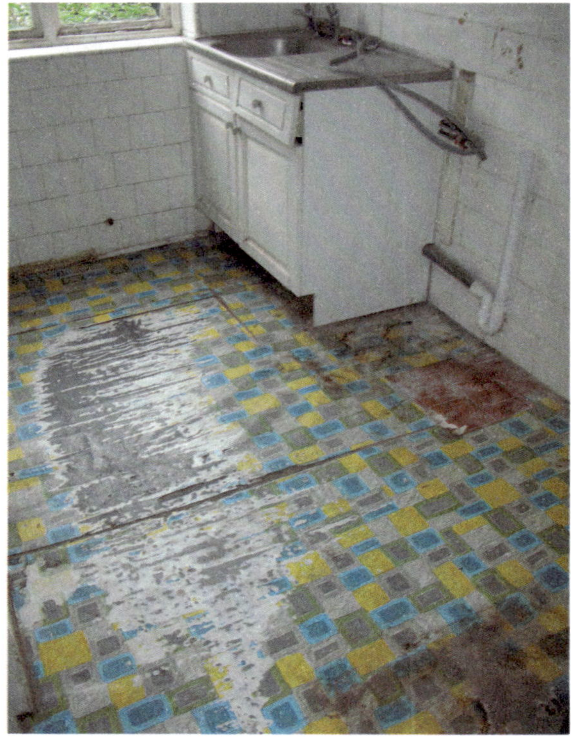

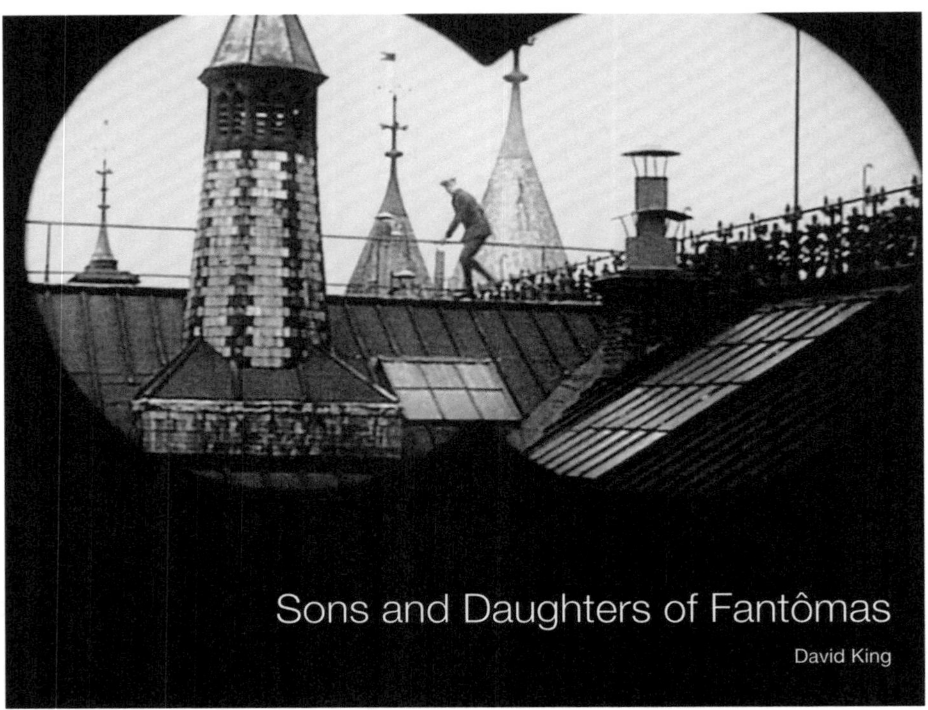
Sons and Daughters of Fantômas
David King

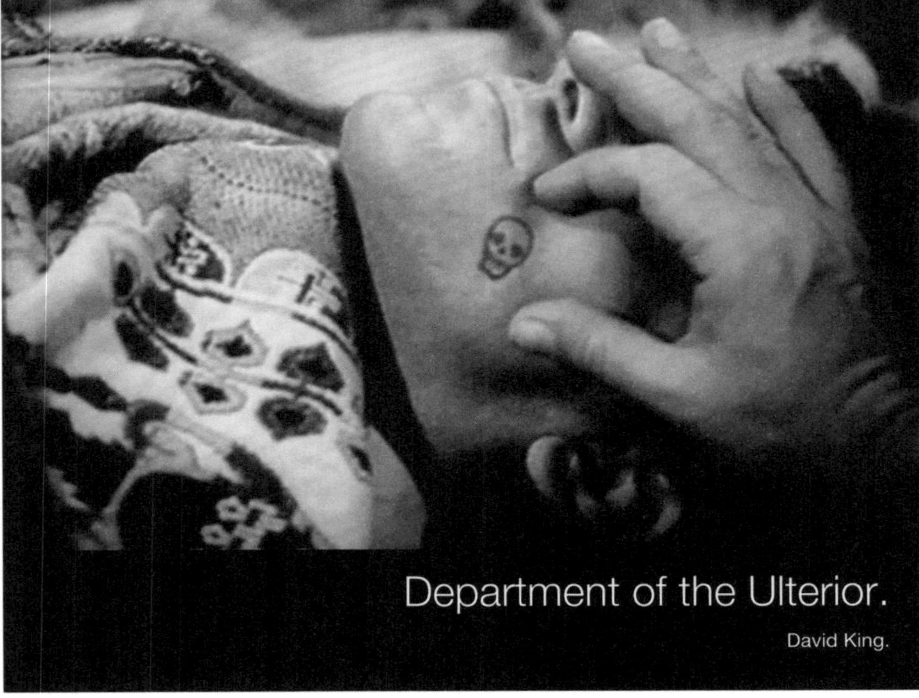
Department of the Ulterior.
David King.

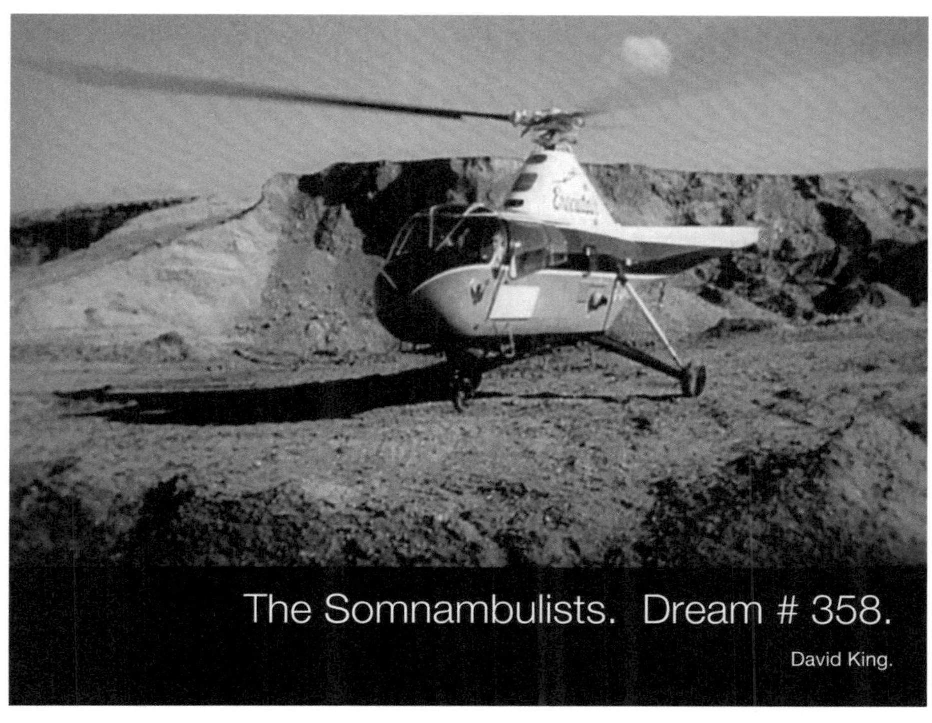

Facing page:
Sons and Daughters of Fantômas, MoST Books, 2011
Apple print-on-demand digital press, perfect bound, 28 pages, 11.25 x 8.75 in. (28.6 x 22.2 cm)

Department of the Ulterior, 2000s
Prototype, never realized, 24 pages, 11.25 x 8.75 in. (28.6 x 22.2 cm)

Above: *The Somnambulists. Dream # 358.*, MOsT Books, 2011
Apple print-on-demand digital press, perfect bound, 22 pages, 11.25 x 8.75 in. (28.6 x 22.2 cm)

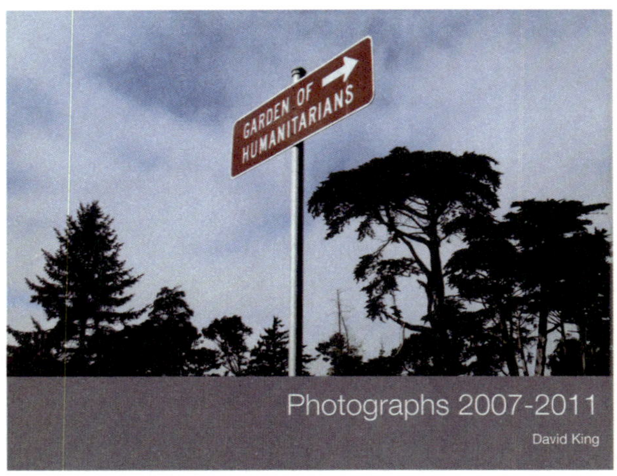

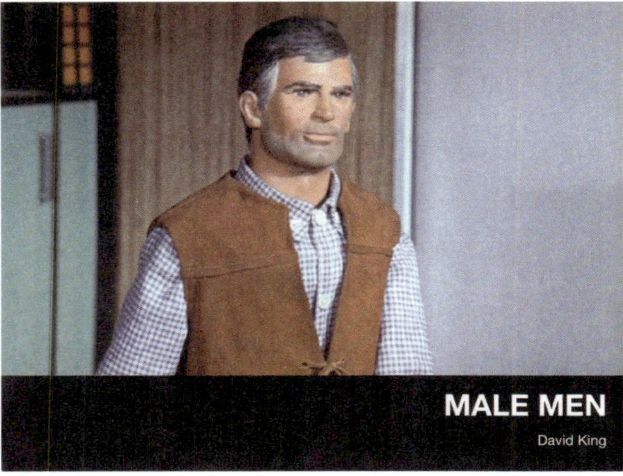

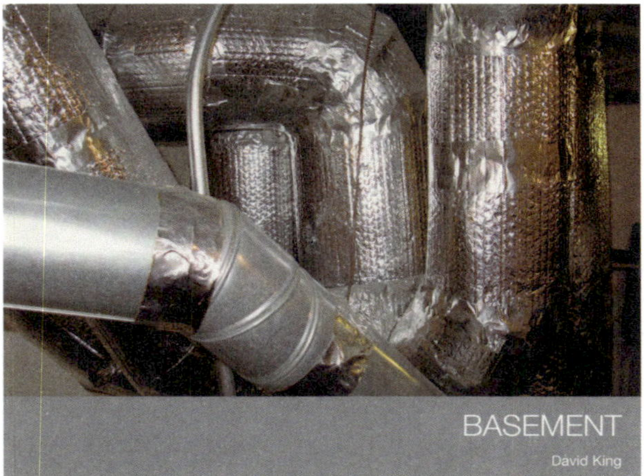

Top to bottom: *Photographs 2007-2011*, MOsT Books, 2011
Apple print-on-demand digital press, perfect bound, 40 pages, hardcover, 11.25 x 8.75 in. (28.6 x 22.2 cm)

Male Men, MOsT Books, revised edition, 2012
Apple print-on-demand digital press, perfect bound, 22 pages, hardcover, 11.25 x 8.75 in. (28.6 x 22.2 cm)

Basement, 2008
Apple print-on-demand digital press, perfect bound, 20 pages, 11 x 8.5 in. (27.9 x 21.6 cm)

Facing page: Interior page, *Doubt*, 2018
Prototype, never realized, 68 pages, 8.5 x 11 in. (21.6 x 27.9 cm)

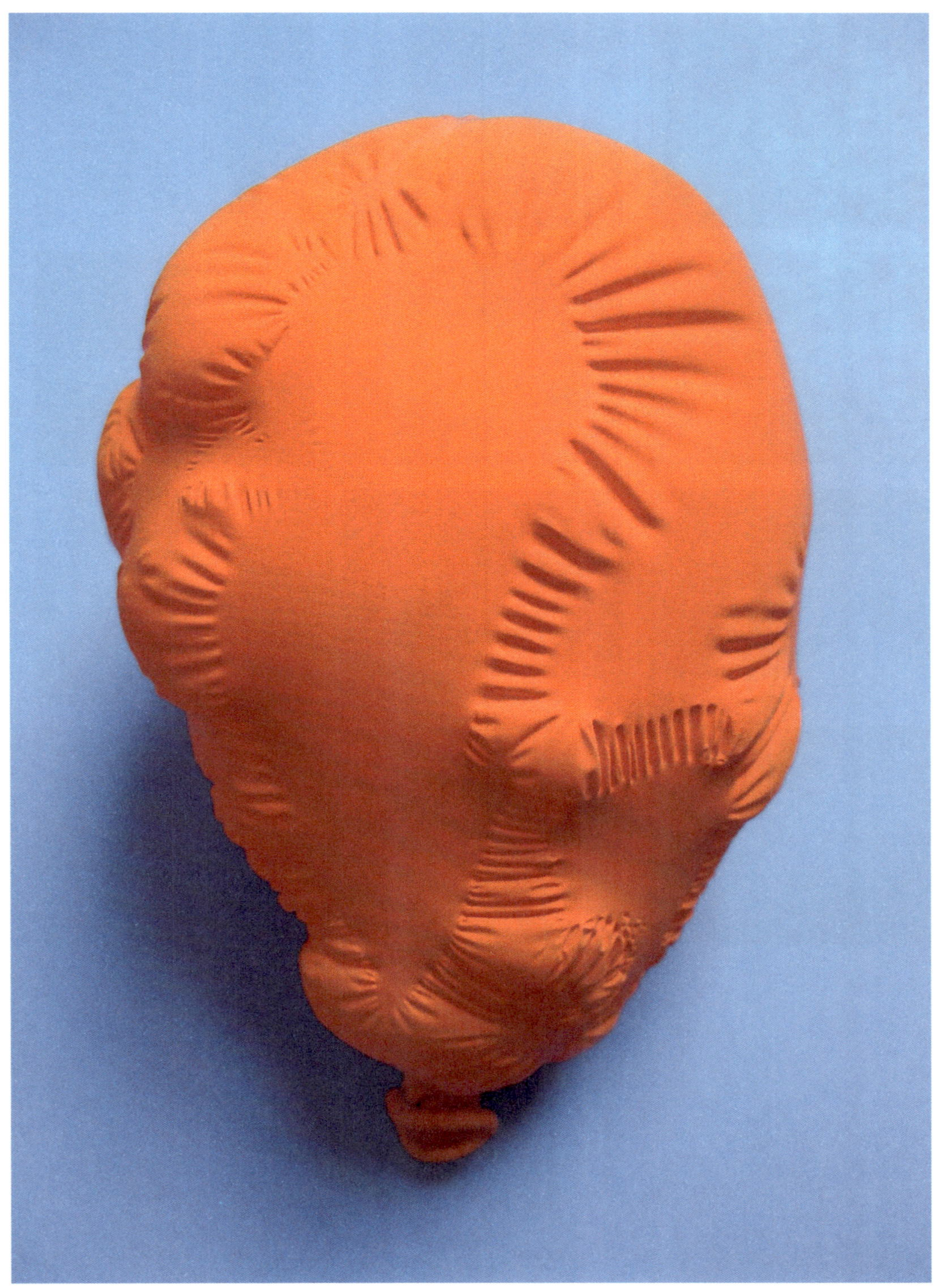

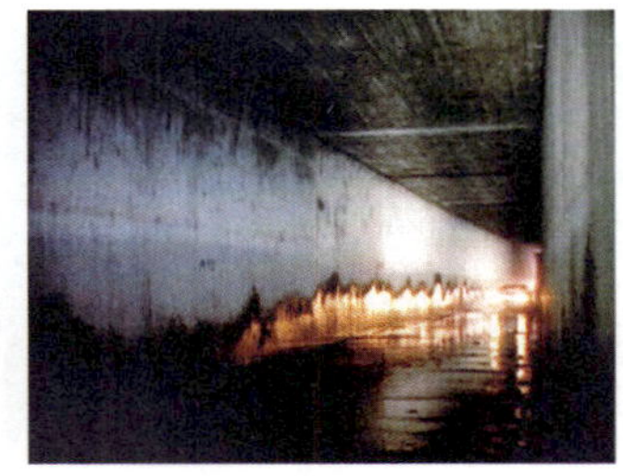

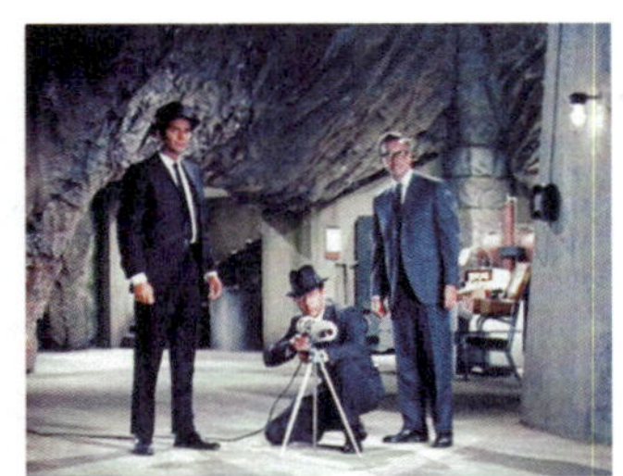

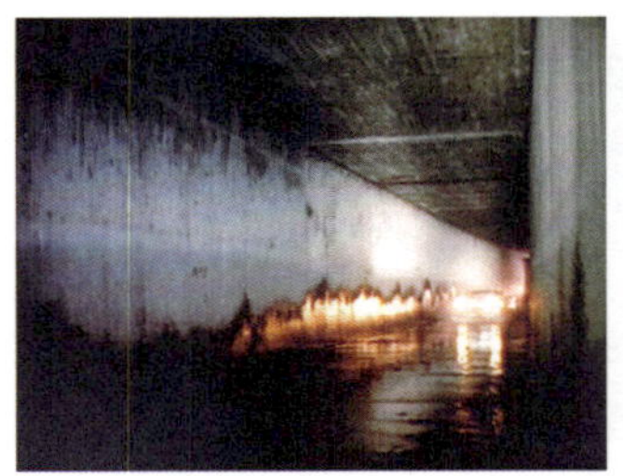

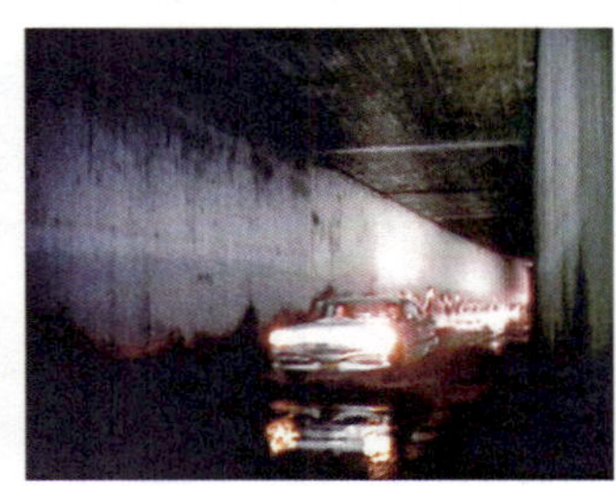

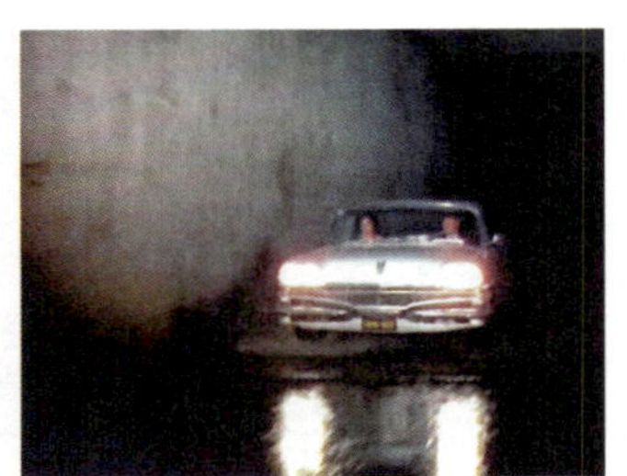

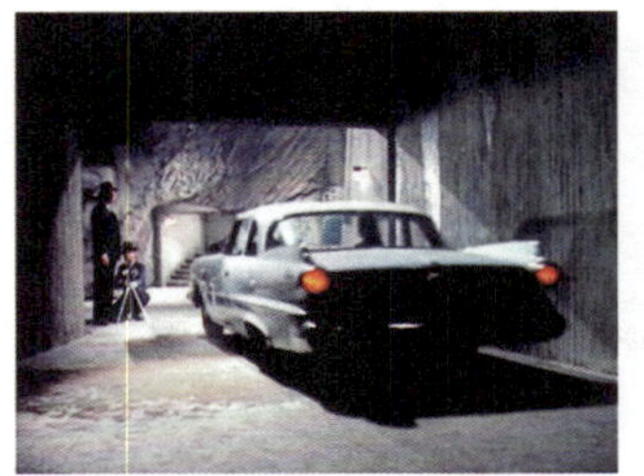

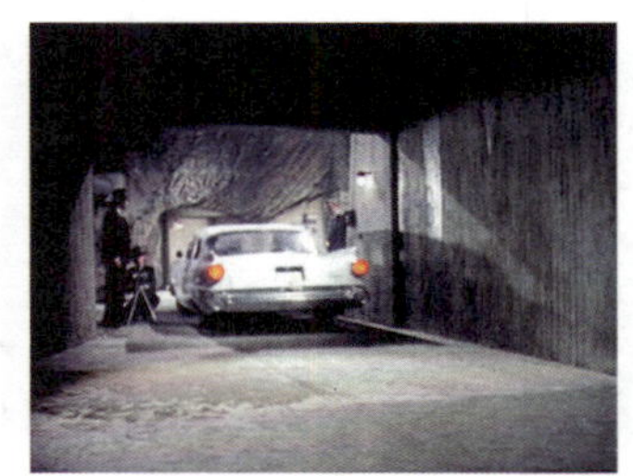

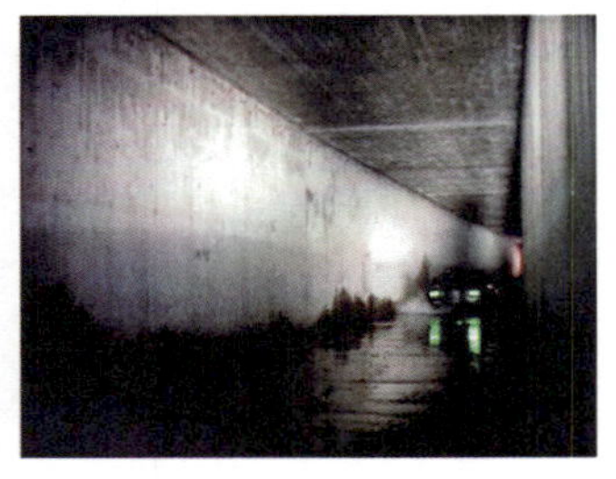

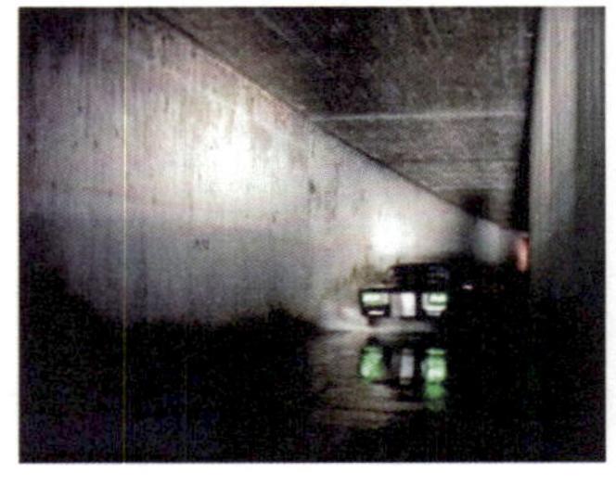

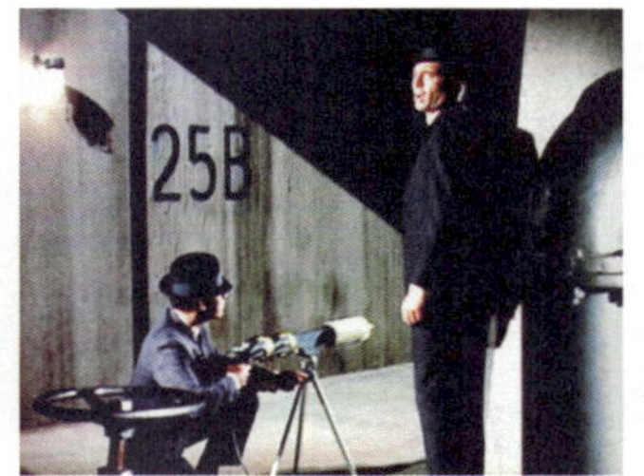
25B

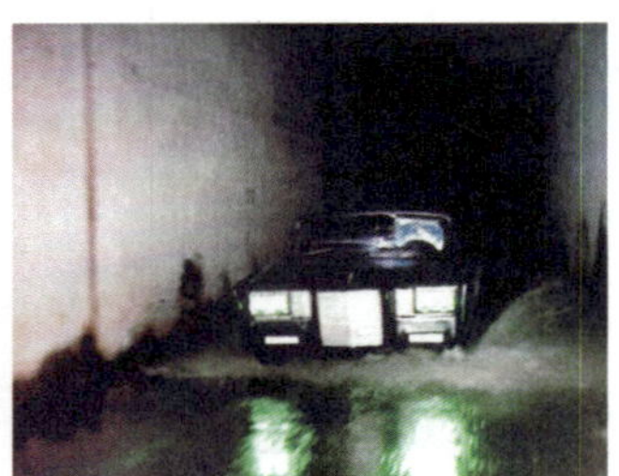

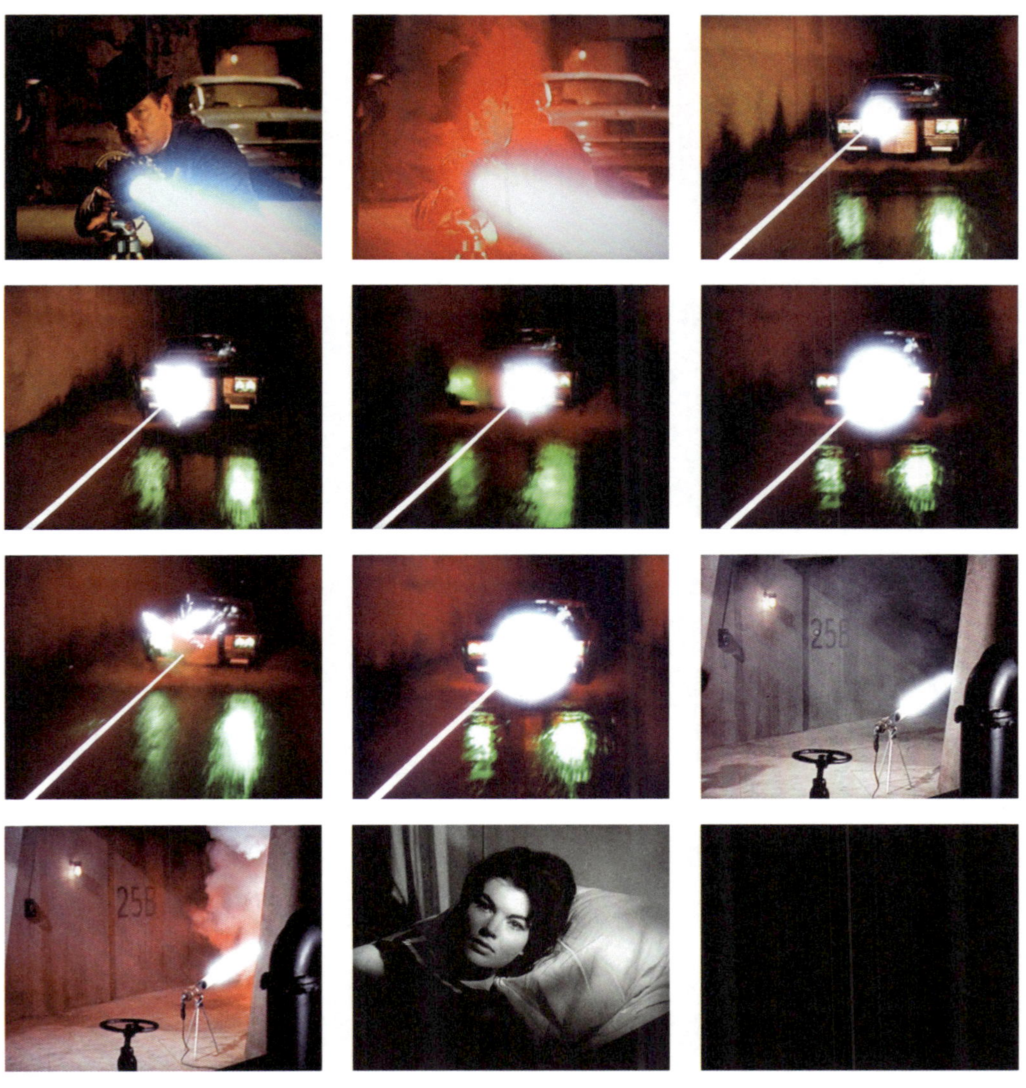

The Somnambulists. Dream # 358., MOsT Books, 2011
Apple print-on-demand digital press, perfect bound,
22 pages, 11.25 x 8.75 in. (28.6 x 22.2 cm)

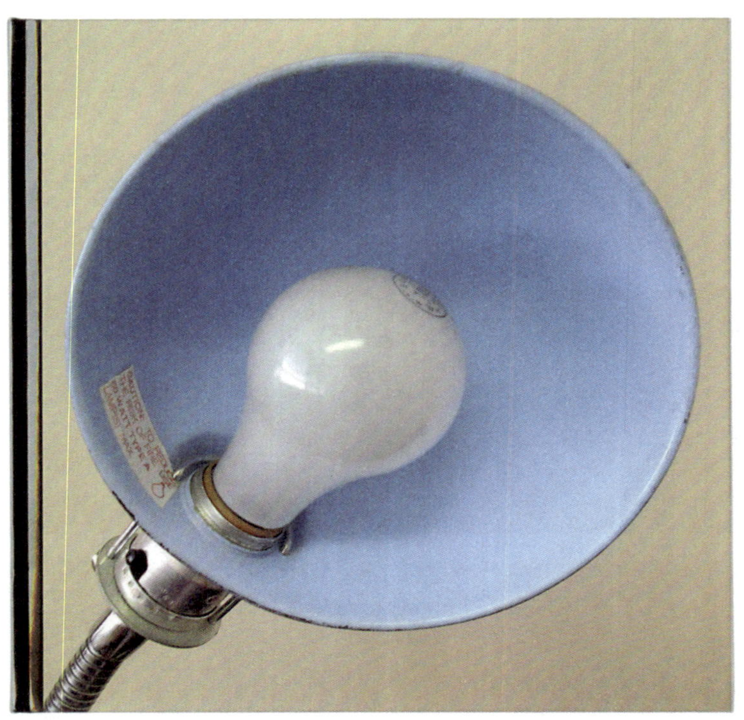

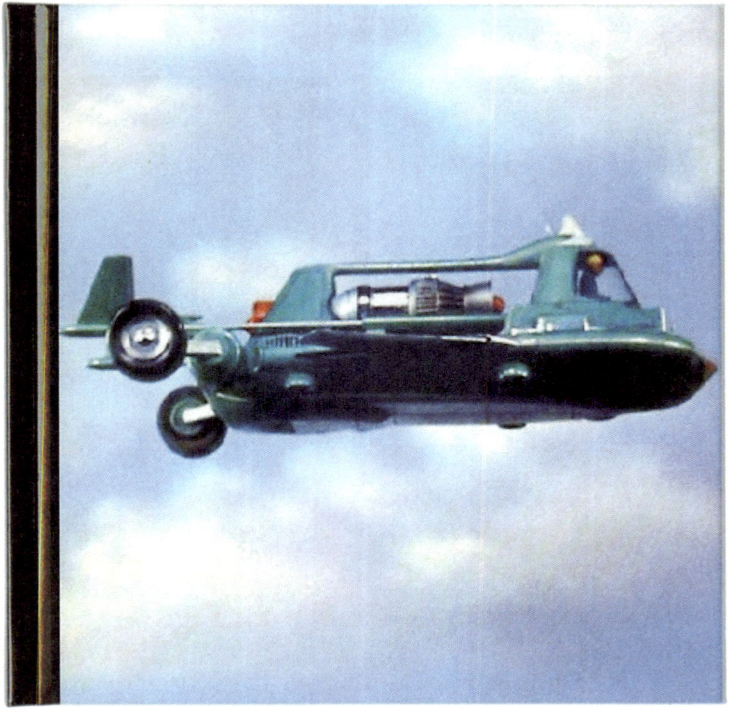

Left: *Several Journeys in One*, 2012
Shutterfly digital press, perfect bound, 22 pages, hardcover, 12 x 12 in. (30.5 x 30.5 cm)

I Dreamt I Dwelt in Marble Halls, 2012
Shutterfly digital press, perfect bound, 22 pages, hardcover, 12 x 12 in. (30.5 x 30.5 cm)

Facing page: *The Sound Mirrors*, 2012
Shutterfly digital press, perfect bound, 22 pages, hardcover, 12 x 12 in. (30.5 x 30.5 cm)

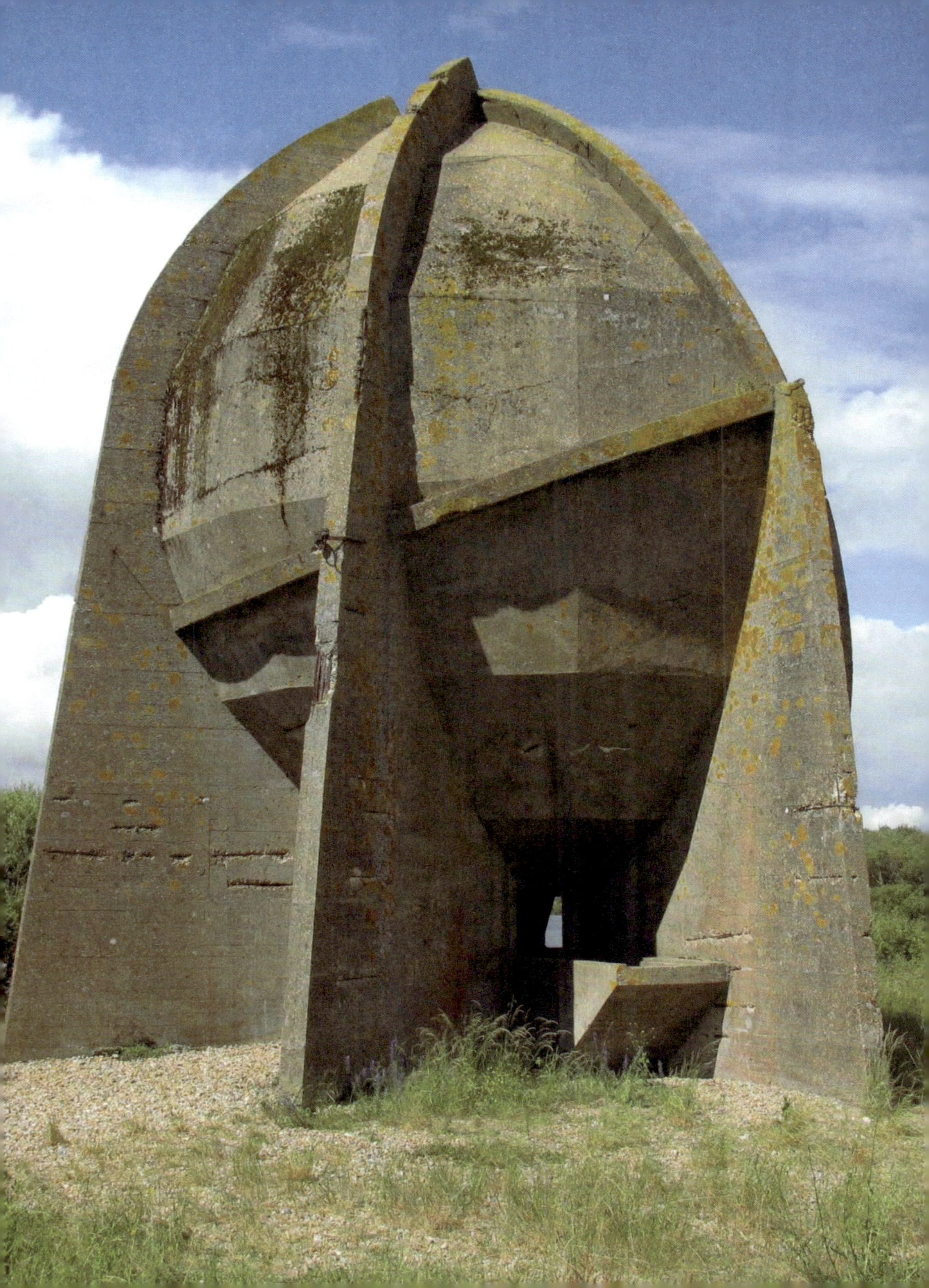

Books published by others, 2010–2019

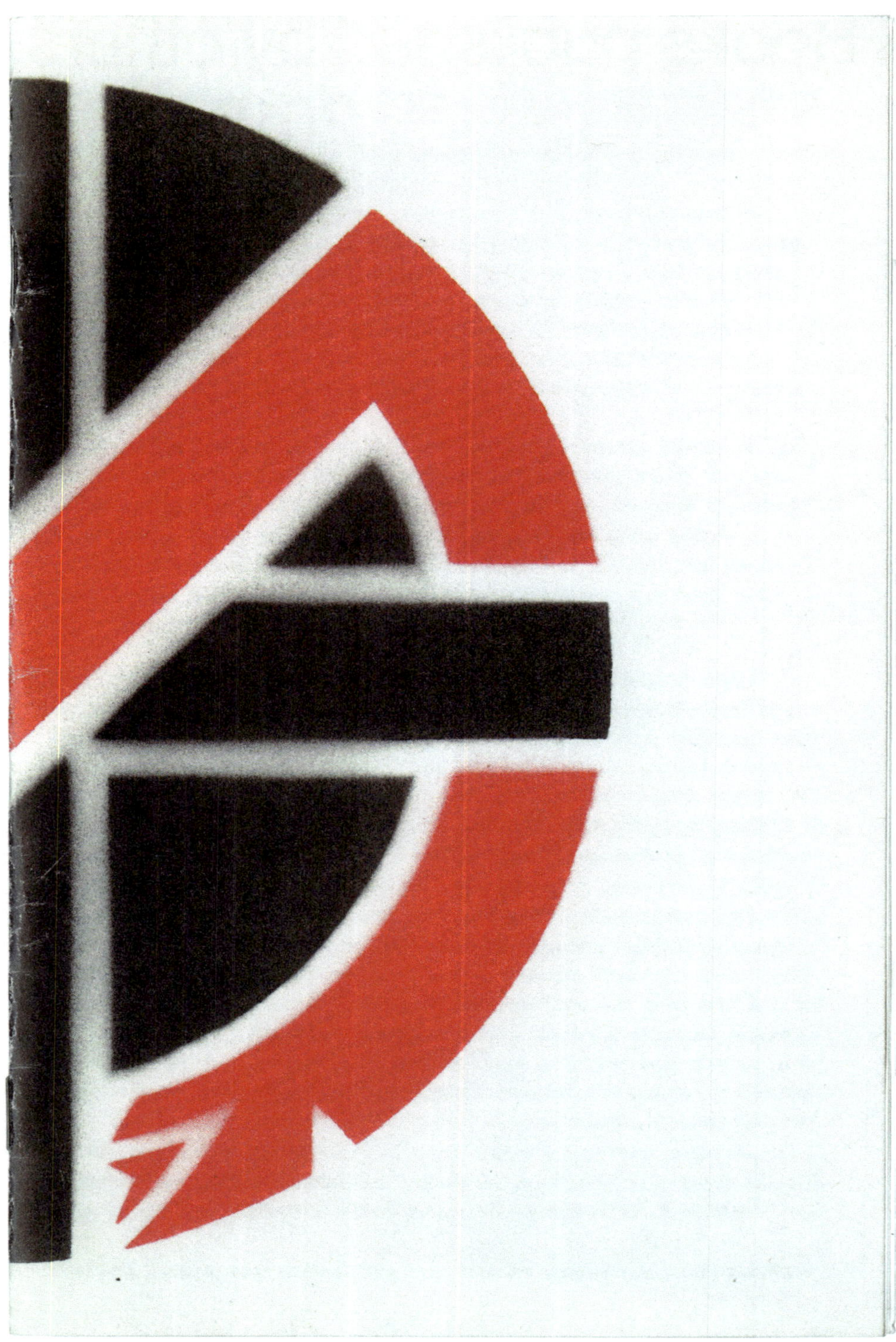

Facing page: *Symbol*, Goteblüd, 2011
Digital press, staple bound, 12 pages,
8.5 x 5.5 in. (21.6 x 14 cm)

Below: *Secret Origins of the Crass Symbol*, &Pens Press, 2013
Offset, perfect bound, 28 pages,
edition of 500, 7 x 7 in. (17.8 x 17.8 cm)

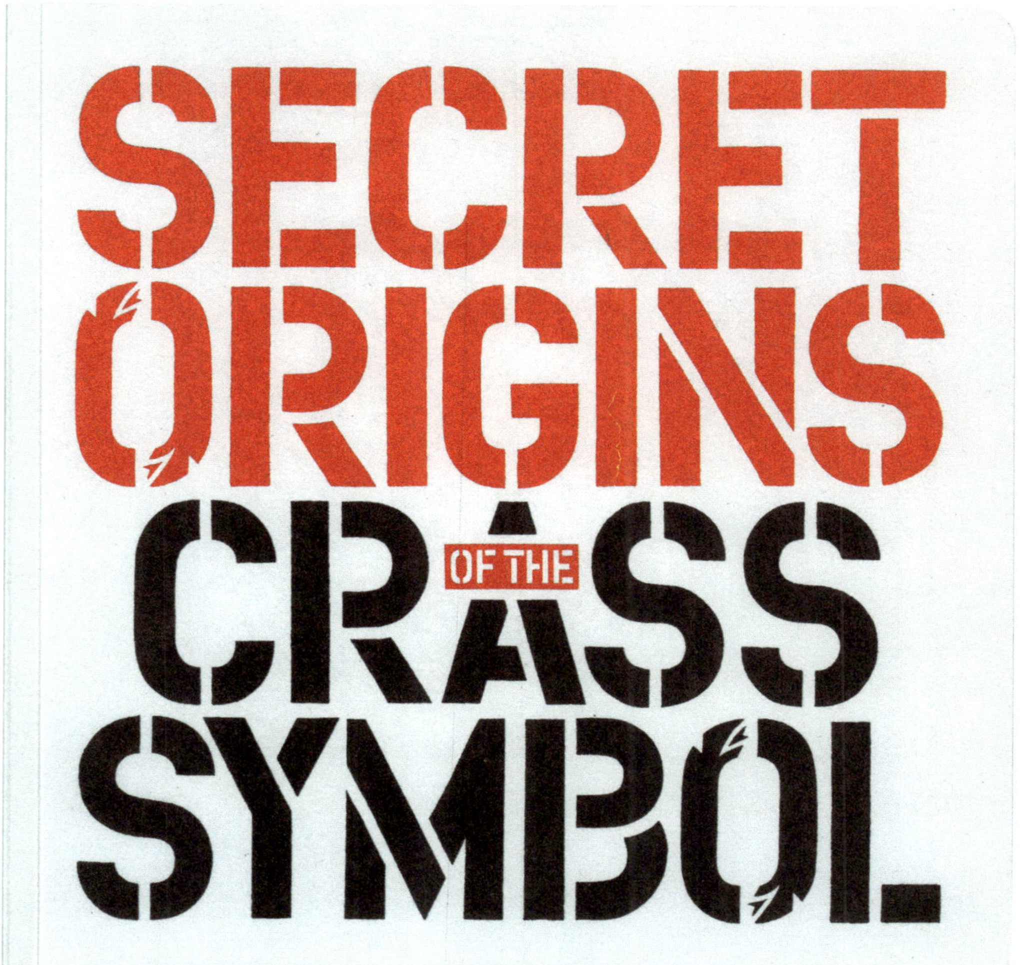

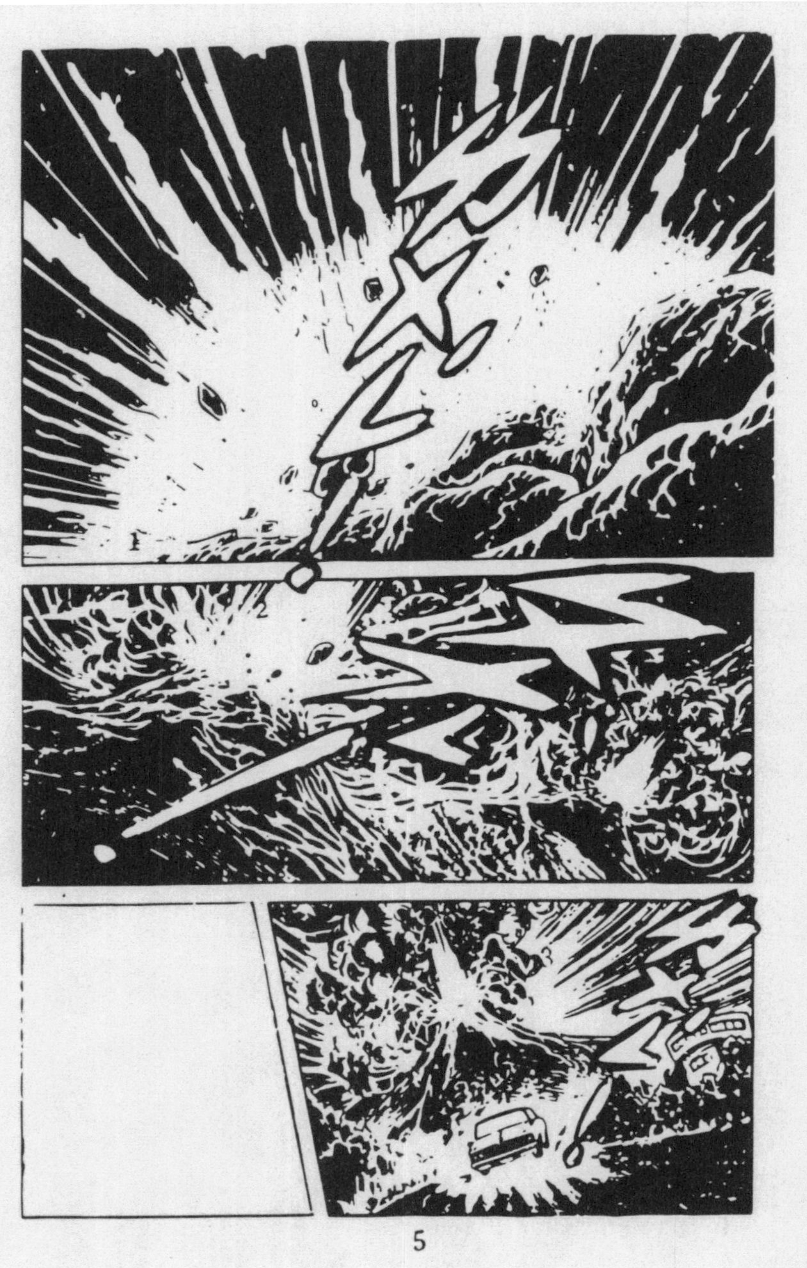
5

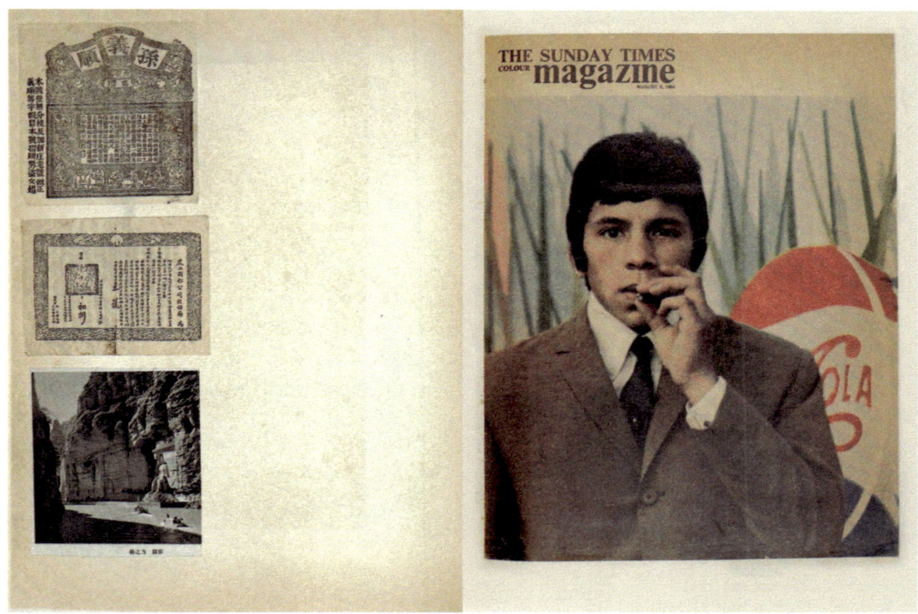

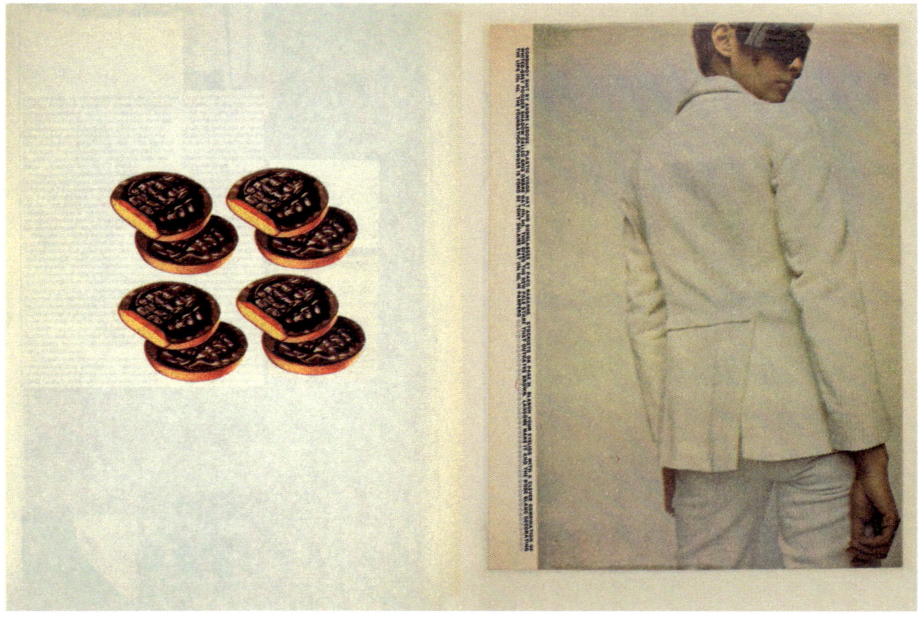

Pages 96–101: *Scrapbook*, Colpa Press, 2017
Digital press, section-sewn and perfect bound, 112 pages, edition of 50, 9 x 12 in. (22.9 x 30.5 cm)

King maintained numerous scrapbooks filled with clippings, comics, typography and graphics that he collected from the 1960s through to the 2000s. Pages from these books were photographed and reproduced in Scrapbook.

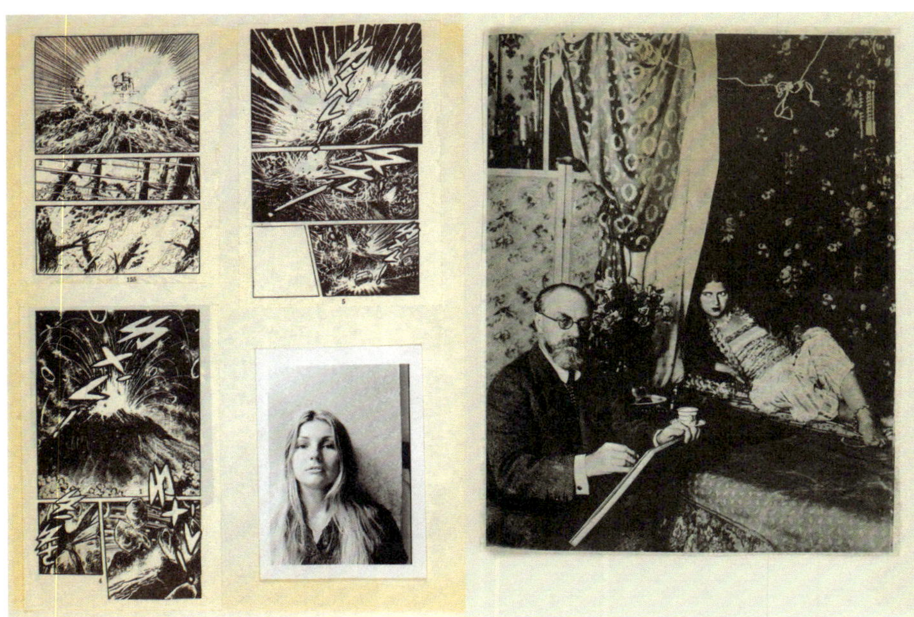

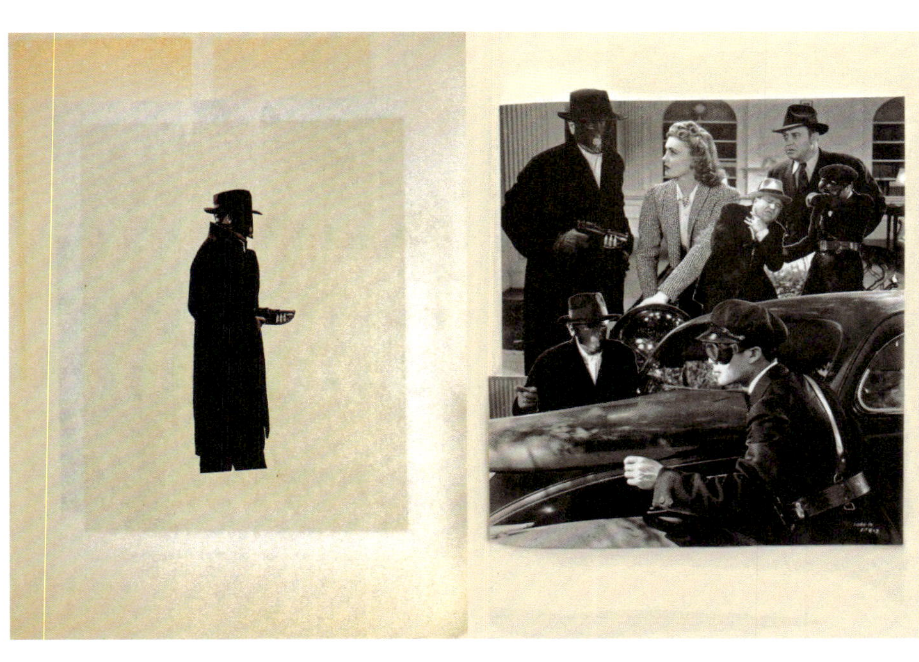

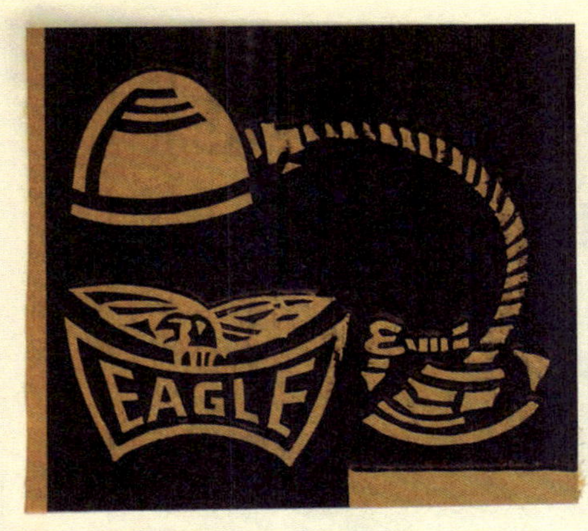

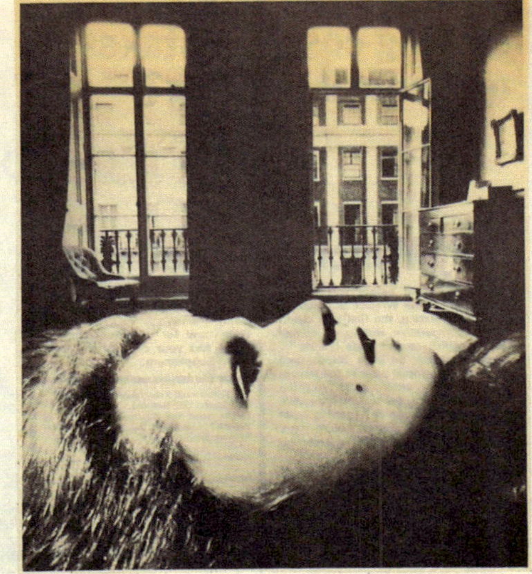

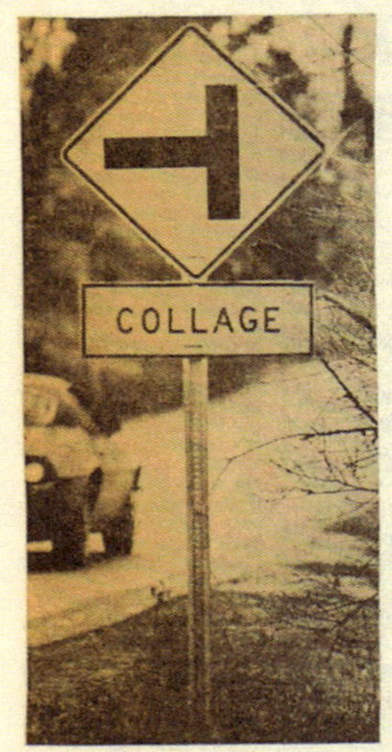

CLOSE COVER BEFORE STRIKING

MAKE
BIG
MONEY

AT
HOME

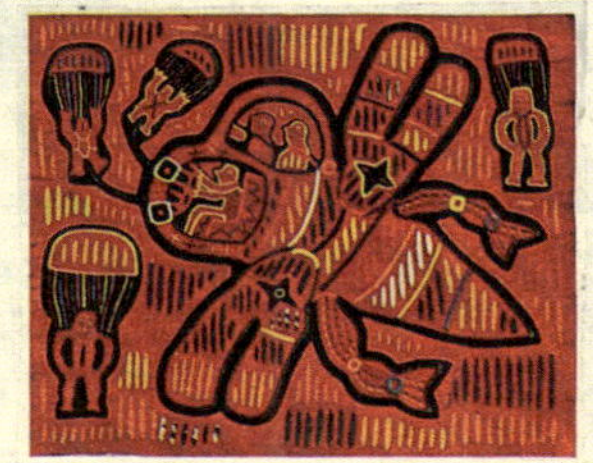

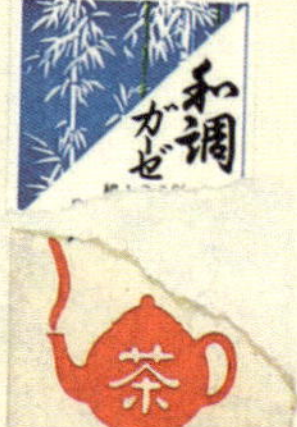

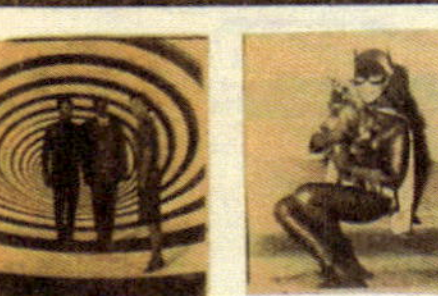

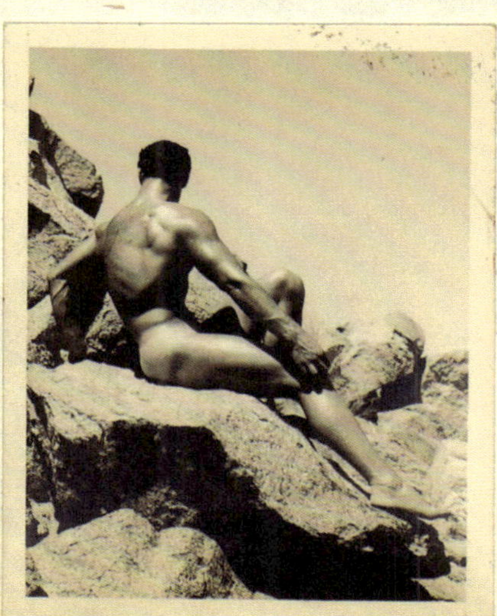

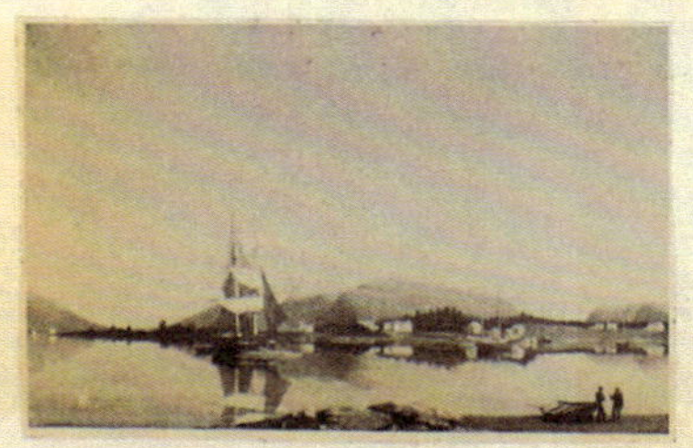

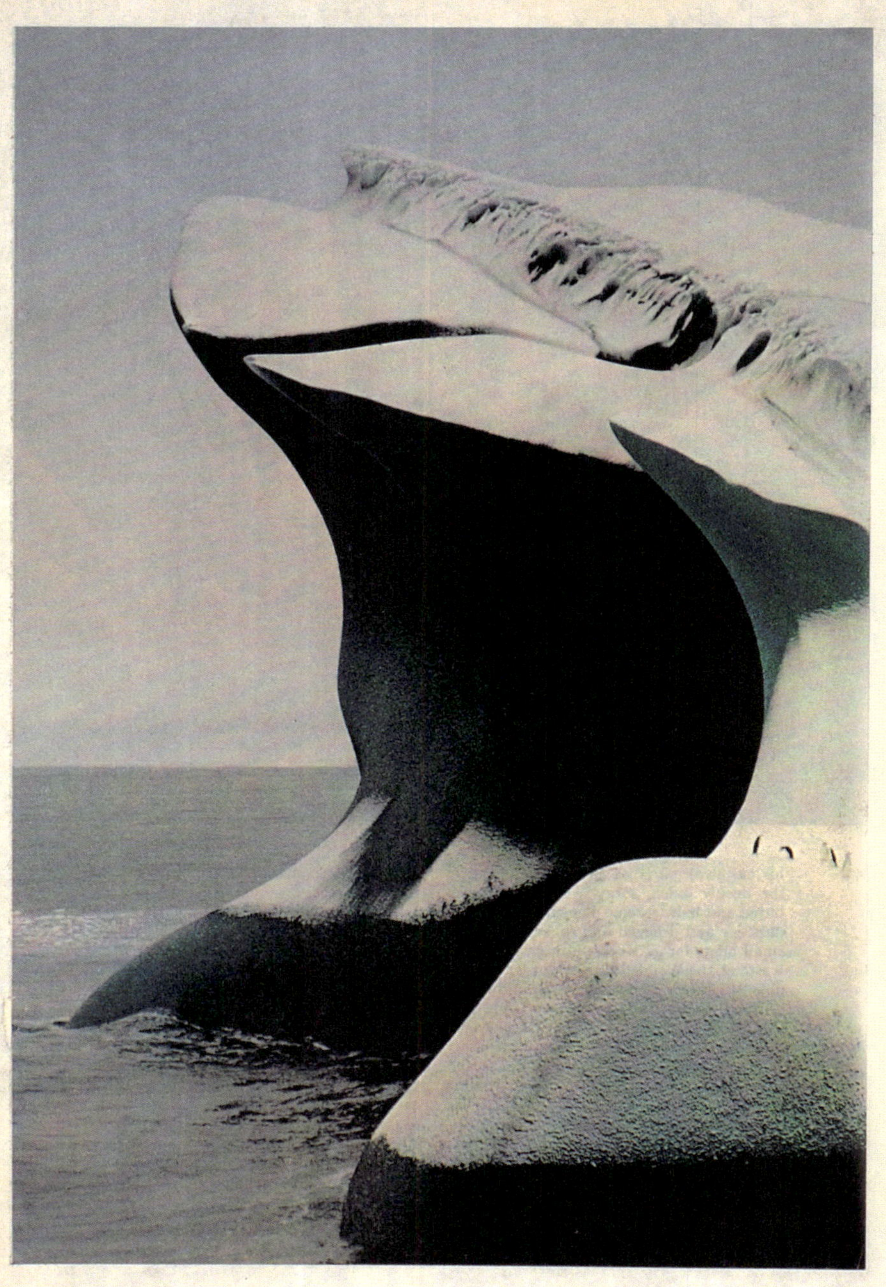

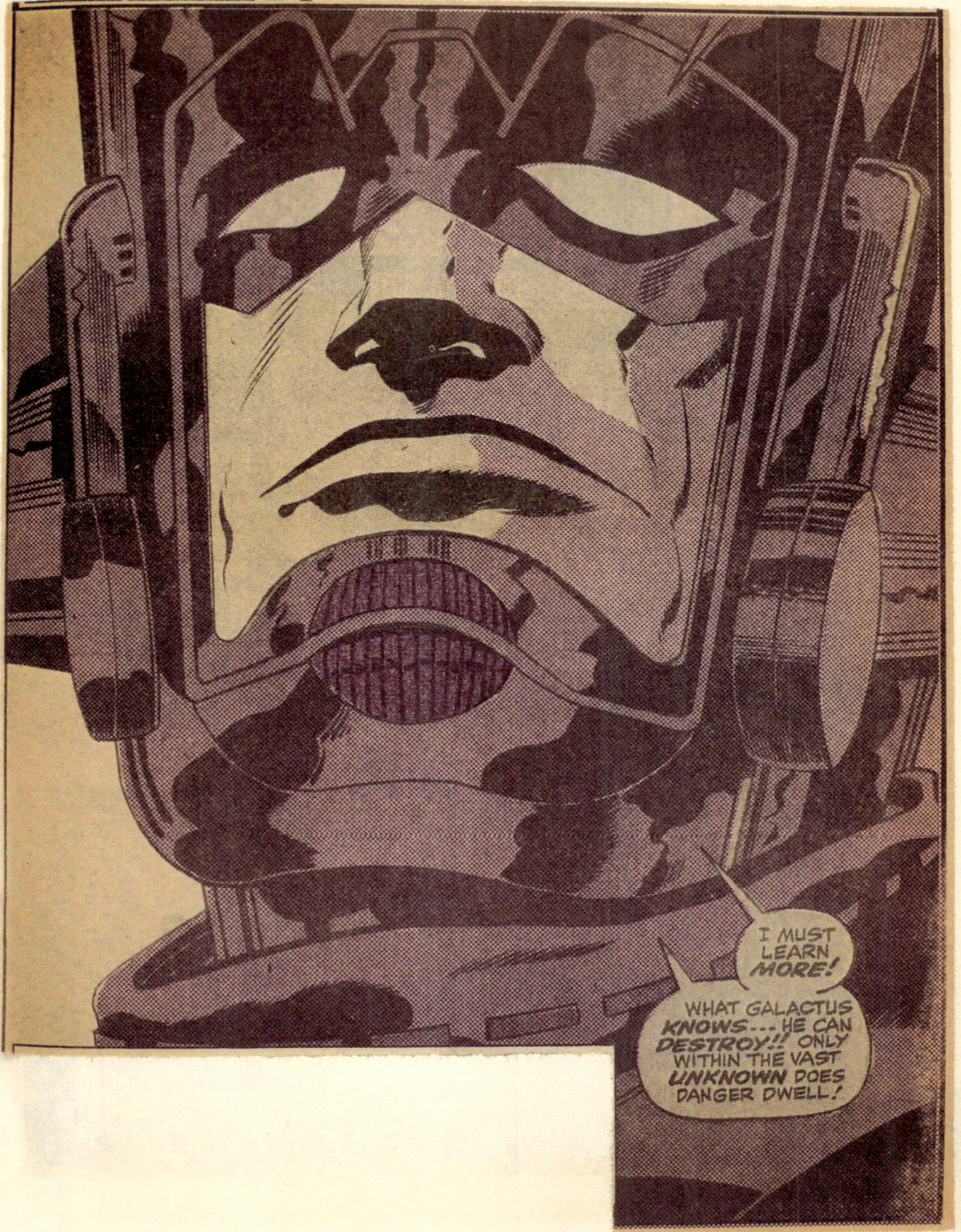
I MUST LEARN MORE!
WHAT GALACTUS KNOWS... HE CAN DESTROY!! ONLY WITHIN THE VAST UNKNOWN DOES DANGER DWELL!

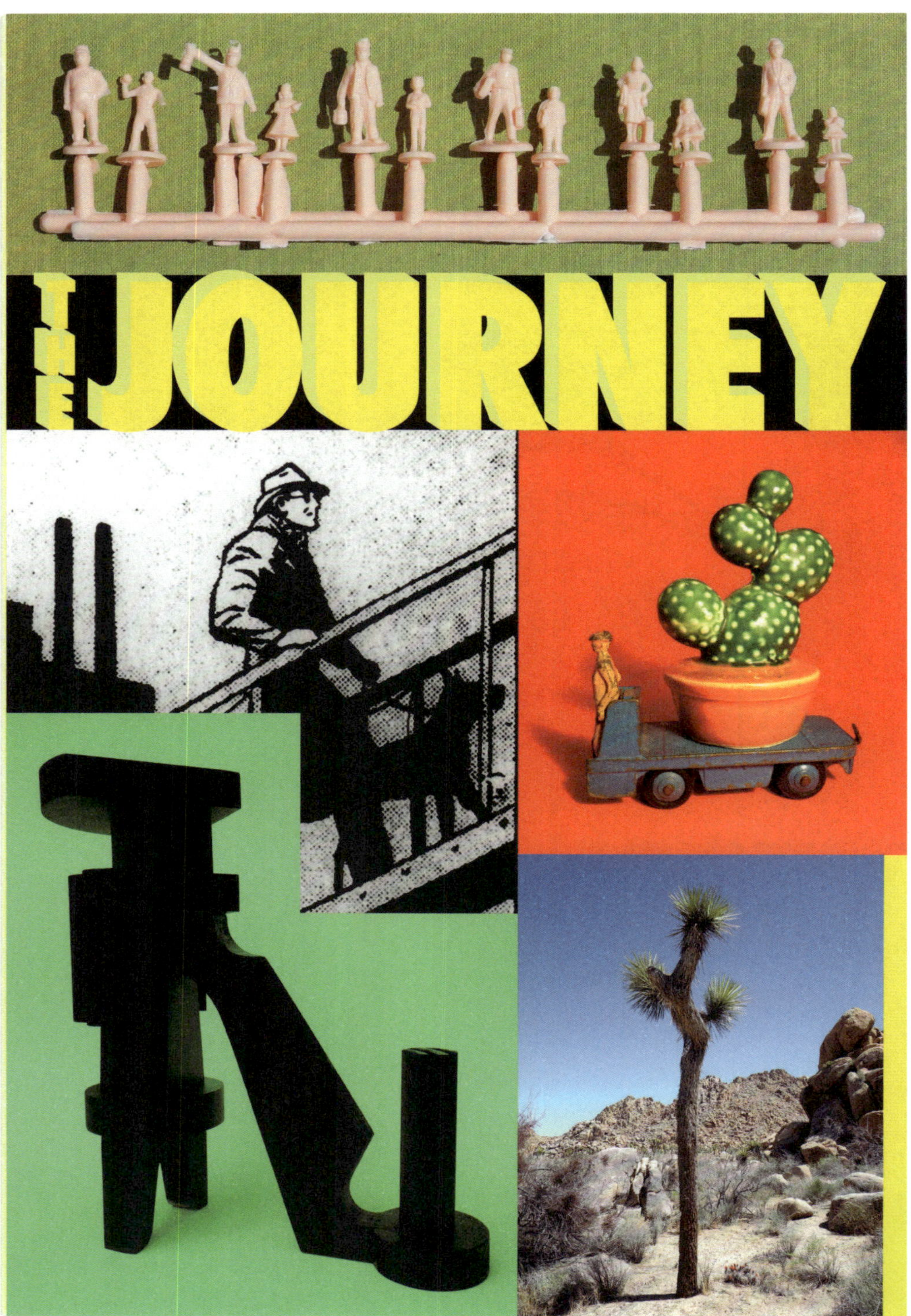
THE JOURNEY

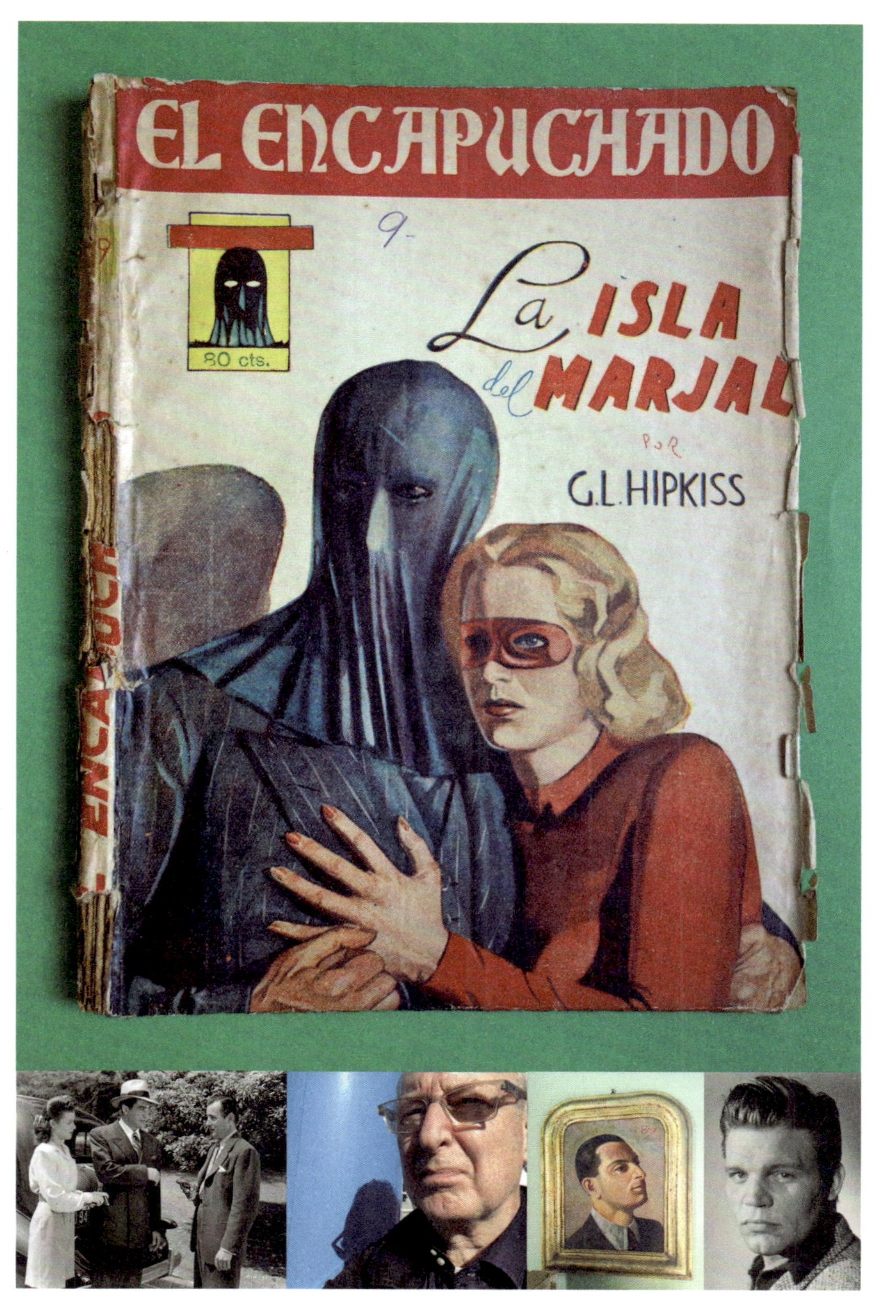

Pages 102-103: *The Journey*, Colpa Press, 2019
Digital press, perfect bound, 124 pages, first edition of 50, Signed and numbered, 7.75 x 11.75 in. (19.7 x 29.8 cm)

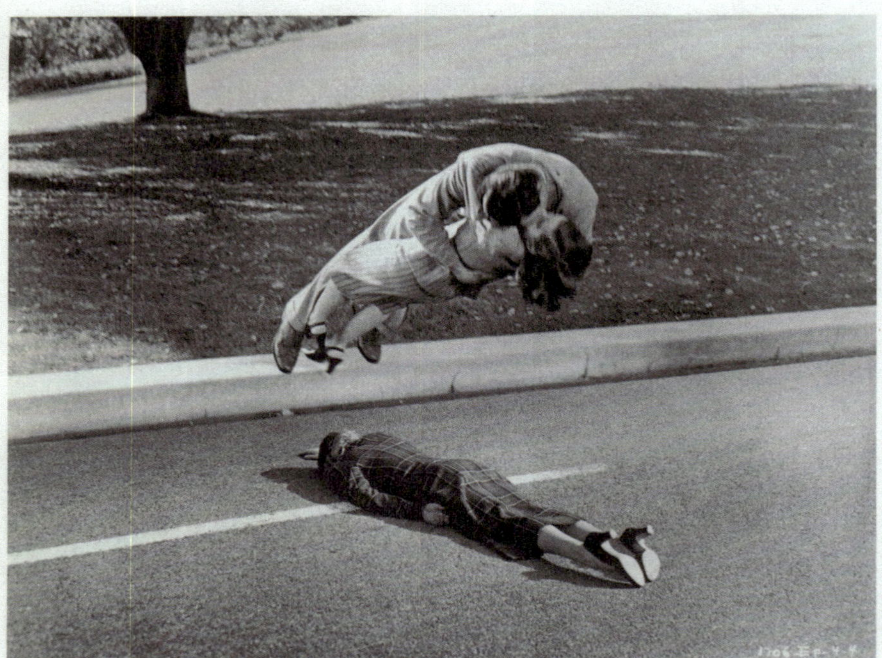

STILL

DAVID KING

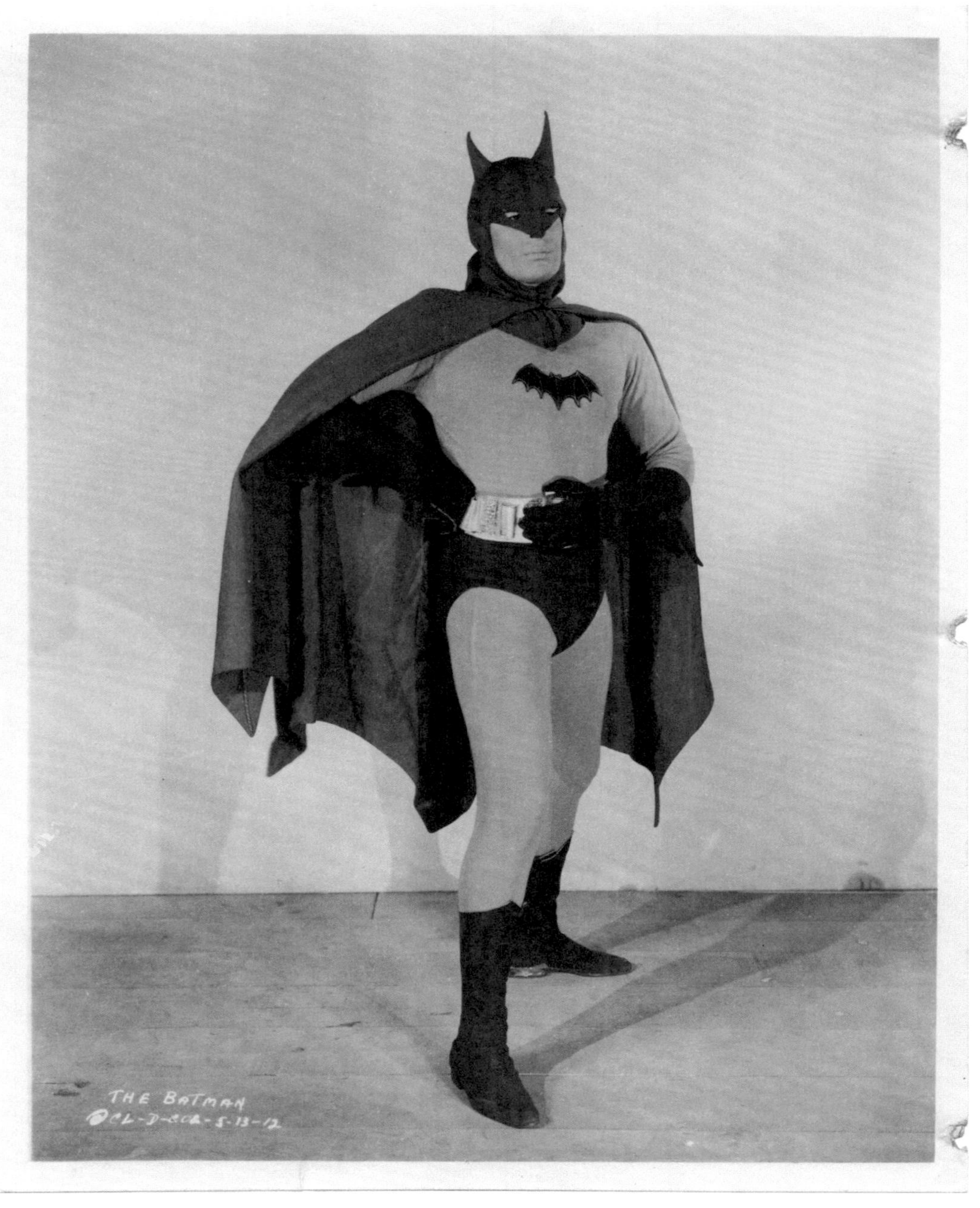

Facing page, above: *Still,* Colpa Press, 2018
Digital press, tape bound, 68 pages,
first edition of 50, 11.75 x 17.75 in.
(29.9 x 45.1 cm)

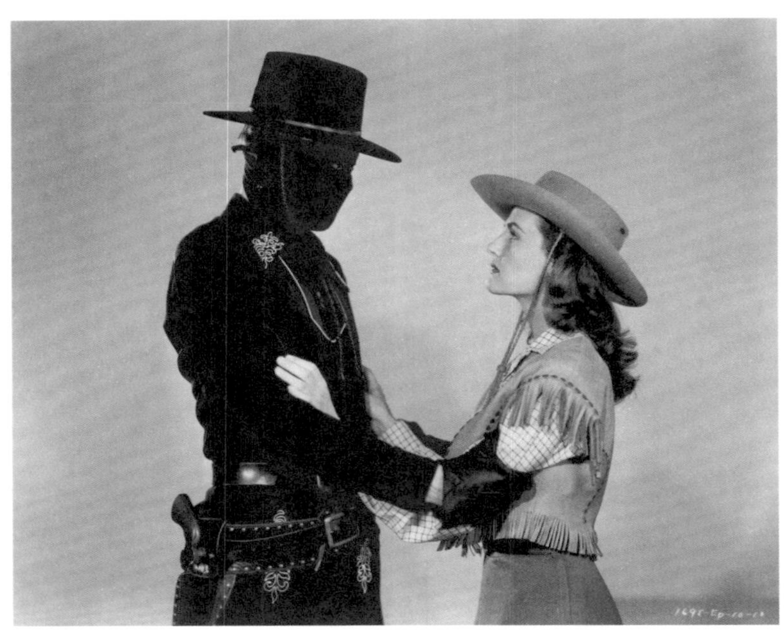

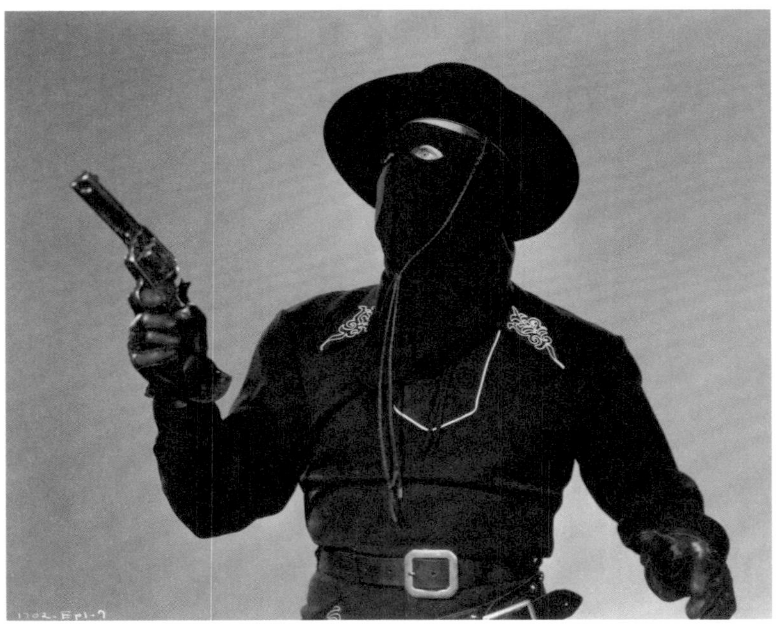

Above, facing page: *Still*, Colpa Press, 2018
Digital press, tape bound, 68 pages, first
edition of 50, 11.75 x 17.75 in. (29.9 X 45.1 cm)

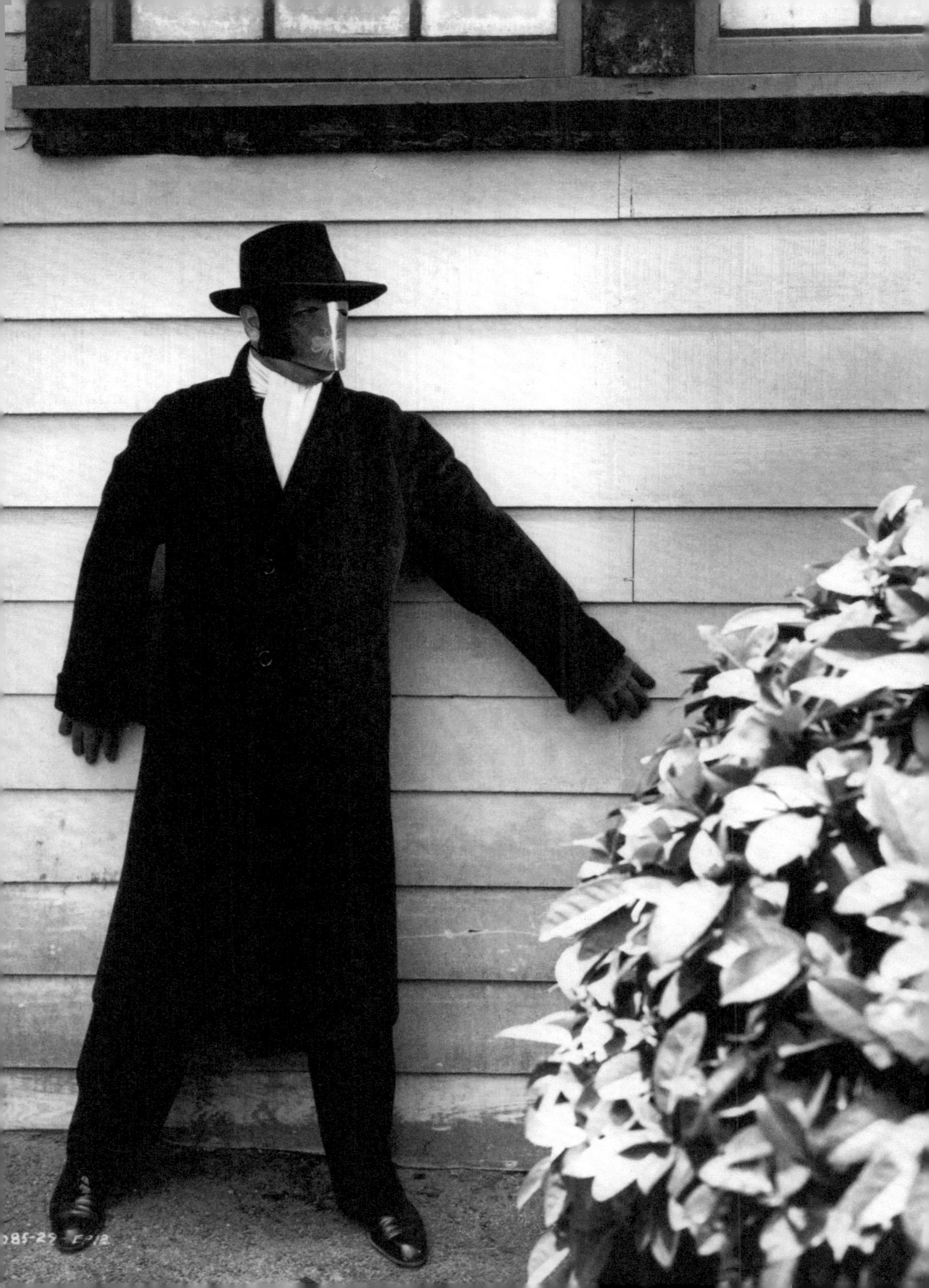
85-29

David King Stencils: Past, Present and Crass!,
Contributors: Matt Borruso, Steven Heller, Howard Rodman, and Barry McGee, Gingko Press with Kill Yr Idols, 2019
Offset, sewn binding, 200 pages, 8 x 10 in. (20.3 X 25.4 cm)

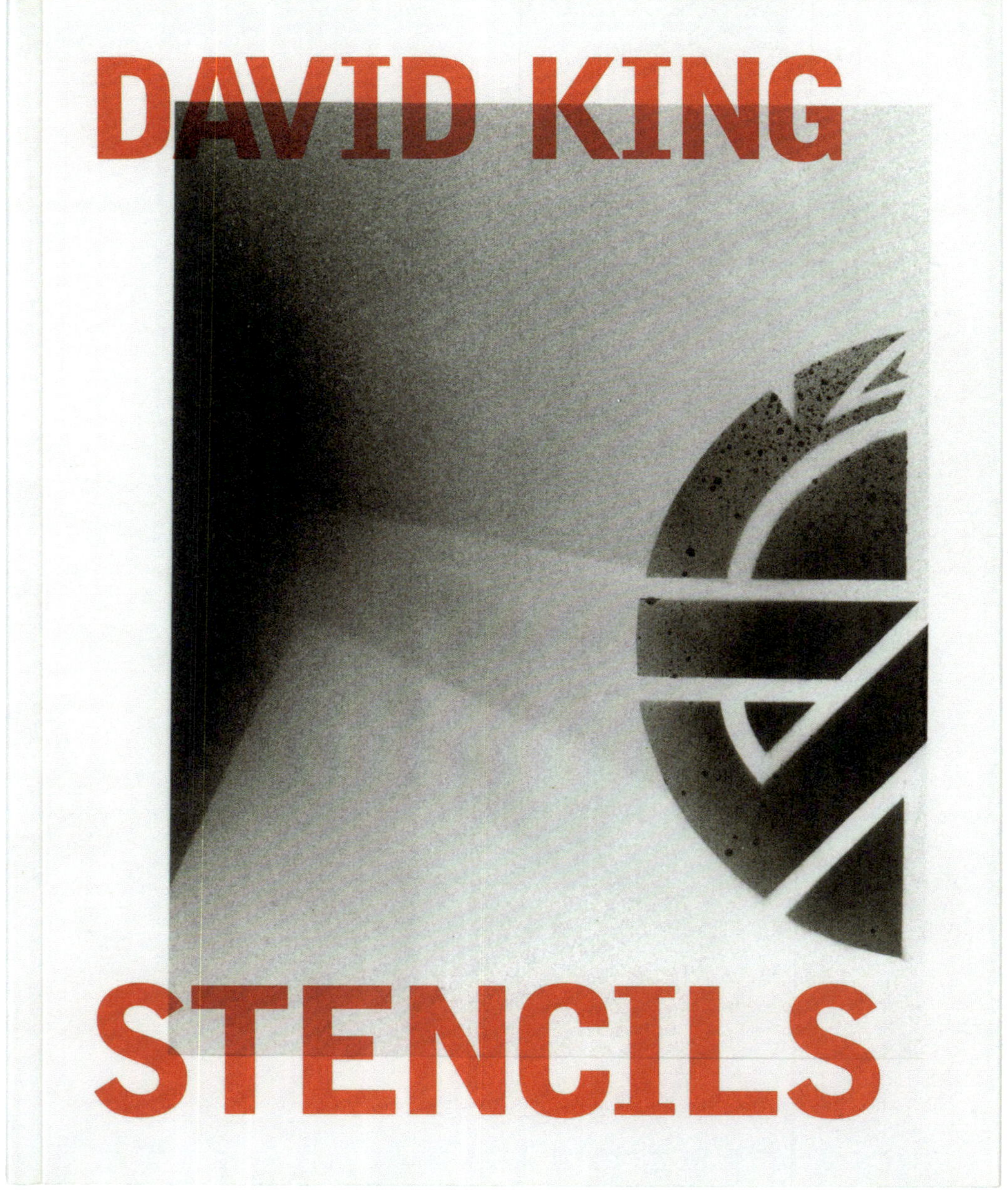

New, Improved?, 2011
Hand cut stencil with spray paint, 11 x 14 in.
(27.9 x 35.6 cm)

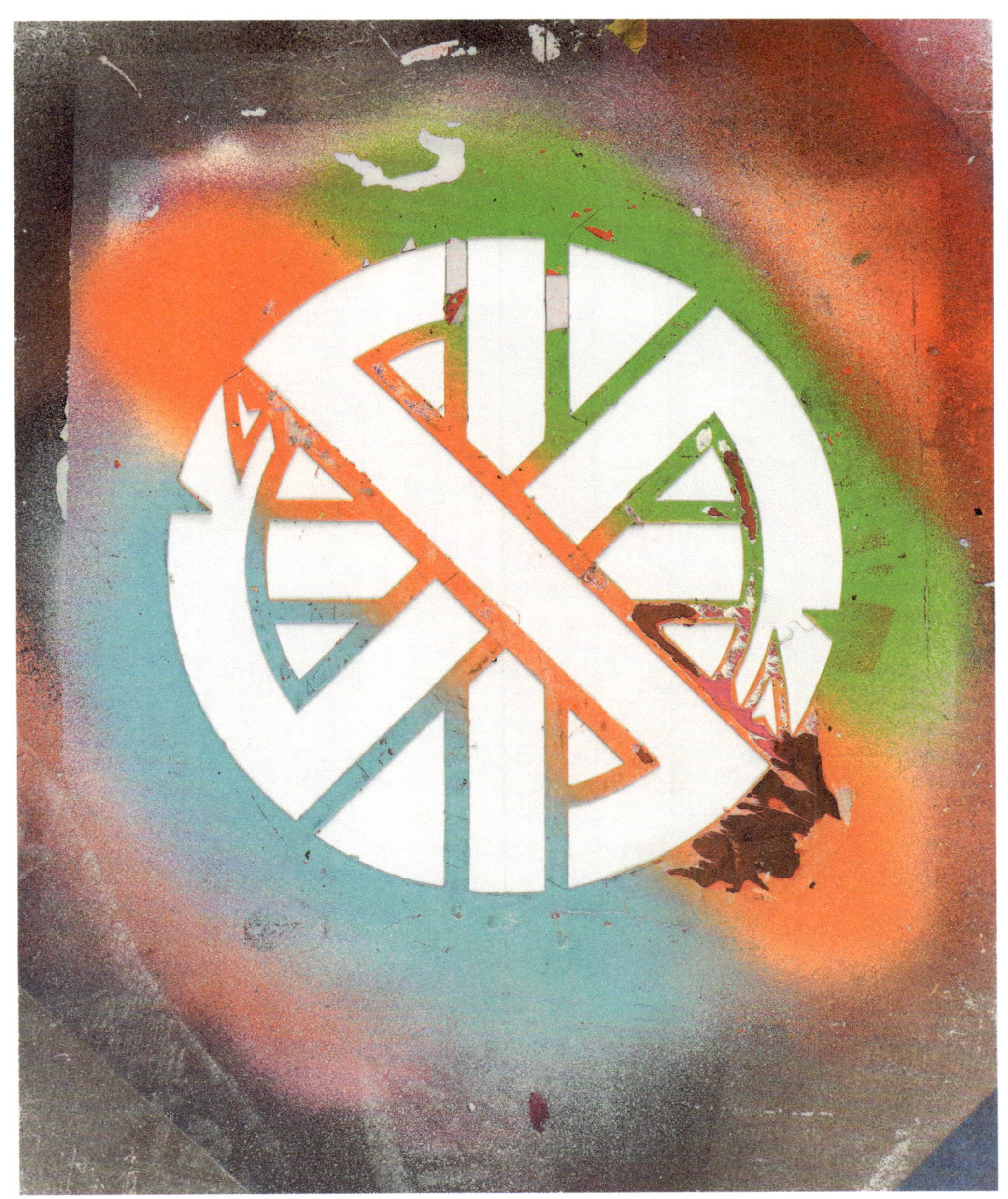

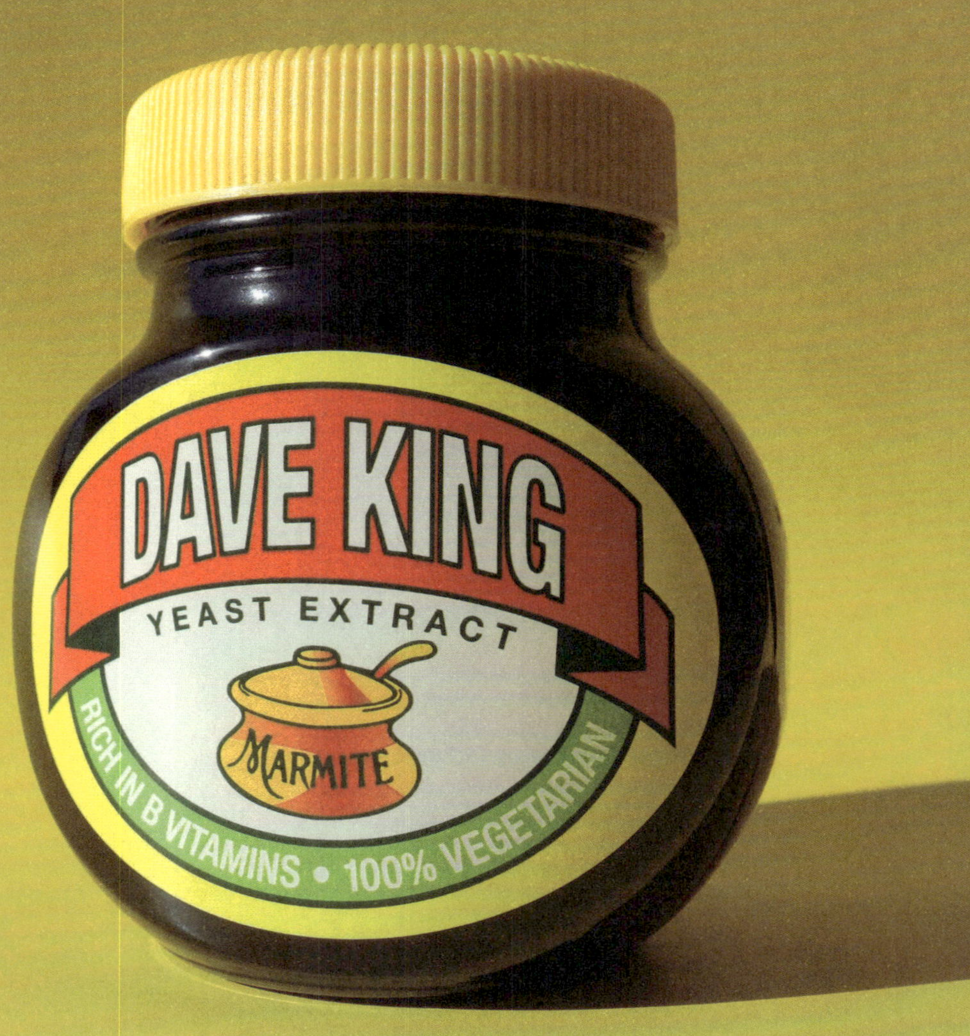
DAVE KING
YEAST EXTRACT
MARMITE
RICH IN B VITAMINS • 100% VEGETARIAN

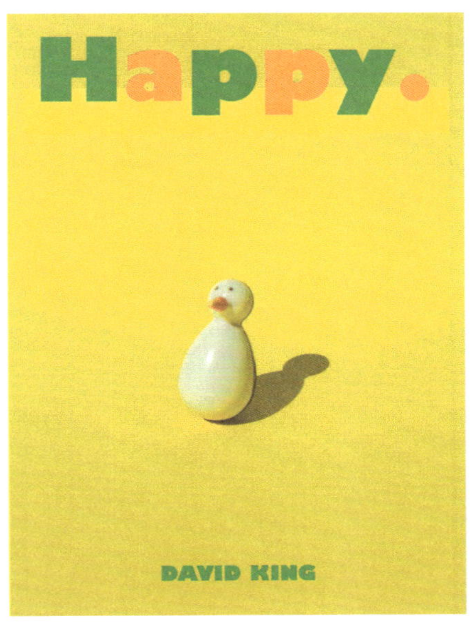

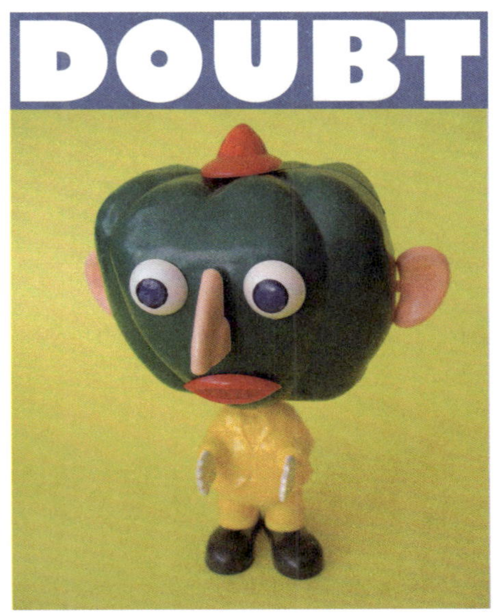

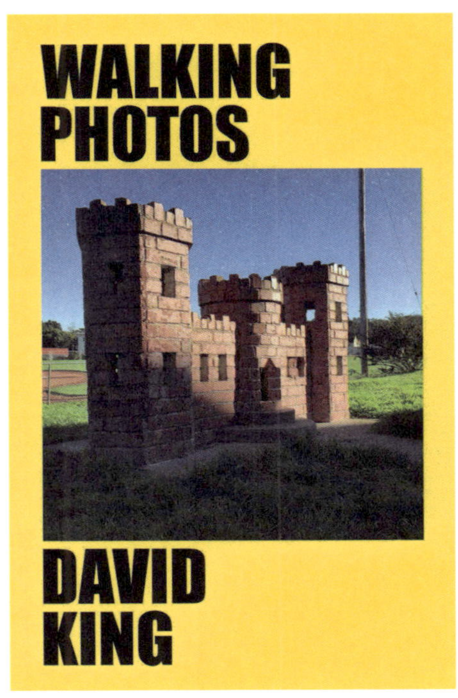

Facing page: Interior page, *Happy*,
Colpa Press, 2020
Digital press, perfect bound, 78 pages,
first edition of 50, 9 x 12 in.
(22.9 x 30.5 cm)

Clockwise from top left:
Happy, Colpa Press, 2020
Posthumous, digital press, perfect bound,
78 pages, first edition of 50, 9 x 12 in.
(22.9 x 30.5 cm)

Doubt, 2018
Prototype, never realized, 68 pages,
8.5 x 11 in. (21.6 x 27.9 cm)

Walking Photos, Forward by
Glen Helfand, Colpa Press, 2019
Digital press, perfect bound, 144 pages,
4.5 x 7 in. (11.4 x 17.8 cm)

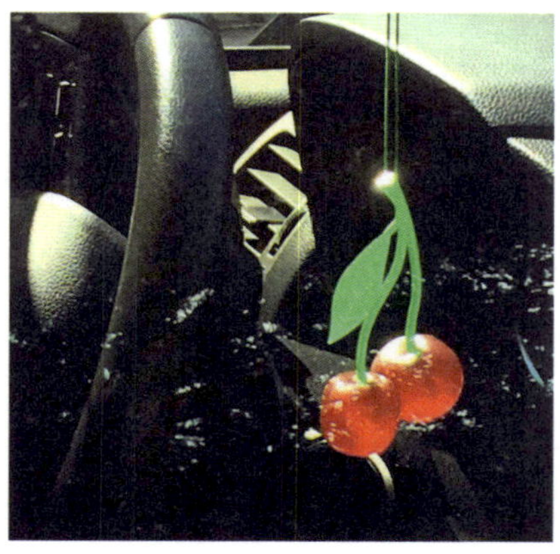

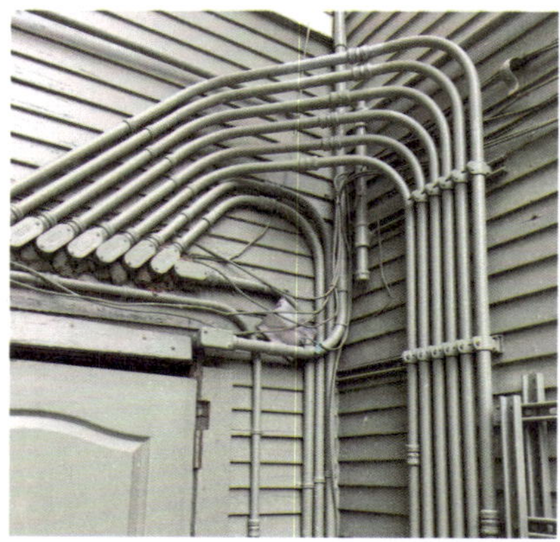

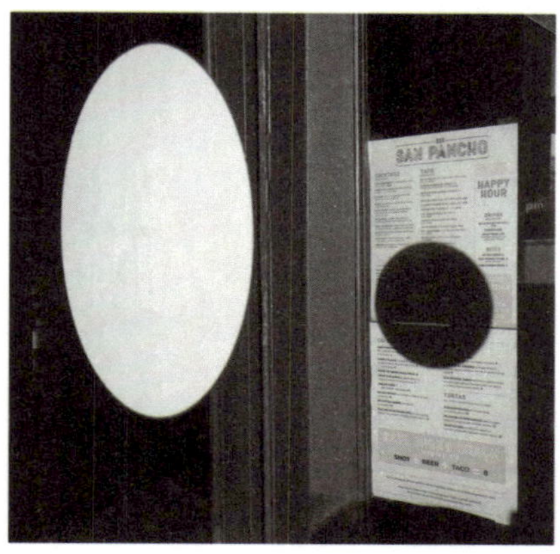

Left, facing page: *Walking Photos*,
Forward by Glen Helfand, Colpa Press, 2019
Digital press, perfect bound, 144 pages,
4.5 x 7 in. (11.4 x 17.8 cm)

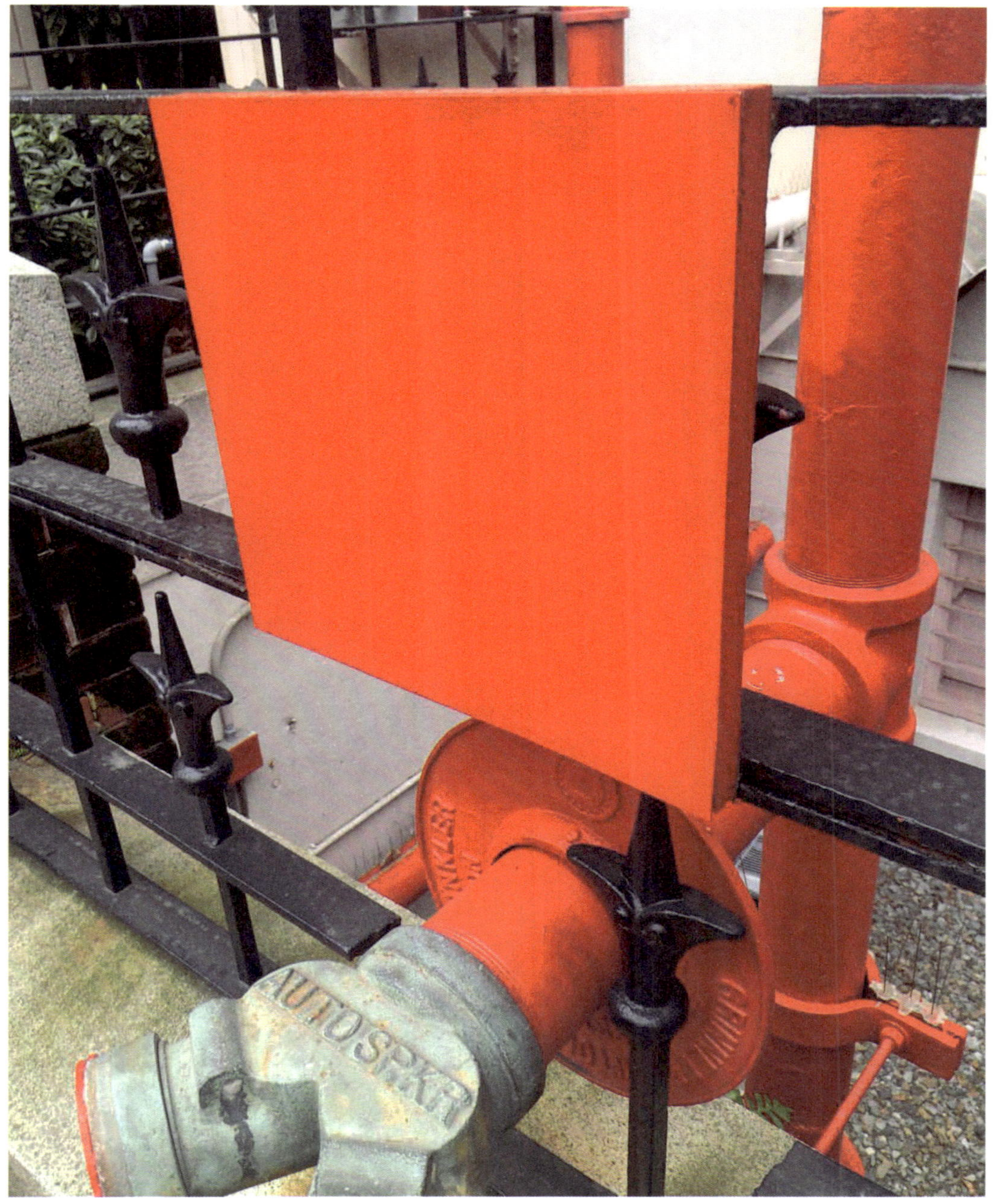
AUTO SPKR

Bibliography

Books / Zines

Non-Stop by Brian Aldiss, cover art by David King, Pan Books, 1977
Mass market paperback, 204 pages, 4.25 x 7 in. (10.8 x 17.8 cm)

Landescapes, 1977/79
Pen, ink, and marker on paper, staple bound, 12 pages, unique, 8.25 x 8.25 in. (21 x 21 cm)

Little People, 1977/79
Pen and ink on paper, staple bound, 28 pages, unique, 5 x 7 in. (12.7 x 17.78 cm)

Beware #1, 1981/82
Photocopy, side stapled, 8 pages, 8.5 x 11 in. (21.6 x 27.9 cm)

Beware #2, 1981/82
Photocopy, side stapled, 12 pages, 8.5 x 11 in. (21.6 x 27.9 cm)

Beware #3, 1981/82
Photocopy, side stapled, 8 pages, 8.5 x 11 in. (21.6 x 27.9 cm)

Beware #4, 1981/82
Photocopy, side stapled, 14 pages, 8.5 x 11 in. (21.6 x 27.9 cm)

Beware #5, 1981/82
Photocopy, side stapled, 20 pages, 8.5 x 11 in. (21.6 x 27.9 cm)

Beware #6, 1981/82
Photocopy, side stapled, 16 pages, 8.5 x 11 in. (21.6 x 27.9 cm)

Beware #7, 1981/82
Photocopy, side stapled, 16 pages, 8.5 x 11 in. (21.6 x 27.9 cm)

Beware #8, 1981/82
Photocopy, side stapled, 14 pages, 8.5 x 11 in. (21.6 x 27.9 cm)

Beware #9, 1981/82
Photocopy, side stapled, 6 pages, 8.5 x 11 in. (21.6 x 27.9 cm)

Beware #10, 1981/82
Photocopy, side stapled, 8 pages, 8.5 x 11 in. (21.6 x 27.9 cm)

Beware #11, 1981/82
Photocopy, side stapled, 8 pages, 8.5 x 11 in. (21.6 x 27.9 cm)

Beware #12, 1981/82
Photocopy, side stapled, 6 pages, 8.5 x 11 in. (21.6 x 27.9 cm)

Beware #14, 1981/82
Photocopy, side stapled, 6 pages, 8.5 x 11 in. (21.6 x 27.9 cm)

Beware #16, 1981/82
Photocopy, side stapled, 6 pages, 8.5 x 11 in. (21.6 x 27.9 cm)

Beware #17, 1981/82
Photocopy, side stapled, 18 pages, 8.5 x 11 in. (21.6 x 27.9 cm)

Beware #18, 1981/82
Photocopy, side stapled, 6 pages, 8.5 x 11 in. (21.6 x 27.9 cm)

Beware #19, 1981/82
Photocopy, side stapled, 10 pages, 8.5 x 11 in. (21.6 x 27.9 cm)

Beware #20, Contributor: Joy DeVivre, 1981/82
Photocopy, side stapled, 10 pages, 8.5 x 11 in. (21.6 x 27.9 cm)

Another Final Morning Extra, Contributors: Sarah Grew, Sin Soracco, Stigg, Arnold Bocklin, Charlie Arsenal, Dirty Dog (David King), Jerry Cornelius, J Neo, A Corn, Ward Abbott, Jagged Canines, Elizabeth Wilhelm,1983
Photocopy, side stapled, 14 pages, 8.5 x 11 in. (21.6 x 27.9 cm)

Final Morning Extra 1, Contributors: Dirty Dog (David King), Elizabeth Wilhelm, Judy D, Bad Boy (Dione King), Cappy Barra, Kiki Felix, Ward Abbott, Sin Suracco, Ann Senuta, Charlie Arsenal, 1983
Photocopy, side stapled, 20 pages, 8.5 x 11 in. (21.6 x 27.9 cm)

Sleeping Dogs #1, 1983
Offset, staple bound, 24 pages, 8.5 x 11 in. (21.6 x 27.9 cm)

Sleeping Dogs #2, 1983
Offset, staple bound, 28 pages,
8.5 x 11 in. (21.6 x 27.9 cm)

Final Morning Extra 3 (Final 3), Contributors: Michael X. King, Terese Svoboda, Peter Mumford, Kurt Flansborg, G.X. Jupiter Larson, Tony Anthony, Megan Jasper, Jacob Reinstein, Willy Idle, Phlegm Pets, Alice Guberman-Carin, Burnt Raisins, Felix Svoboda-Bull, 1983/84
Photocopy, side stapled, 14 pages,
8.5 x 11 in. (21.6 x 27.9 cm)

Don't Believe Them, promo zine for *Sleeping Dogs: Don't Believe Them*, a video by Steve Bull, 1984
Photocopy, side stapled, 6 pages,
8.5 x 11 in. (21.6 x 27.9 cm)

Final Morning Extra 4 (Final 4), Contributors: Bunny Hubcap, Mat Lock, Rippstirl, Nazik Malika and Bad Boy, Ward Abbott, Sean, 1984
Photocopy, side stapled, 20 pages, 8.5 x 11 in. (21.6 x 27.9 cm)

Final Morning Extra 5, Contributors: Burnt Raisins and Phlegm Pets (Lissa and Stephen), J.N. Skellman. PL.1, Wee Doggies, Tragic Mulatto, 1984
Photocopy, side stapled, 8 pages, 8.5 x 11 in. (21.6 x 27.9 cm)

Final Morning Extra 6: Free Poetry, Contributors: Gatsby, Caroliner, KR and Chris/ Altamont, 1984
Photocopy, side stapled, 16 pages, 8.5 x 11 in. (21.6 x 27.9 cm)

Final Morning Extra 8, Contributors: Carol A. Sohneck, Bean Church, Morse, Oven Hickey, 1984
Photocopy, side stapled, 26 pages, 8.5 x 11 in. (21.6 x 27.9 cm)

Brain Rust Zine #1, 1984
Photocopy, side stapled, 4 pages,
8.5 x 11 in. (21.6 x 27.9 cm)

Dead Men's Clothes as Too Many Zombies, 1984/85
Photocopy, side stapled, 14 pages,
8.5 x 11 in. (21.6 x 27.9 cm)

Too Many Zombies at New Method Industries Warehouse, (flyer) Emeryville, CA. Nov. 24, 1984
Photocopy, 8.5 x 11 in. (21.6 x 27.9 cm)

Too Many Zombies #2, Contributors:
David King, Charlie Nash, 1984/85
Photocopy, side stapled, 6 pages, 8.5 x 11 in. (21.6 x 27.9 cm)

Too Many Zombies #4, Contributors:
David King, Charlie Nash, 1984/85
Photocopy, side stapled, 10 pages, 8.5 x 11 in. (21.6 x 27.9 cm)

Too Many Zombies #5, Contributors:
David King, Charlie Nash, 1984/85
Photocopy, side stapled, 14 pages, 8.5 x 11 in. (21.6 x 27.9 cm)

Too Many Zombies #6, Contributors:
David King, Charlie Nash, 1984/85
Photocopy, side stapled, 12 pages, 8.5 x 11 in. (21.6 x 27.9 cm)

Too Many Zombies #9, Contributors:
David King, Charlie Nash, 1984/85
Photocopy, side stapled, 10 pages, 8.5 x 11 in. (21.6 x 27.9 cm)

Too Many Zombies #11, Contributors:
David King, Charlie Nash, 1984/85
Photocopy, side stapled, 4 pages, 8.5 x 11 in. (21.6 x 27.9 cm)

Too Many Zombies #22, Contributors:
David King, Charlie Nash, 1984/85
Photocopy, 2 pages, 8.5 x 11 in.
(21.6 x 27.9 cm)

Too Many Zombies #33: Election Issue, Contributors: David King, Charlie Nash, 1984/85
Photocopy, side stapled, 6 pages, 14 x 8.5 in. (35.6 x 21.6 cm)

Too Many Zombies Mailer, Contributors:
David King, Charlie Nash, 1984/85
Photocopy, side stapled, 4 pages, 7 x 8.5 in. (17.8 x 21.6 cm)

Too Many Zombies Zoo Books Issue, Contributors: David King, Charlie Nash, 1984/85
Photocopy, side stapled, 8 pages, 8.5 x 11 in. (21.6 x 27.9 cm)

Brain Rust Zine #2, 1984/88
Photocopy, side stapled, 12 pages,
5.5 x 8.5 in. (14 x 21.6 cm)

Some Brain Rust Songs, 1984/88
Photocopy, staple bound, 8 pages, 5.5 x 8.5 in. (14 x 21.6 cm)

Too Many Final Morning Zombies Extra 107, Contributors: David King, Charlie Nash, Shagnasty, Barrington Bailey, Denver Tucson, Stigs, assorted anonymous, 1985
Photocopy, side stapled, 28 pages, 8.5 x 11 in. (21.6 x 27.9 cm)

Songs of Death by Bad Boy, Illustrations by Kris Force, Cover and Art Direction by Dirty Dog (David King), Typesetting by Catastrophe Graphics, published by Squash Press, 1986
Photocopy, staple bound, 20 pages, 5.5 x 8.5 in. (14 x 21.6 cm)

No 1 #1, Contributors: Beate Prido, Margot Koch, Dirty Dog (David King), 1987
Photocopy, staple bound, 10 pages, 8.5 x 11 in. (21.6 x 27.9 cm)

No 1 #2, Contributors: Beate Priolo, Dirty Dog (David King), 1987
Photocopy, side stapled, 10 pages, 8.5 x 11 in. (21.6 x 27.9 cm)

No 1 #3, Contributors: Nicole, Dirty Dog (David King), Dan Personoid, Mary, 1987
Photocopy, side stapled, 8 pages, 8.5 x 11 in. (21.6 x 27.9 cm)

No 1 #4, Poems by Edward Mycue, Illustrations: Dirty Dog (David King), Typography: Freddie Baer, 1987
Photocopy, side stapled, 12 pages, 8.5 x 11 in. (21.6 x 27.9 cm)

Souvenir 001, 1987
Photocopy, side stapled, 6 pages, 8.5 x 11 in. (21.6 x 27.9 cm)

No 1 #5, Contributors: Paul Weinman and Dirty Dog (David King) 1987/88
Photocopy, side stapled, 4 pages, 8.5 x 11 in. (21.6 x 27.9 cm)

No 1 #6, Poems by Edward Mycue, Production: Dirty Dog (David King), 1987/88
Photocopy, side stapled, 16 pages, 8.5 x 11 in. (21.6 x 27.9 cm)

Brandenburg Gate, 1980s
Photocopy, slide bound, 32 pages, 8.5 x 11 in. (21.6 x 27.9 cm)

Breaking Through to the Grey Room, 1980s
Photocopy, side stapled, 20 pages, 8.5 x 11 in. (21.6 x 27.9 cm)

Found Guns,1980s
Photocopy, slide bound, 26 pages, 11 x 8.5 in. (27.9 x 21.6 cm)

Let Them Eat Cake, 1980s
Photocopy, side stapled, 8 pages, 8.5 x 11 in. (21.6 x 27.9 cm)

Suburbs of Hell, 1980s
Photocopy, slide bound, 38 pages, 8.5 x 11 in. (21.6 x 27.9 cm)

Dreaming in a Colossus by Rodney Relax, Published by .xtrasensual. Press, Type: Freddie Baer, Graphics: Skazoo & Dirty Dog (David King), 1990
Two color Xerox, staple bound, 6 pages with foldout, 8.5 x 11 in. (21.6 x 27.9 cm)

Poems!, Poetry zine made for Diane DiPrima's poetry class at the San Francisco Art Institute. Contributors: George Andrews, Cameron Bamberger, Gregory Cruikshank, Django Golden, Rebekah Horne, Ron W. Ibon, David King, Leah Korican, Philip McGaughy, Asako Sumii, Quillon Swane, Dave Warnke, Spring 1992
Photocopy, side stapled, 40 pages, 8.5 x 11 in. (21.6 x 27.9 cm)

Whatever!, Cover design by Dirty Dog (David King), 1994
Photocopy, staple bound, 16 pages, 8.5 x 11 in. (21.6 x 27.9 cm)

Untitled (Photographs), 1990s
Digital press, Wire-O bound, acetate cover, 32 pages, 8.5 x 11 in. (21.6 x 27.9 cm)

Yesterday Will Not Die: A Tribute to Cornell Woolrich, Cover design by David King and David Holloway, 1990s
Photocopy, staple bound, 34 pages, 8.5 x 11 in. (21.6 x 27.9 cm)

The Green Photographs, 2002
Digital press, acetate cover, slide bound, 48 pages, 8.5 x 11 in. (21.6 x 27.9 cm)

Modus Operandi, The Adventures of Mo, 2005
Apple print-on-demand digital press, perfect bound, 28 pages, 7.88 x 5.88 in. (20 x 14.9 cm)

Photos the Phone Made, MoST Books, 2007
Digital press, perfect bound, 40 pages, 10 x 8 in. (25.4 X 20.3 cm)

Airship, MOsT Books, 2008
Apple print-on-demand digital press, perfect bound, 20 pages, 11.25 x 8.75 in. (28.6 x 22.2 cm)

Basement, 2008
Apple print-on-demand digital press, perfect bound, 20 pages, 11 x 8.5 in. (27.9 X 21.6 cm)

The Good Photos, MOsT Books, 2008
Apple print-on-demand digital press, perfect bound, 20 pages, 11.25 x 8.75 in. (28.6 x 22.2 cm)

Inexplicable Book One, MOsT Books, 2008
Apple print-on-demand digital press, perfect bound, 20 pages, 11.25 x 8.75 in. (28.6 x 22.2 cm)

Light the Blue Touch Paper #1, 2008
Digital press, coil bound, acetate cover, 52 pages, 5 x 7 in. (12.7 x 17.8 cm)

Light the Blue Touch Paper #2, 2008
Digital press, coil bound, acetate cover, 56 pages, 5 x 7 in. (12.7 x 17.8 cm)

Light the Blue Touch Paper #3, 2008
Digital press, coil bound, acetate cover, 54 pages, 5 x 7 in. (12.7 x 17.8 cm)

The Somnambulists. Homage to California, MOsT Books, 2008
Apple print-on-demand digital press, perfect bound, 38 pages, 11.25 x 8.75 in. (28.6 x 22.2 cm)

2009!, MOsT Books, 2009
Apple print-on-demand digital press, perfect bound, 24 pages, 11.25 x 8.75 in. (28.6 x 22.2 cm)

Dreaming of Istanbul, MOsT Books, 2009
Apple print-on-demand digital press, perfect bound, 30 pages, hardcover, 11.25 x 8.75 in. (28.6 x 22.2 cm)

Goodnight New York, MOsT Books, 2009
Apple print-on-demand digital press, perfect bound, 24 pages, hardcover, 11.25 x 8.75 in. (28.6 x 22.2 cm)

Miscellany, 2009, Apple print-on-demand digital press, Wire-O binding, 20 pages, 8.5 x 11 in. (21.6 x 27.9 cm)

More Photos the Phone Made, MOsT Books, 2009
Apple print-on-demand digital press, perfect bound, 20 pages, 11.25 x 8.75 in. (28.6 x 22.2 cm)

Photos the Phone Made in England, MOsT Books, 2009, Digital press, perfect bound, 20 pages, 8 x 6 in. (20.3 x 15.2 cm)

Sea Birds, MOsT Books, 2009
Digital press, perfect bound, 20 pages, 8 x 6 in. (20.3 x 15.2 cm)

Turkish Skulls, MoST Books, 2009
Digital press, Wire-O binding, 20 pages, 8 x 6 in. (20.3 x 15.2 cm)

At The End of J.G Ballard's Street, 2010
Prototype, never realized, 32 pages, 11.25 x 8.75 in. (28.6 x 22.2 cm)

Buildings. Mostly Houses, MOsT Books, 2010
Apple print-on-demand digital press, perfect bound, 22 pages, hardcover, 11.25 x 8.75 in. (28.6 x 22.2 cm)

Catalog #1, MOsT Books, 2011
Digital press, staple bound, 20 pages, 8 x 6 in. (20.3 X 15.2 cm)

Passages, MOsT Books, 2011
Apple print-on-demand digital press, perfect bound, 20 pages, 8 x 6 in. (20.3 x 15.2 cm)

Photographs 2007–2011, MOsT Books, 2011
Apple print-on-demand digital press, perfect bound, 40 pages, hardcover, 11.25 x 8.75 in. (28.6 x 22.2 cm)

The Somnambulists. Dream # 358., MOsT Books, 2011
Apple print-on-demand digital press, perfect bound, 22 pages, 11.25 x 8.75 in. (28.6 x 22.2 cm)

Sons and Daughters of Fantômas, MoST Books, 2011
Apple print-on-demand digital press, perfect bound, 28 pages, 11.25 x 8.75 in. (28.6 x 22.2 cm)

Symbol, Goteblüd, 2011
Digital press, staple bound, 12 pages, 5.5 x 8.5 in. (14 x 21.6 cm)
I Dreamt I Dwelt in Marble Halls, 2012
Shutterfly digital press, perfect bound, 22 pages, hardcover, 12 x 12 in. (30.5 x 30.5 cm)

I Dreamt I Dwelt in Marble Halls, (small), 2012
Shutterfly digital press, perfect bound, 22 pages, hardcover, 8 x 8 in. (20.3 x 20.3 cm)

London Light, 2012
Shutterfly digital press, perfect bound, 20 pages, hardcover, 12 x 12 in. (30.5 x 30.5 cm)

Male Men, MOsT Books, revised edition, 2012
Apple print-on-demand digital press, perfect bound, 22 pages, hardcover, 11.25 x 8.75 in. (28.6 x 22.2 cm)

Odd, 2012
Shutterfly digital press, perfect bound, 24 pages, hardcover, 12 x 12 in. (30.5 x 30.5 cm)

Photos the Phone Made, 2012
Shutterfly digital press, perfect bound, 22 pages, hardcover, 12 x 12 in. (30.5 x 30.5 cm)

Photos the Phone Made (small), 2012
Shutterfly digital press, perfect bound, 26 pages, hardcover, 8 x 8 in. (20.3 x 20.3 cm)

Several Journeys in One, 2012
Shutterfly digital press, perfect bound, 22 pages, hardcover, 12 x 12 in. (30.5 x 30.5 cm)

The Sound Mirrors, 2012
Shutterfly digital press, perfect bound, 22 pages, hardcover, 12 x 12 in. (30.5 x 30.5 cm)

The Sound Mirrors (small), 2012
Shutterfly digital press, perfect bound, 22 pages, hardcover, 8 x 8 in. (20.3 x 20.3 cm)

Towards the Ness, 2012
Shutterfly digital press, perfect bound, 20 pages, hardcover, 12 x 12 in. (30.5 x 30.5 cm)

Who Was That Masked Man?, davidanthonyking.com, 2012, Digital press, staple bound, 20 pages, 11 x 8.5 in. (27.9 X 21.6 cm)

3/3/2013, 2013
Apple print-on-demand digital press, perfect bound, 20 pages, hardcover, 11.25 x 8.75 in. (28.6 x 22.2 cm)

The Corner of Sage and Sage, 2013
Shutterfly digital press, perfect bound, 32 pages, hardcover, 12 x 12 in. (30.5 x 30.5 cm)

The Corner of Sage and Sage (small), 2013
Shutterfly digital press, perfect bound, 26 pages, hardcover, 8 x 8 in. (20.3 x 20.3 cm)

Internet Scrapbook 001, MOsT Books, 2013
Apple print-on-demand digital press, perfect bound, 20 pages, 11.25 x 8.75 in. (28.6 x 22.2 cm)

J.G. Ballard's Inner Space, MoST Books, 2013
Shutterfly digital press, perfect bound, 22 pages, hardcover, 12 x 12 in. (30.5 x 30.5 cm)

KING, 2013
Shutterfly digital press, perfect bound, 22 pages, hardcover, 8 x 8 in. (20.3 x 20.3 cm)

Secret Origins of the Crass Symbol,
&Pens Press, 2013
Offset, perfect bound, 28 pages, edition of 500, 7 x 7 in. (17.8 x 17.8 cm)

Net Book 2, MOsT Books, 2015
Apple print-on-demand digital press, perfect bound, 28 pages, hardcover, 11.25 x 8.75 in. (28.6 x 22.2 cm)

Every Red Death, MOsT Books, 2016
Apple print-on-demand digital press, perfect bound, 20 pages, hardcover, 11.25 x 8.75 in. (28.6 x 22.2 cm)

7 Teen, MoST Books, 2017
Digital Press, plastic slide binding, 32 pages, edition of 15, 8.5 x 11 in. (21.6 x 27.9 cm)

Scrapbook, Colpa Press, 2017
Digital press, section-sewn and perfect bound, 112 pages, edition of 50, 9 x 12 in. (22.9 x 30.5 cm)

Doubt, 2018
Prototype, never realized, 68 pages, 8.5 x 11 in. (21.6 x 27.9 cm)

Intrusions, MOsT Books, 2018
Apple print-on-demand digital press, perfect bound, 40 pages, hardcover, 11.25 x 8.75 in. (28.6 x 22.2 cm)

Penumbra, MOsT Books, 2018
Apple print-on-demand digital press, perfect bound, 62 pages, hardcover, 11.25 x 8.75 in. (28.6 x 22.2 cm)

Still, Colpa Press, 2018
Digital press, tape bound, 68 pages, first edition of 50, 11.75 x 17.75 in. (29.9 x 45.1 cm)

David King Stencils: Past, Present and Crass!,
Contributors: Matt Borruso, Steven Heller, Howard Rodman, and Barry McGee,
Gingko Press with Kill Yr Idols, 2019
Offset, sewn binding, 200 pages, 8 x 10 in. (20.3 x 25.4 cm)

El Rayo X, MoST Books, 2019
Digital press, perfect bound, 20 pages, 8 x 10 in. (20.3 x 25.4 cm)

Gas Gun, MoST Books, 2019
Digital press, perfect bound, 26 pages, hardcover, 8.25 x 10.25 in. (21 x 26 cm)

Gas Gun (soft cover), MoST Books, 2019
Digital press, perfect bound, 26 pages, hardcover, 8 x 10 in. (20.3 x 25.4 cm)

The Journey, Colpa Press, 2019
Digital press, perfect bound, 124 pages, first edition of 50, Signed and numbered, 7.75 by 11.75 in (19.7 x 29.8 cm)

Walking Photos, Forward by
Glen Helfand, Colpa Press, 2019
Digital press, perfect bound, 144 pages, 4.5 x 7 in. (11.4 x 17.8 cm)

What is Your Favorite Comic Strip,
Blisterzine / MoST Books, 2019
Digital press, perfect bound, 64 pages, 8.5 x 11 in. (21.6 x 27.9 cm)

Every Red Death Volume 2, MOsT Books, 2000s
Apple print-on-demand digital press, perfect bound, 20 pages, hardcover, 11.25 x 8.75 in. (28.6 x 22.2 cm)

Green House, 2000s
Apple print-on-demand digital press, perfect bound, 24 pages, hardcover, 11.25 x 8.75 in. (28.6 x 22.2 cm)

Museum of Small Things by the Two Davids, 2000s
Apple print-on-demand digital press, perfect bound, 20 pages, hardcover, 11.25 x 8.75 in. (28.6 x 22.2 cm)

Museum of Small Things, 2000s
Apple print-on-demand digital press, perfect bound, 28 pages, hardcover, 11.25 x 8.75 in. (28.6 x 22.2 cm)

The Rock Wall, 2000s
Mockup, laser prints, clip bound,102 pages, 5 x 7 in. (12.7 x 17.8 cm)

Department of the Ulterior, 2000s
Prototype, never realized, 24 pages, 11.25 x 8.75 in. (28.6 x 22.2 cm)

Happy, Colpa Press, 2020
Posthumous, digital press, perfect bound, 78 pages, first edition of 50, 9 x 12 in. (22.9 x 30.5 cm)

Credits

Published by

Colpa Press
771B Capp Street
San Francisco, CA 94110

colpapress.com

In association with

San Francisco Center for the Book
375 Rhode Island Street
San Francisco, CA 94103

sfcb.org

Editor: Matt Borruso
Essay: Experimental Jetset
Design: Visible Publications
Copy editor: Sarah Hotchkiss

First printing of 1000, 2024

ISBN 979-8-218-46101-0

Printed by die Keure, Belgium

This publication accompanies the exhibition *David King Publications 1977–2019*, on view at San Francisco Center for the Book, San Francisco, October 25, 2024–December 22, 2024.

Exhibition curated by Luca Antonucci
and Matt Borruso
Organized by Jennie Hinchcliff

With thanks to Dione King, Marci Washington, John Borruso, Alex Arzt, Chris Grunder, Gwenaël Rattke, Marieke Stolk, Erwin Brinkers and Danny van den Dungen, Jeff Khonsary, and David Senior.

This catalog and the exhibition *David King Publications 1977–2019* are supported in part by the National Endowment for the Arts.

San Francisco Center for the Book is a 501(c)(3) non-profit organization. Focusing on the history, artistry, and importance of books as a medium of self-expression, SFCB offers workshops, exhibitions, and public programs about printing, bookbinding, and book-related arts.

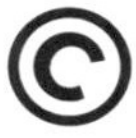

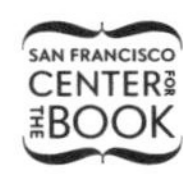

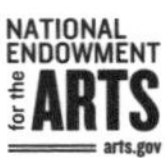